THE OLYMPICS' STRANGEST MOMENTS

THE OLYMPICS' STRANGEST MOMENTS

Extraordinary but true tales from the history of the Olympic Games

Geoff Tibballs

ROBSON BOOKS

To Carol, Nicki and Lindsey

First published in Great Britain in 2004 by Robson Books,
The Chrysalis Building, Bramley Road, London W10 6SP

An imprint of Chrysalis Books Group plc

Copyright © 2004 Geoff Tibballs

British Library Cataloguing in Publication Data
A catalogue record for this title is available from the British Library

ISBN 1 86105 711 3

Typeset by SX Composing DTP, Rayleigh, Essex
Printed and bound in Great Britain by Creative Print & Design (Wales), Ebbw Vale

Contents

INTRODUCTION

The Olympic Games were the wonder of the ancient sporting world. Athletics played a major role in the religious festivals of the ancient Greeks, who believed that competitive sports pleased the spirits of the dead, and so what better way to gain the gods' approval than by arranging a showcase for the finest talent? Staged every four years in the valley of Olympia in south-west Greece from 776BC, the Olympics ran for more than 1,100 years until eventually being banned by the zealous Roman Emperor Theodosius in AD393 on the grounds that they were a pagan ritual. At their height they drew competitors not only from Greece itself but also from across the Roman and Macedonian empires and were initially considered so sacred that for their duration all hostilities were ceased. When Sparta attacked a rival city during an Olympic truce, it was fined the equivalent of one million dollars. Among the illustrious entrants in AD66 was none other than Emperor Nero of Rome who, accompanied by 5,000 bodyguards, was – predictably, perhaps – declared the winner in every event in which he took part.

For the first thirteen Olympiads the sole event was a 200 yards foot race, but soon the programme was expanded to include events over a longer distance. Aside from these traditional races on foot and in chariots, there were competitions in the javelin, the discus, the long jump and wrestling. Centurions displayed their speed and strength in races run in full suits of armour, and there was even a contest for kissing! At first the ancient Olympics were very much a men-only affair – indeed, women caught so much as watching the events were liable to execution – but in time the rules were relaxed to the extent that women were eventually allowed to take part . . . which must have come as a bonus to the men who had put their names down for the kissing competition. The prestige associated with Olympic victory was enormous. With Olympia considered holy ground, winners gave public thanks to the gods. Three-time winners had statues erected in their honour and were offered exemption from taxation – a welcome incentive, as ordinarily first prize was often nothing more valuable than a stick of celery. However, these rewards ultimately corrupted the Games and the idealistic amateur competitors gave way to foreign mercenaries who were granted the citizenship necessary to take part and were paid by Greek gamblers.

Following their cancellation, the Olympics lay dormant for 1,500 years until a French nobleman, Baron Pierre de Coubertin, began admiring a model of ancient Olympia that was on show at the 1889 Paris Exposition. The model inspired de Coubertin to attempt to revive the Games, but at first few seemed to share his enthusiasm. However, he persisted and in June 1894 twelve countries attended a special conference dedicated to relaunching the Olympics and a further 21 sent messages of support. As president of the newly formed International Olympic Committee, de Coubertin earmarked the first modern Olympics for his home city of Paris in 1900, but the Greeks were so excited by the prospect of bringing back the Games that Athens was swiftly inserted for 1896.

Backed by private donations, notably from wealthy Greek businessman Georgios Averoff, the Greek organising committee raised sufficient money to rebuild the city's famous Panathenaic Stadium, constructed originally in 330BC, and on the afternoon of 6 April 1896 the first modern Olympics were officially opened by King George I of Greece. A total of 245 athletes (164 of them Greek) took part, from fourteen different nations. Women were not permitted to compete. Although there were no national teams as such, the British Athletic Association sent a party, as did the German Gymnastics Society and, from across the Atlantic, the Boston Athletic Association. The Americans had a most unfortunate introduction to the Olympics. Having spent sixteen and a half days at sea, they arrived in the Greek capital at 9 p.m. on 5 April, believing that they still had another twelve days to prepare for the competition. But to their horror they were awoken at 4 a.m. the following morning by the sound of a brass band heralding the start of the Games. For the Americans had forgotten that Greece still used the Julian calendar and was therefore eleven days in advance.

An even sadder case was that of Italian Carlo Airoldi, who set off from his home in Milan on 28 February and reached Ragusa in Yugoslavia on 19 March, having covered the 695 miles on foot. Giving his feet a well-deserved rest, he boarded a boat on 23 March and sailed via Corfu to Patrasso, where he arrived four days later. He then resumed the great trek, walking the 136 miles to Athens over the next five days. Leg-weary but delighted to have finally reached his goal, he duly handed in his Olympic entry for the marathon, only for it be refused because he was believed to be a professional. It must have been a long walk home.

A number of the competitors at the 1896 Olympics were simply people who happened to be on holiday at the time, including Irish tennis player John Boland, who ended up winning the singles and partnering Germany's Friedrich Traun to victory in the doubles. There were no gold medals. Each winner was awarded a silver medal, a crown of olive branches and a diploma. The runner-up received a bronze medal, a crown of laurel and a diploma. Third place earned nothing. But above all it was the Olympic spirit that prevailed. Although soldiers armed with rifles were positioned at the entrance to each row in the stadium in order to prevent overcrowding, the Games were conducted in a friendly manner, in keeping with de Coubertin's vision for nations and people to be united by sport and for the taking part to be more important than the winning. That spirit was personified by French cyclist Léon Flameng part-way through the 300-lap, 100-km track race. When his solitary opponent, Georgios Kolettis of Greece, was forced to stop for urgent repairs, Flameng also stopped and waited for him. Although the Frenchman fell in the closing stages, his sportsmanship was rewarded with a victory by eleven laps. Meanwhile, on the running track a French sprinter insisted on competing in gloves because he was appearing before royalty.

The first modern Olympics proved an unqualified success. At the closing banquet, the Greek monarch expressed the hope that the Games would be held permanently in Greece, but de Coubertin stuck to his plan of awarding the 1900 Olympics to Paris. In the course of the twentieth century, the Olympic movement travelled the world – from Montreal to Melbourne, Stockholm to Seoul – but it never returned officially to Greece. Now, 108 years after their resurrection, the Olympics are finally coming back to their spiritual home.

Countless words have been written about the Summer Olympic Games, the vast majority, quite understandably, devoted to gold medallists. However, in this book I have looked at some of the more obscure, bizarre moments in Olympic history, featuring not only the greats such as Paavo Nurmi, Emil Zátopek and Greg Louganis, but also forgotten participants such as Philip Plater, the unlucky British shooter of 1908, Konrad von Wangenheim, the courageous German horseman of 1936, and Polin Belisle, the dual-nationality marathon fraudster of 1992. And to prove that even in these days of big-money sport the Olympics can still produce offbeat stories, we only have to hark back four years to the exploits in Sydney of Eric Moussambani from Equatorial Guinea, who has entered Olympic folklore as 'Eric the Eel' after being acknowledged as the slowest swimmer in the history of the Games. His tale is just one of the Olympics' strangest moments.

As ever, I am indebted to the enthusiasm and expertise of Jeremy Robson and to my editors at Robson Books, Jane Donovan and Rob Dimery, and to the helpful staff at both the British Newspaper Library and Nottinghamshire Library Services.

Geoff Tibballs

A LEAP INTO THE UNKNOWN

ATHENS, 6 APRIL 1896

The distinction of becoming the first Olympic champion in over 1,500 years went to an American student, James B Connolly, but only after he had overcome all manner of adversities. Indeed, the authorities at Harvard University did their utmost to prevent Connolly even travelling to Greece and in the end the headstrong athlete only made it to Europe by paying his own way.

Born in south Boston in 1868 to Irish-Catholic parents, Connolly was one of twelve children. A keen sportsman, he dropped out of school at fifteen and worked as a clerk for an insurance company before deciding to further his education at university. In 1895 he was accepted by Harvard to study the classics but struggled to cope with academic life. So when, as the national triple jump champion, he heard about the Olympics that were to take place in Europe, he resolved to seek permission to take eight weeks' leave of absence in order to travel to Athens and compete in the Games. He approached both the head of the university, Dean Shaler, and the chairman of the Harvard Athletic Committee, but both turned him down flat. The chairman implied that the trip was nothing more than a 'junket', while the dean was distinctly unimpressed by Connolly's claim that it would yield 'educational advantages'. They told him that his only course of action would be to resign and reapply to Harvard on his return, a suggestion that apparently infuriated Connolly who raged: 'I am not resigning and I'm not making application to re-enter on my return. I am through with this college right now. Good day.' To add to Connolly's sense of injustice, a fellow student, Ellery H Clark, was granted leave by Harvard to journey to Athens.

Denied permission, Connolly formally withdrew from Harvard in readiness for the adventure of a lifetime. He was part of an eleven-man United States contingent, but whereas his fellow Americans travelled all expenses paid – mostly under the banner of the Boston Athletic Association – Connolly was considered too poor to be accepted by such an elite, upper-class establishment and was obliged instead to travel under the auspices of the tiny Suffolk Athletic Club. He spent all his life savings – around $700 – on a ticket aboard the German freighter SS *Fulda*, but two days before he was due to sail, a back injury threatened to wreck his plans. Fortunately it cleared up on the seventeen-day voyage from New York to Naples where, however, he had the misfortune to have his wallet stolen.

As I mentioned in the introduction, the Americans arrived in Athens (having completed the journey from Italy by rail) thinking they had twelve days to train but discovered that the difference between the Greek and Western calendars meant that the Games were actually starting the following day. Connolly blamed American provincialism for the blunder. Even worse for Connolly, he read in the programme that his event would be the hop, hop and jump (as opposed to the traditional hop, step and jump) – a variation that he had not practised since childhood.

The brief opening ceremony was followed by the first round of the 100 metres, which saw three Americans advance to the finals. Next it was the triple jump, to be decided by the best of three jumps per competitor. Connolly was the last to jump. After the others had finished, he walked out of the sandpit and contemptuously threw his cap to a point a yard beyond their best effort, indicating how far he would jump. Promising to anyone within earshot that his leap would be 'one for the honour of County Galway', he sped down the runway, did two hops and a jump and landed well beyond his marker cap. Connolly's effort of 44ft 11¾in (13.71m) – although short of his own best and of the world record he would set later in the year – still outdistanced his nearest rival by over a yard and was good enough to make him the first modern Olympic champion.

Connolly recalled the event in a 1906 edition of *The Outing Magazine* – a curious account in which he refrained from mentioning himself by name. He wrote: 'The glorified youth of a dozen nations took their turns, until it simmered down to a Greek, a Frenchman and an American. And the final winning of it by the American led up to an occasion that he has been able since to recollect without greatly straining his faculties. The 140,000 throats roared a greeting, and the 140,000 pairs of eyes, as nearly as he could count, focused themselves on his exalted person. And then, when his name went up on the board, to the crest of the hills outside the multitude re-echoed it . . . it was a moment to inspire!'

Connolly was not finished yet. He went on take second place in the high jump (clearing 5ft 5in [1.65m]) and third place in the long jump (20ft 0½in [6.11m]), both events being won by Ellery Clark. Indeed, Connolly's opening-day victory inspired the Americans to win nine of the twelve track and field events.

He was very much the black sheep of the party, deemed socially inferior to his compatriots. One of the few surviving photographs of the time shows him sitting apart from the other American athletes on board the SS *Fulda*, while some contemporary accounts pointedly referred to every American competitor except him by their first name. The triple jump winner, however, was simply 'Connolly'. In a bid to recoup some of his outlay, Connolly took the opportunity to endorse a brand of medication from the scene of the 1896 Olympics. 'Johnson's Anodyne Liniment,' he stated, 'greatly helped my back which is now entirely well . . . I am nearly out of Johnson's Anodyne Liniment, as the boys have been calling on me for some.' Daley Thompson would have been proud of him.

On his return to the United States, Connolly accepted a post as editor of the journal *Land and Water: the Authority of American Athletic Sports*. He served as a soldier in the Spanish–American War of 1898, publishing his accounts in the *Boston Globe* as 'Letters from the Front in Cuba', and revisited Europe in 1900 to defend his Olympic triple jump title in Paris, but this time had to be content with second place. He became a prolific writer about the sea – penning over two hundred short stories and fifty novels – but continued to harbour a grudge against Harvard for attempting to deny him his chance of Olympic glory. In 1949 the university tried to bury the hatchet by offering him an honorary doctorate, but he turned it down. He died in New York in 1957, the culmination of a life that had seen him defy the odds to stake a unique place in Olympic history.

THE FIRST OLYMPIC MARATHON

ATHENS, 10 APRIL 1896

It was in 490BC that the Greek soldier Pheidippides ran nearly 25 miles from the battlefield of Marathon to Athens with the news of a Greek victory over the Persians. The story passed into folklore and so when it was announced that Athens would be hosting the first modern Olympics, French historian and linguist Michel Bréal, a friend of Baron de Coubertin, proposed a race from Marathon to Athens to commemorate Pheidippides' run. Naturally the Greeks reacted enthusiastically to a race celebrating one of their heroes, all the more so when Bréal offered a cup to the winner. Moreover a Greek bearing gifts, wealthy collector Ionnis Lambros, then offered an antique vase as an additional prize to the first man home.

Although there was some disquiet among medical experts as to whether a 25-mile run along the hot and dusty roads of Greece would endanger the health of the competitors (it is said that three Greek athletes died while training for the Olympic marathon), the Greeks were determined to claim first prize. To this end, they arranged a trial race over the full distance and, on 10 March 1896, Charilaos Vasilakos beat eleven other local runners in a time of 3hr 18min. Keen to field the best possible team, officials arranged for a second trial to take place two weeks later. This was won by Ioannis Laventis in 3hr 11min 27sec and, despite the fact that entries for the Games were officially closed, several additional names were added to the Greek team, including that of Spiridon Louis, who had finished fifth in the second trial in 3hr 18min 27sec.

Louis's job as a water carrier required him to walk several miles daily. The 24-year-old had dreamed beforehand that he would win the Olympic marathon and he is believed to have fasted on the eve of the race, concentrating instead on his prayers. On the actual race day he compensated for his strict diet by eating a whole chicken.

Thirteen of the seventeen starters for the Olympic marathon were Greek. Principal among the foreigners was Edwin Flack, an Australian accountant who lived in London, and who had already won both the 800 metres and the 1,500 metres – the former just the day before the marathon. However, he had never raced over a distance of more than ten miles. Arthur Blake of the United States had finished second in the 1,500 metres, with Albin Lermusiaux of France third. These two clearly represented a threat, as did the fourth outsider, Gyula Kellner of Hungary, the only non-Greek entrant to have previously run such an extreme distance.

In spite of their numerical superiority, Greek athletes had so far failed to cover themselves in glory at the Athens Olympics, prompting a wave of fresh incentives to secure a home win in the marathon. Among the gifts offered to the winner (in addition to the official cup and vase) were a barrel of sweet wine and free clothing and haircuts for life. The owner of a chocolate factory promised over 2,000lb of chocolate to the winner, while the Games' benefactor, Georgios Averoff, went so far as to promise his daughter's hand in marriage, along with a dowry of one million drachma. So much for amateurism . . .

The night before the race the competitors were transported to Marathon Bridge by wagon and housed at an inn. As a crowd in excess of 100,000 gathered in and around Athens' Panathenaic Stadium in anticipation of a Greek triumph, 25 miles away a small group of villagers watched the starter, Major Papadiamantopoulos, make a short speech (which took less time than to introduce him by name) and then fire his pistol in the air to set the runners on their way at 2 p.m.

The Frenchman Lermusiaux set a frenetic pace from the off, preceded only by the flotilla of bicycles and horse-drawn wagons that ferried officials and doctors along the course. He reached the village of Pikermi, more than halfway into the race, in the astonishing time of 55 minutes and led his nearest rival, Flack, by almost two miles. With Blake third and Kellner fourth, the Greeks were well off the pace but appeared to be quietly biding their time, confident that the leading quartet would wilt long before Athens. When Louis, running in shoes donated by his home village, arrived in Pikermi back in sixth place, he enjoyed a glass of wine and told spectators: 'Everything is going to plan. My turn will come yet.'

The road out of Pikermi turned uphill and the leaders began to regret the early pace. Blake retired less than a mile out of the village, Kellner was passed by Vasilakos and Lermusiaux also started to suffer. Nevertheless, he still led at the village of Palini, where the excited villagers crowned him with a victory wreath. Their actions proved decidedly premature as shortly afterwards Lermusiaux weakened alarmingly, his cause not helped by an accidental collision with a French cyclist, which caused him to fall and be passed by Flack. Even an alcohol rubdown failed to revive him and, although he continued the race, he collapsed before the twenty-mile mark and had to be carried to a medical carriage.

Meanwhile, Flack was so sure of victory that he sent a cyclist off to the stadium to announce his impending triumph. The news was received with glum resignation by the Greek spectators waiting in the Panathenaic, unaware that Louis, having timed his run to perfection, was rapidly closing on the Australian. Five miles from the finish, Louis swept past the exhausted Flack, who gamely kept in touch for the next two miles before finally succumbing to fatigue when the Greek raised the pace outside the village of Ambelokipi. As Flack began to reel, his helper asked a Greek spectator to stop the runner from falling over while he went in search of a wrap. But in a state of delirium, Flack thought he was being attacked and rewarded the Good Samaritan with a punch in the face. Flack promptly dropped out and had to be revived with a drink of egg and brandy.

Ahead at the stadium a dust-covered Major Papadiamanto-poulos rode up to the royal box to deliver a message to the King. The news spread around the crowd in an instant: a Greek runner looked like winning the Olympic marathon. As a mighty roar went up, the sound of a cannon announced that the leader was approaching. Battling his way through ecstatic well-wishers, the small figure of Louis appeared through the marble entrance to the stadium. 'It seemed that all of Greek antiquity entered with him,' de Coubertin later wrote in his memoirs. 'Cheers went up such as have never been heard before.' Prince George and Crown Prince Constantine rushed down to the track and accompanied him to the finish. Up in the VIP stand, women tore off their jewellery and showered it upon the victor. Although exhausted as he crossed the finish line, Louis summoned enough energy to bow to the King, who responded with a joyous wave of his naval cap.

With a time of 2hr 58min 50sec, Louis had run the first official sub-three-hour marathon. Vasilakos finished second – seven minutes in arrears – and it appeared that the host nation had achieved a clean sweep when Spiridon Belokas crossed the line in third place. However, Kellner accused Belokas, who had passed him near the end, of taking a ride in a carriage and when the Crown Prince investigated the allegation, Belokas confessed to the deception and was disqualified; the Hungarian was promoted to third.

A national hero, Louis was feted wherever he went. At the awards ceremony a few days later he duly received the cup and the antique vase on which was painted a runner in a foot race at the ancient Olympic Games. Louis generously donated the vase to a museum. A grateful nation continued to attempt to shower him with gifts. As he was already married (with two children) he was unable to accept the offer of Miss Averoff's hand in marriage and when the King insisted on rewarding him somehow, he contented himself with a horse and cart to facilitate the transport of fresh water from his village, Maroussi, to Athens.

A new Greek mythology grew up around the unassuming Louis. His story inspired a novel and expressions such as 'to take off like Louis' became part of the Greek language. Yet after his epic victory he quietly returned to Maroussi – declining all the offers of free clothes, meals and haircuts – and never ran again. In 1936 he emerged from anonymity as a guest of honour at the Berlin Olympics. Four years later he died, but his legend lives on.

THE BIG CHILL

ATHENS, 11 APRIL 1896

Alfred Hajos decided to learn to swim at the age of thirteen after his father had tragically drowned in the River Danube. In 1895 Hajos won the 100 metres freestyle at both the Hungarian national championships and the European swimming championships, a feat he repeated the following year to acquire the nickname of 'the Hungarian Dolphin'. In fact, he was an exceptional all-round athlete, representing Hungary at soccer while in track and field he captured national titles in the 100 metres, 400 metres hurdles and discus. Yet it was as a swimmer of supreme courage that he left an indelible mark at the Athens Olympics.

At the time he was an eighteen-year-old architecture student and, like James Connolly, had to seek permission from his university before being allowed to compete. Whereas Connolly's plea was rejected, the Dean of Budapest's Polytechnical University gave Hajos his blessing to miss classes . . . albeit grudgingly.

The swimming competition at the first modern Olympics was a far cry from the comfort of today. There was no heated indoor pool in Athens – instead, the races took place in the open waters of the Mediterranean Sea, in the Bay of Zea, near Piraeus. Not only did the swimmers have to cope with the cold – the sea temperature was no more than 13 degrees Celsius (55 degrees Fahrenheit) – but the waters were also decidedly choppy. After overcoming the elements to win the 100 metres freestyle in 1min 22.2sec, Hajos attempted the double a few hours later in the 1,200 metres freestyle.

9

Three small boats ferried the nine starters out to sea and then left them to swim the 1,200 metres back to shore. Hajos recalled: 'My body had been smeared with a half-inch-thick layer of grease, for I was more cunning after the 100 metres event, and tried to protect myself against the cold. We jumped into the water at the start of a pistol, and from that point on the boats left the competitors to the mercy of the waves, rushing back to the finish line to inform the jury of the successful start.' The course was marked out by a series of hollowed-out pumpkins floating on the surface but quickly became almost impossible to follow as the swimmers were lashed by soaring, twelve-foot waves. 'The icy water almost cut into our stomachs,' said Hajos. 'I must say I shivered from the thought of what would happen if I got cramp from the cold water. My will to live completely overcame my desire to win.'

A number of his rivals gave up, but as the boats returned to fish distraught competitors, numb from the cold, out of the water, Hajos pressed on bravely towards the shore. He finally reached the safety of dry land in 18min 22.2sec, finishing over two and a half minutes ahead of the runner-up. When, at the dinner honouring the Olympic winners, the King of Greece asked him where he had learned to swim so well, Hajos coolly replied: 'In the water.'

The dean at his university was less impressed, refraining from congratulating Hajos on his two titles. 'Your medals are of no interest to me,' he snapped, 'but I am eager to hear your replies in your next examination.'

Hajos obviously heeded the dean's words, for in 1924 he won the silver medal at the Paris Olympics in the special arts competition for architecture. He was only denied the gold medal because the French did not want to award it to a foreigner.

DUFFEY'S DISASTER

PARIS, 14 JULY 1900

The 1900 Paris Olympics were a long drawn-out affair, beginning in May and not ending until October. In his eagerness for his home city to host the Games, Baron de Coubertin had allowed them to be incorporated with the Fifth Universal Exposition, which was also being held in Paris. As a result the Olympics became little more than a sideshow and many competitors, even medal winners, did not realise until later that they had actually been competing at the Olympic Games. Not only did some athletes die without ever knowing that they had participated in the Olympics, but also it has been estimated that these were the only Olympics where the athletes outnumbered the spectators.

For the first time women were allowed to compete, although they made up only nineteen of the 1,225 competitors and there were no track events for them. Instead, they concentrated on sports such as croquet and tennis, which, along with golf and cricket, were mainstays of the 1900 Olympics. The cricket competition consisted of a solitary match between Britain (represented by the Devon and Somerset Wanderers Cricket Club) and France, made up of staff from the British Embassy. In the circumstances it was little surprise that Britain won by 158 runs.

The swimming events took place in the River Seine and, because the races were swum with the current, times were remarkably fast. Among the more unusual events was a swimming obstacle race in which competitors had to climb a

11

pole, scramble over a row of boats and swim under another line of boats. The track and field events were staged on rough ground at Croix-Catelan in the Bois de Boulogne, where facilities were so basic that the jumpers had to dig their own pits. And the obstacles for the men's 400 metres hurdles were 30ft-long telephone poles! The marathon was run in a heat of 38.9 degrees Celsius (102 degrees Fahrenheit), with only seven of the thirteen starters finishing. Victory went to France's Michel Théato, a baker's deliveryman, but only after the clear leader, Sweden's Ernst Fast, had taken a wrong turning three miles from the finish. Cursing his luck, Fast had to settle for third place.

Instead of medals, competitors were presented with *objets d'art*. In foot races, these prizes were to the value of 400 francs for first place, 200 francs for second, and 50 francs for third; in other events, they were to the value of 250 francs for first place and 80 francs for runners-up.

A vociferous American college contingent (said to make up over half of the support in the main stadium) frequently antagonised the locals, who somewhat uncharitably described the visitors from across the Atlantic as 'a band of savages'. Meanwhile, the *San Francisco Chronicle* sniffed at the amateurish approach of the Europeans, writing: 'The natty college costumes of the Americans were a decided contrast to the home-made attire of some of the best European athletes, who, instead of donning a sweater or a bathrobe after the trials, walked about in straw hats and light overcoats.' Given the degree of ill-feeling on view, every American reversal could easily have been greeted with delight by European spectators, but even they were dismayed by the misfortune that befell crack US sprinter Arthur Duffey in the final of the 100 metres.

At barely 5ft 7in tall, the Georgetown University student was a veritable pocket dynamo. He was the strong favourite to win the Olympic sprint, particularly since he had beaten his two principal rivals, Frank Jarvis of Princeton and John Tewksbury of Pennsylvania, in London the week before. The only factor counting against the American trio was that they had never previously run on a grass track, but they had soon made light of the new surface, Jarvis and Tewksbury both equalling the world record of 10.8sec on their way to the final. However, the general consensus of opinion was that Duffey had not stretched himself to date and was keeping plenty in reserve for the big race.

Sure enough, Duffey got a flying start and by halfway had established what looked to be an unassailable lead; then, suddenly and inexplicably, he collapsed in a heap on the track, allowing Jarvis to burst through and beat Tewksbury by two feet with Australia's Stanley Rowley back in third. The *New York Times* described the drama: 'Duffy [sic] was selected by practically everybody as a certain winner. When the pistol was fired for the final he left the mark like a shot and had already assumed what appeared to be a decisive lead when he was seen to wobble and a moment later he fell heavily to the ground. A groan of disappointment and sympathy rose from the crowd of Americans, which changed almost immediately into a shout of victory as Jarvis breasted the tape.'

Some observers concluded that Duffey's left foot had become entangled in the ropes that divided the lanes, but the runner himself revealed that he had suffered some form of injury, probably a strained tendon. 'I do not know why my leg gave way,' he told reporters. 'I felt a peculiar twitching after going twenty yards. I then seemed to lose control of it, and suddenly it gave out, throwing me on my face. But that is one of the fortunes of sport.'

NEVER ON A SUNDAY

PARIS, 15 JULY 1900

Although the desire for victory was less tangible in the early Olympics, not every defeat was met with a polite handshake. Indeed, so intense was the rivalry between two American long jumpers at Paris in 1900 that they physically came to blows amid accusations of betrayal and treachery.

The athlete who considered himself the injured party was Myer Prinstein. Born into a family of Polish-Russian Jews in 1878, he was just five when his parents brought the Prinstein clan from Poland to settle in Syracuse, New York. Young Myer's sporting and academic ability eventually earned him a place studying Law at Syracuse University, where he took part in all manner of track and field events, from hurdles and sprints to the high jump and pole vault. At 5ft 7¾in tall, Prinstein was not an obvious candidate for the Syracuse basketball team but his sturdy shoulders, allied to a fierce competitive spirit, adequately compensated for his lack of height. Yet it was the triple jump and long jump (or 'broad jump' as it was often known in those days) that were to become his specialist events and he developed a reputation for producing the goods on the big occasion.

In 1898, still a freshman and having been jumping for only two years, he won the long jump at a major meet in New York and in June of that year set a new world record of 23ft 9in (7.23m) at the New York Athletic Club Games. His great rival was Alvin Kraenzlein from the University of Pennsylvania, a man two years his senior. The pair tackled the long jump with differing styles. New York sports journalist Malcolm Ford wrote of Prinstein: 'He does not approach the takeoff with as much speed as Alvin Kraenzlein, but he gets higher up in the air and also in better shape . . . He has an unusually pretty style and impresses one that he always knows what he is doing.' However, it was Kraenzlein who seized the upper hand in 1899 with a world record leap of 24ft 4½in (7.43m), only for Prinstein to reclaim his record the following year at the Penn Relays in Philadelphia by jumping 24ft 7¼in (7.50m). Kraenzlein had the excuse that he was recuperating from malaria, but the ongoing battle between the two was heading for a showdown at the Paris Olympics. First the combatants had to get to Europe. Unable to afford the transatlantic tickets, Prinstein and three Syracuse team-mates accepted the generous offer of an oil baron who allowed them to travel free on one of his tankers. It was hardly a luxury voyage, but at least they were able to train on board the ship.

The qualifying round for the Olympic long jump took place on Saturday 14 July – Bastille Day in France – with Prinstein leaping 23ft 6½in (7.17m) to put himself in the lead. From the outset, Syracuse and several other Methodist-affiliated universities whose rules forbade their student athletes from competing on the Christian Sabbath had begged the French authorities not to schedule any events on a Sunday, but now it emerged that the final of the long jump would indeed take place on Sunday 15 July. The announcement was met with horror by the Syracuse contingent. After trying unsuccessfully to persuade the French to change their mind, the American athletes entered into a gentleman's agreement among themselves that none would compete on the Sunday. Prinstein agreed to this pact even though he was Jewish and the Sunday was not his Sabbath. He was apparently under the impression that Kraenzlein, too, was willing to pull out.

Yet when it came to the crunch, Kraenzlein showed up for the final and, by virtue of six unopposed jumps, pipped Prinstein's mark by a quarter of an inch to win the event. Although he did not compete in the final, the organisers sympathised with Prinstein's predicament and ruled that his qualifying jump should enable him to take second prize.

This was scant consolation for someone who believed his fellow countryman had betrayed him. On the Monday a furious Prinstein, convinced that he had been tricked out of Olympic glory, challenged Kraenzlein to a jump-off. When the man from Pennsylvania refused, Prinstein reportedly punched him in the face. Being a qualified dentist, Kraenzlein at least knew how to repair the damage.

The following day Prinstein took out his anger on the triple jump runway, powering down it to win the Olympic title with a leap of 47ft 5¾in (14.49m), defeating reigning champion James Connolly in the process. But he never forgave Kraenzlein, their feud becoming, according to the *Encyclopedia of Jews in Sports*, 'one of the most fabled in the early history of track and field'. Prinstein's sense of injustice was further fuelled by the fact that Kraenzlein was subsequently perceived as the hero of the Paris Olympics. For Kraenzlein's controversial victory in the long jump brought him his fourth Olympic title in the space of just two days (following on from the 60 metres dash, the 110 metres hurdles and the 200 metres hurdles). His achievement of four individual track and field triumphs at a single Olympics remains unsurpassed to this day.

Before their rivalry could produce further bloodshed, Kraenzlein retired from competition and Prinstein profited from his absence to pick up gold medals at both the long jump and triple jump on the same day at the 1904 Olympics, his leap of 24ft 1in (7.34m) in the long jump proving particularly satisfying as it eclipsed Kraenzlein's contentious Olympic record of four years earlier. By now a fully fledged lawyer, Prinstein also won gold in the long jump at the interim Athens Games of 1906, but these were later declared unofficial.

He died in 1925 at the age of 45 from a heart condition, leaving behind a wife and a young son. In its obituary Syracuse's *Post-Standard* described him as 'one of the greatest athletes developed at Syracuse University'. He was inducted post-humously into the International Jewish Sports Hall of Fame, his Olympic record standing as a monument to his talent . . . even though he was robbed of an additional title by what was, in his eyes anyway, the underhand behaviour of a compatriot.

THE BOY CHAMPION

PARIS, 26 AUGUST 1900

At the 1896 Games a Greek gymnast, Dimitris Loundras, finished third in the parallel bars at the tender age of 10 years and 218 days. Yet his achievement was surpassed at the Paris Olympics when a young boy – perhaps as young as seven – helped Dutch rowers Antoine Brandt and Roelof Klein to victory in the pair-oared shell with coxswain competition.

Brandt and Klein, representing the Minerva Club, Amsterdam, were warm favourites for the event but in their qualifying heat surprisingly finished more than eight seconds adrift of the French pair of Martinet and Waleff. It did not take a genius to work out the problem. For whereas the French teams reduced the weight in their boats by using children as coxes, the Dutch duo employed an adult coxswain, Dr Hermanus Brockmann, who weighed 132lb. So when it came to the final the Dutch decided to follow the French example and found a local boy who weighed barely half as much as Dr Brockmann. Incredibly, although the boy weighed a mere 72¾lb, he had already been rejected by the French teams as being too heavy! On the other hand, when they put the new cox into their boat, Brandt and Roelof discovered that he was too light to force the rudder under water, as a result of which they were obliged to attach a lead weight to the rudder.

With their youthful cox on board, Brandt and Roelof made a flying start to the final, determined to offset possible French underhand tactics whereby one boat would deliberately impede the Dutch by cutting in front early on in the race, thereby allowing the other to sprint ahead. The Dutch plan worked to perfection and although they inevitably tired in the closing stages, they held on to win by a couple of feet from the fast-finishing Martinet and Waleff, just 0.2sec separating the crews at the finish.

The young French cox stayed around long enough to have his photograph taken with the Olympic champions before vanishing into thin air. His name was never recorded and all attempts to trace him proved fruitless, but it seems certain that he is the youngest-ever winner of an Olympic competition. He certainly set the standard for young coxes in that event. When France's Raymond Salles and Gaston Mercier won in 1952, they used a fourteen-year-old coxswain, Bernard Malivore, and in 1960 the German gold medallists – Bernard Knubel and Heinz Renneberg – were accompanied by a thirteen-year-old cox, Klaus Zerta.

THE MARATHON IMPOSTOR

ST LOUIS, 30 AUGUST 1904

The 1904 Olympics were originally scheduled for Chicago but, at the request of United States President Theodore Roosevelt, who was also President of the US Olympic Committee, they were switched to St Louis to coincide with the Louisiana Purchase Exposition. Sadly the Americans reneged on their promise to send a ship to collect competitors from European ports, with the result that 85 per cent of those taking part in the Games were from the host nation. The few Europeans who did attend were forced to exist on a diet of boiled potatoes and milk because the main food on offer – buffalo meat – was deemed unpalatable.

For the first time gold, silver and bronze medals were awarded to the first three finishers, which was good news for William Dickey of the United States who won the 1904 Olympics' most unusual event – the plunge for distance. The competitors made a standing dive into a pool and then glided underwater as far as they could until being forced up for air! Dickey's winning distance was 62ft 6in (19.05m), but the event proved so tedious to spectators that it was dropped from future Olympics.

By contrast, Olympic marathons are rarely dull and the 1904 race was no exception. Among the favourites were Michael Spring, Thomas Hicks (an English-born brass worker from Massachusetts) and Fred Lorz, who had finished first, second and fifth respectively in that year's Boston Marathon. The 32-runner field also featured the first two black Africans to take part in the Olympics – Zulu tribesmen Lentauw and Mashiani, who were in St Louis as part of the Boer War exhibit at the Louisiana Purchase Exposition! Another entry was a 5ft-tall Cuban postman, Felix Carvajal, whose exploits even in getting to St Louis were worthy of recognition. After running the length of his own country, he caught a boat to the United States, only to lose all his travel money in a game of craps at New Orleans. Forced to hitch-hike all the way to St Louis, he arrived at the start line wearing his everyday clothes – a beret, a long-sleeved white shirt, long trousers and heavy boots. Even though discus thrower Martin Sheridan kindly cut off Carvajal's trousers at the knees, the little moustachioed Cuban still constituted a singular sight as he mingled with the immaculately turned out American college runners.

The race was to start and finish in the main stadium but the course in between was one of bumpy, dusty country roads and no fewer than seven stamina-sapping hills. In their wisdom, the organisers had decided to run the marathon in the afternoon, when temperatures would top 32.2 degrees Celsius (90 degrees Fahrenheit), and to incorporate just one water stop – a well some twelve miles from the stadium. Small wonder that only fourteen made it to the finish.

Some 5,000 spectators watched the runners set off at three minutes past three in hot, sultry conditions that suggested a thunderstorm was imminent. Hicks jostled for the early lead but it was Lorz, representing the Mohawk Athletic Club of New York, who was the first to pass through the east gate of the stadium into Olympian Way after the stipulated five laps of the track.

Once out on the open roads, where the route was marked by red flags, the runners began to suffer – none more so than Lorz who, hit by a combination of cramps and exhaustion, stopped after nine miles and climbed into a car. Fellow Americans Arthur Newton and Sam Mellor took over at the head of affairs, but soon Mellor was reduced to walking pace while John Lordon, another fancied home runner, began vomiting and was forced to drop out. By now the roads were deep in dust, the situation exacerbated by the legion of horsemen who galloped ahead to clear the thoroughfares for the athletes, hotly pursued by officials, physicians and journalists, all travelling in cars. At times the runners were scarcely visible through the clouds of dust, and at one point an official car swerved off the road and down an embankment, seriously injuring the two occupants, after the driver failed to spot one of the runners.

By the eleven-mile mark Mellor had recovered from his sticky patch and managed to catch the fading Newton. Hicks had moved up to third, followed by the Frenchman Albert Corey, a professional strike-breaker who had arrived in Chicago during a 1903 butchers' strike and, quickly aware that he would never be short of work there, decided to stay. Corey was running in tandem with San Francisco's William Garcia and they were pursued by the inimitable Carvajal, despite the fact that the Cuban stopped occasionally to chat to spectators along the route.

As Corey began to tire over the next few miles, Garcia suffered a considerably worse fate and was discovered lying unconscious at the side of the road following a stomach haemorrhage caused by the dust. Fortunately, medics were able to treat him in time. Mellor finally surrendered to the elements at sixteen miles, while the unlucky Lentauw lost valuable ground when he was chased off the road and through a cornfield by two wild dogs! With ten miles remaining Hicks found himself in the lead but he, too, was nearing exhaustion. Briefly revived by a sponge-down, he soon weakened again, although his advantage over his nearest rival was now an imposing one and a half miles. Hicks begged his helpers to allow him to lie down and rest but they refused and instead his attendant, Charles Lucas, administered an oral dose of strychnine mixed with raw egg white. Ironically beef tea was also available but Lucas thought better of it for fear of upsetting Hicks's stomach! A mile or so later, Hicks was given more strychnine – this time with egg and brandy – and his body was bathed in water warmed by being kept next to the boiler of the steam-powered automobile that accompanied him along the route. Despite suffering from hallucinations, Hicks pushed on. When a spectator asked him how he was feeling, Hicks replied:

'I want something to eat as soon as I get there. I'm nearly starved.'

Hicks must have thought he had survived everything that nature – and his helpers – could throw at him, but fate had one last nasty trick up its sleeve. With victory almost in sight, he was suddenly passed by Lorz, looking remarkably fresh. As Lorz sped off into the distance, negotiating the final two hills with remarkable ease, Hicks had to rely on more strychnine and brandy just to maintain some form of forward momentum. Indeed, he walked much of the last few miles before raising a defiant jog on entering the stadium.

That was 15 minutes after Lorz had crossed the finish line in a time of 3hr 13min. The New Yorker was immediately declared the winner and, milking the moment, had his photograph taken with Alice Roosevelt, the President's daughter. He was just about to be presented with the gold medal when the officials who accompanied the runners lodged a protest. It emerged that after dropping out at nine miles, Lorz had hitched a ride in a car for the next eleven miles but when the car had broken down some four miles from the stadium, he had decided to resume running. Lorz readily admitted the practical joke and insisted that he would have confessed . . . eventually. The Amateur Athletic Union failed to see the funny side and imposed a lifetime ban. However, the ban was soon lifted and Lorz went on to win the 1905 Boston Marathon by more conventional means.

Belatedly declared the Olympic champion, Hicks, still in a state of delirium, revealed that he would rather have won the race than be President of the United States. Having shed 16lb during the course of the marathon, he happily announced his retirement.

Corey finished second and Newton third, although the bronze medal would surely have gone to Carvajal had he not compounded his error of stopping to chat to spectators by making a short detour in the closing stages to pick some thirst-quenching apples from an orchard. Sadly for the Cuban, they were unripe and gave him severe stomach pains, which left him in agony and greatly hindered his progress. Thus he had to make the long journey home broke and without the medal that his endeavours surely deserved. Further back in the field, Lentauw recovered from his ordeal by dog to finish a creditable ninth . . . the highest-placed exhibit in Olympic history.

THE MAN WITH THE WOODEN LEG

ST LOUIS, 28 OCTOBER 1904

Given their overwhelming numerical superiority, it was hardly surprising that American competitors monopolised the medals table. One that got away, however, was the 50 metres freestyle. Hungary's Zoltan Halmay (winner of three swimming medals in 1900) clearly beat the American J Scott Leary by a foot, only for the American judge to declare Leary the winner. The result sparked an unseemly brawl between the two swimmers, a truce only being declared when the judges ordered a rematch. This time Halmay won easily.

But there was no stopping the Americans in the gymnastics competitions, where their star turn was one of the most remarkable individuals ever to grace the Olympic stage. Born in 1871, George Eyser had his left leg amputated after he was run over by a train, but this did not prevent him from participating in sport at the highest level . . . with a wooden left leg. In St Louis he represented a local club, Concordia Turnverein, and proceeded to pick up no fewer than six medals, three of them gold. Displaying remarkable strength and dexterity on a wide variety of apparatus, Eyser proved more than a match for his able-bodied opponents. He collected two gold medals in one day (28 October), on the long horse vault (in which he tied with fellow countryman Anton Heida) and the parallel bars, and also triumphed in the rope climb. He finished second in the pommel horse and the combined event, and picked up a bronze in the horizontal bar. To round things off, his club won the team

24

championship, although no medals were awarded for that particular feat.

Even though precious little is known about Eyser's later career, he did go on to represent Concordia at an international meeting in Frankfurt in 1908 and at a 1909 national meet in Cincinnati. He was, in short, an amazing gymnast who made light of his disability.

THE CHAMPION WHO NEVER WAS

LONDON, 11 JULY 1908

The 1908 Olympics were earmarked for Rome, but the eruption of Mount Vesuvius in 1906 brought about a hasty rethink. Faced with a massive bill to rebuild Naples, the Italian government decided that it could no longer finance the Olympics and so the Games were moved to London, where it was hoped that Britain's experience in staging such prestigious events as the Henley Regatta and the All-England Tennis Championships at Wimbledon would augur well for a smooth, trouble-free Olympics. As it turned out, the London Games were among the most controversial ever.

National pride was at the root of most of the recriminations. Even before the Games a number of Irish athletes withdrew in protest at being ordered to compete on behalf of Great Britain rather than their own country. Then at the opening ceremony Finland, which was then under Russian rule, refused to obey instructions to march under the Russian flag and instead opted to march under no flag at all. There were other mutterings of discontent but by far the deepest hostility was reserved for relations between Britain and the United States. The ill-feeling began when the US delegation noticed that the American flag was missing from the array of national flags decorating London's White City Stadium for the opening ceremony. At the official march past the US team's flag bearer, shot-putter Ralph Rose, pointedly refused to dip the Stars and Stripes to the royal box, as other countries had done. It was a calculated snub, and Rose did little to repair the damage by commenting famously and tersely: 'This flag dips to no earthly king.' From then on, the British were intent on taking their transatlantic visitors down a peg or two.

One of the worst clashes took place in a first-round tug-of-war contest between the USA and a British team from Liverpool Police. The stunned Americans were pulled over the line in a matter of seconds and promptly complained that the police had used illegal boots, adapted with steel spikes and heels in order to obtain a better grip. The Liverpudlians maintained that they were wearing regulation police boots and the protest was rejected, whereupon the Americans withdrew from the remainder of the competition. Liverpool eventually finished second to a team from the City of London Police whose captain, in an honourable attempt to build bridges, challenged the Americans to a friendly pull in stockinged feet, although there are no reports of the offer ever being taken up.

Amid all the acrimony with America, the British managed to contrive one controversy among themselves. The rules for the small-bore rifle, prone, event stated that each nation was restricted to twelve entries. When the entry form of Britain's George Barnes was mislaid, reserve Philip Plater was entered in his place. However, Barnes's form was then found and, because the USA had been granted an extension of the closing date for entries, the same courtesy was extended to the British, with the result that Barnes was readmitted to the team. Alas, it appears that nobody bothered to inform Plater and so Britain went into competition day with thirteen entries. It would prove unlucky for one.

As the competition drew to a close, chaos reigned as the British team officials completely lost count of the number of British marksmen who had shot. In the belief that only eleven had fired, Plater was allowed to start even though there was barely half an hour remaining. Flitting from mat to mat, Plater put in an inspired performance and managed to fire off his allotted eighty rounds within the time limit. In his forty rounds from 50 yards he dropped a mere five points and from a distance of 100 yards he fell just four short of the maximum.

The result was that Plater was declared Olympic champion with a world record total of 391 points.

But then it dawned on the bumbling Brits that all twelve members of the official team had already shot before Plater came to the mat. As arguments raged, they tried to decide whether it should be the score of Plater or that of Barnes to be erased from the records. A few days later they solemnly declared that Barnes was the official British entrant, thus ensuring that Plater's achievement would not be recognised and that he would lose his gold medal. Instead his compatriot Arthur Carnell took gold with 387 points – four fewer than the unfortunate Plater. By way of scant consolation, the British Olympic Council subsequently presented Plater with a special gold medal and a diploma of his score, but his performance was expunged from the Games records and he remains the Olympic champion who never was.

THE JOSTLING MATCH

LONDON, 23 JULY 1908

In the early years of the twentieth century running races in the United States could sometimes be roughhouse affairs. They were not always run in lanes and it was by no means uncommon for athletes to interfere with fellow competitors in the course of a race. Nudging, pushing, blocking – indeed, almost anything short of tripping – was considered fair game. But when the Americans tried to bring these dubious tactics to the 1908 Olympics, a fearful furore ensued as the British cried 'foul'.

Having swept all before them in the sprints at the three previous Games, the Americans were confident of a repeat performance in London. But standing in their way in the 400 metres was a stubborn Briton, Lt Wyndham Halswelle, a 26-year-old London-born Scot whose speed had first been spotted during the Boer War. It was while serving with the Highland Light Infantry in South Africa that Halswelle impressed former professional athlete Jimmy Curran who, on the regiment's return to Edinburgh at the end of the war, persuaded Halswelle to take up the sport seriously. At the unofficial 1906 Olympics in Athens, Halswelle repaid Curran's faith by collecting a silver medal in the 400 metres and a bronze in the 800 metres. Two years later and his form was even better. He set the fastest time in both the Olympic heats and in the semi-finals, where he set a new Olympic record time of 48.4sec to earn a place in the final alongside three Americans – John Taylor, William Robbins and John Carpenter.

Before the final (which was actually run over 440 yards rather than the metric equivalent) British officials expressed concern that the American trio might gang up on Halswelle and employ what could be euphemistically described as 'team tactics' to secure the gold medal at the expense of a clearly superior opponent. With the race not being run in lanes, these fears were heightened and officials were accordingly stationed every 20 yards around the track in case of foul play. Furthermore, the starter made a point of warning the four finalists about jostling.

In anticipation of a British victory, a large crowd assembled but it was Robbins who stormed into the lead and held an advantage of some twelve yards at the halfway point. However, the early pace took its toll and rounding the final bend he was overtaken by Carpenter and Halswelle, the latter looking ominously strong and full of running. Entering the home straight, Halswelle decided to make his move but as he tried to pass Carpenter on the outside, the American deliberately veered across his path, severely hampering Halswelle's progress and, in the space of twenty yards, forcing him to within eighteen inches of the surrounding bicycle track. At that point one of the British umpires intervened and ordered the judges to break the finishing tape before Carpenter could reach it. As confusion reigned, a protesting Taylor was dragged from the track by officials. It was half an hour until the track could be cleared properly and another thirty minutes before a verdict of 'no race' was announced and Carpenter disqualified for 'boring'.

The Times correspondent had no doubt as to his guilt, writing: 'It certainly seemed as if the Americans had run the race on a definite and carefully thought-out plan. It was not as if Carpenter, the one who forced Halswell [sic] to run wide, and elbowed him severely as he tried to pass him, had himself taken a wide curve at the bend and then run straight on. He appeared rather to run diagonally, crossing in front of the Englishman [sic] so that he was obliged to lose several yards, and finally could only run on the extreme outside edge of the track.'

It was decreed that the final should be re-run two days later – without Carpenter – and that this time strings should be laid out to divide the lanes in order to prevent a repeat of the unsavoury incident. However, Robbins and Taylor were so aggrieved at their team-mate's treatment that they flatly refused to take part. Halswelle himself had no desire to run unless the two Americans were present and was even willing to sacrifice gold but British officials persuaded him to forsake his principles. Thus on 25 July Halswelle completed the formalities, being cheered to a hollow victory in a time of 50sec. It was all very unsatisfactory.

The *New York Press* newspaper certainly thought so. Beneath the headline 'BAD LOSERS', it wrote: 'Our uncousinly competitors have to learn how to win from American athletes, and they still more need to learn how to lose.' In London *The Times* countered: 'Interfering with another runner is considered fair in America and Carpenter saw nothing wrong in acting on that principle. However, as the race was run in England, where tactics of this kind are contrary alike to the rules that govern sport and to our notions of what is fair play, the committee had no option but to punish the offender.'

As a result of this – and other controversies at the Games – the International Olympic Committee decided that in future judges would be drawn from an international pool rather than be provided by the host nation. And to combat the discrepancy in track and field rules in different countries, the International Amateur Athletics Association was formed in 1912 with a view to standardising rules and regulations. Interference on the track would no longer be tolerated, even in America.

The unhappiest gold medallist of the Games, Wyndham Halswelle was so disgusted by the whole affair that he quit athletics and returned to his regiment. On 31 March 1915 he was killed by a sniper's bullet while serving in France during the First World War.

THE PERILS
OF THE POOL

LONDON, 24 JULY 1908

Four years after being involved in an Olympic brawl at St Louis, Hungarian swimmer Zoltan Halmay faced a fresh peril in the pool at London . . . and this time it nearly cost him his life. Swimming the final leg of the 4×200 metres freestyle relay, Halmay looked certain to seal gold for his country until he suddenly began to lose consciousness over the last 50 metres. As Halmay started flailing in the water, Henry Taylor capitalised on the Hungarian's plight to swoop past and snatch an unlikely gold for Britain. Halmay just about managed to struggle to the finish, but had to be dragged from the pool before he drowned.

Halmay was not the first casualty in the pool at the 1908 Games. In the preliminary round of the platform diving, Britain's George Cane dived in with his mouth open and, as he hit the water awkwardly, ruptured a small blood vessel in his chest, causing him to lose consciousness. Luckily Cane was saved by the quick thinking of Sweden's Hjalmar Johansson, who dived in and pulled him from the water. Artificial respiration was administered and Cane soon recovered.

Johansson was rewarded for his efforts by going on to take gold, but even that was tinged with bitterness. George Gaidzik of the United States achieved the highest score in the preliminary round but was disqualified in the semi-finals after one of the judges accused him of receiving coaching signals from a team-mate. Not for the first time – nor the last – the

American team protested and Gaidzik was allowed through to the final as an additional qualifier. But the controversy had taken its toll and Gaidzik could finish only fifth.

HER MAJESTY'S PLEASURE

LONDON, 24 JULY 1908

In the course of the first four Olympics the marathon distance varied at the whim of the organisers. At Athens in 1896 it measured 250 yards short of 25 miles. The 1900 race in Paris was 'about 25 miles' and at St Louis in 1904 it again fell fractionally short of 25 miles at 24 miles and 1,500 metres. When the Games came to England, officials wanted to put on a race fit for a queen – Queen Alexandra, wife of Edward VII – and intended that the marathon course should be one of 25 miles with the last third of a mile run inside the White City Stadium in West London. To underline the royal connection, they selected the grounds of Windsor Castle as a suitable starting-point, only to discover that this would extend the marathon to considerably in excess of 25 miles. Throwing caution to the wind, the organisers agreed to start the race on the East Terrace of the castle and outlined a course that would measure precisely 26 miles to the entrance of the stadium. An additional lap of White City would have made the total distance 26 miles and 586 yards, but it was decided instead that the ideal finish point was directly opposite the royal box. And it was this distance – 26 miles, 385 yards – that would in years to come be adopted as the official length of the marathon.

If any concerns were raised about forcing the athletes to run an extra mile and a quarter, they were overridden by the desire to stage a royal spectacle, to give the Queen an afternoon to remember. As it turned out, it was one she would never forget.

Fifty-five runners lined up at the start, among them the Onondoga Indian teenager Tom Longboat, from Toronto, Canada, winner of the 1907 Boston marathon; John Hayes of the United States, fresh from winning the inaugural Yonkers marathon in New York; British ace Alex Duncan who, in appalling April conditions, had won the official national trial over 22½ miles of the Olympic route; Charles Hefferon of South Africa; and a little Italian pastry cook from Capri whose name was printed in the programme as Pietri Dorando. However, it subsequently emerged that the editor had inadvertently transposed the names and that the Italian should have been listed as Dorando Pietri.

Born in 1885, Pietri's chosen sport was cycling but he soon turned to running and won his first national title over a distance of fifteen miles in 1905. On 3 June 1908 he was one of only three athletes competing in the inaugural Italian marathon championship in Rome – a race that doubled as the country's Olympic trial. Despite being the favourite on the strength of his previous runs, Pietri dropped out at twenty miles but was still selected for the Games after running creditably in a 25-mile race just seventeen days before the Olympic marathon. He arrived in London virtually unknown outside his homeland but would soon be elevated to the status of national treasure – England's favourite foreigner at a time when outsiders were invariably viewed with deep suspicion.

The Polytechnic Harriers Club had made such a good job of organising the April trial from Windsor to Wembley Park that it was entrusted with staging the Olympic marathon. The Oxo Company was awarded the role of official caterer and undertook to provide refreshments for the runners along the route in the form of hot and cold Oxo, Oxo and soda, rice pudding, raisins, bananas and milk. The Oxo representatives were also on hand to offer eau de Cologne and wet sponges, as a result of which the competitors have been described as 'the best fed and most fragrant marathon runners in history'. The rules stipulated that the athletes had to wear 'complete clothing from the shoulder to the knees (i.e. jersey sleeved to the elbows and loose drawers with slips)' and they were allowed to use the waiting rooms at Windsor railway station for the purpose of changing into their running gear. To protect his head from the heat, Pietri decided to top off his outfit with that most English of fashion accessories, the white knotted handkerchief.

On a sultry Friday afternoon, the prospect of hot Oxo must have seemed about as welcome as an attack of cramp as the runners lined up in four rows in the shadow of the castle. In keeping with the royal theme, the race was started by the Princess of Wales, who set the competitors underway at 2.30 p.m. prompt. Vast numbers of Eton schoolboys turned out to watch as the runners headed past the college on their way to Slough. The heat was particularly intense across Uxbridge Common and, as *The Times* wrote, 'It was a relief to get into the more shady roads near Ickenham and Ruislip.'

The early pace was set by the Scotsman Thomas Jack, who ran the first mile in a little over five minutes, a standard he maintained for the next two miles. In such humid conditions it was inevitable that this exertion would take its toll and after five miles an exhausted Jack began to drop back through the field. Another Briton, Jack Price, took over and at the halfway stage at Ruislip he led by 200 yards from Hefferon, Fred Lord of Great Britain and Pietri. Hefferon, who had previously finished fourth in the Olympic five-mile race, had kept a watching brief in the early stages and was now looking ominously strong. Shortly after fourteen miles he swept into the lead and at fifteen miles led Lord by two minutes, Price having retired. Lord, too, was feeling the strain and when he stopped for a rest, both Pietri and Longboat passed him. Lord eventually finished a remote fifteenth. With Longboat reduced to walking, the race seemed set to become a straight fight between the powerful Hefferon and the 5ft 3in Italian.

At twenty miles, the South African held an advantage of almost four minutes but, ignoring the heat, Pietri started to close the gap as countryside gave way to city. Behind him the Americans, led by John Hayes, were also beginning to make a move. The US team were still aggrieved over their treatment in the previous day's controversial 400 metres and Hayes, in particular, had a point to prove, having been robbed of a possible victory in the 1907 Boston marathon (the race won by Longboat) after being delayed crucially at a level crossing while waiting for a train to pass.

At the 22-mile mark Pietri had reduced the deficit to less than three minutes and by the time Hefferon reached the Clock Tower, Harlesden, at 24 miles, his lead had been cut to just two minutes. Foregoing the plentiful supplies of Oxo on offer, Hefferon instead sought urgent refreshment by accepting a drink of champagne. It was to prove a fatal error, for almost immediately he started getting cramps and feeling dizzy. The fast-closing Italian spotted his prey for the first time in Old Oak Common Lane, where the enthusiastic crowds repeatedly slapped Hefferon on the back in a bid to encourage him – actions that merely served to drain his last remaining reserves of energy. At the same time the spectators urged Pietri on to even greater efforts and a mile from the stadium he duly took the lead for the first time.

Behind, Hayes, too, was about to pass Hefferon. The American, who had enjoyed a light lunch of two ounces of beef and two slices of toast washed down by a cup of tea, had eschewed any refreshment along the route and, having run comfortably within himself, was still relatively fresh. However, he had little hope of catching the leader over the remaining mile unless, of course, some dramatic fate were to befall Pietri.

Out in front, Pietri began to feel increasingly weary. The encouragement of the crowd had prompted him to sprint for home sooner than he would have wished and now as he crossed Wormwood Scrubs with the giant White City Stadium within sight, he was paying the price. With timekeepers buzzing around in front of him, Pietri staggered towards the stadium, his frail body wilting in the oppressive, relentless heat. Inside, 75,000 seated spectators peered expectantly in the direction of the entrance, ready to acclaim the victor, and another 25,000 stood shoulder to shoulder around the perimeter of the track. In the royal box, the Queen waited. At last the small, moustachioed Italian came into view, wandering aimlessly down the ramp that led on to the cinder track. *The Times* described the scene: 'A tired man, dazed, bewildered, hardly conscious, in red shorts and white vest, his hair white with dust, staggers on to the track. It is Dorando, the Italian. He looks about him, hardly knowing where he is.'

Instinctively he turned right instead of left on to the track and had to be pointed in the correct direction by officials. The blunder not only sapped his energy yet further but also left him increasingly disorientated. A few yards on, his legs gave way completely and he crumbled to the ground in a heap. The crowd screamed. As officials and doctors rushed to his aid, he managed to scramble to his feet, only to fall three more times. On each occasion he was helped to his feet by concerned officials, who sponged him down in an effort to revive him. One correspondent described him as 'simply a flounder, with arms shaking and legs tottering'. Gallantly he battled on, drawing upon uncharted reserves. It was painful to watch. Still surrounded by officials (among them Sir Arthur Conan Doyle, creator of Sherlock Holmes) hovering over his every faltering step, Pietri tottered towards the tape. Suddenly, fifty yards from the finish, he suddenly burst into what *The Times* called 'a pathetic, almost a horrible, parody of a sprint'. It came to an abrupt halt ten yards from the tape when he fell yet again. As the Official Report of the Games later noted: 'It was impossible to leave him there, for it looked as if he might die in the very presence of the Queen.' Sensing that such an occurrence might mar Her Majesty's enjoyment of the day, chief race organiser Jack Andrew jumped to Pietri's aid and helped him across the line.

While the Italian contingent celebrated a glorious victory, the stricken Pietri was taken away on a stretcher and Hayes crossed the line as runner-up, 32 seconds adrift in a time of 2hr 55min 18.4sec. Hefferon finished another 48 seconds back in third, ahead of the Americans Joseph Foreshaw and Alton Welton. With the home athletes paying the price for their suicidal early pace, none finished in the top ten. Only 27 runners – less than half the field – finished.

The Italian flag was immediately run up the victory pole but not surprisingly the American team lodged a formal protest on the grounds that Pietri had been helped across the finish line. The protest was upheld and the plucky Italian disqualified.

For two and a half hours Pietri hovered between life and death. He later recounted: 'I was literally a dead man. My heart had moved half an inch out of place with the strain of the run, and I did the last stretch by instinct. They brought me back to life by massaging my heart into place.'

Remarkably, by the following day he had made a full recovery and was well enough to chastise the officials for dashing to his rescue, insisting that he could have finished unaided. Jack Andrew defended himself against criticism by maintaining that he had not actually helped Pietri but had simply caught him as he fell at the tape.

Although the Italian's criticism seems unjustified and perhaps a shade ungrateful, he was accorded a hero's welcome on 25 July when he returned to the stadium to receive a special gold cup from the Queen, who had been so moved by his bravery of the previous day. The inscription read: 'For Pietri Dorando, In remembrance of the Marathon Race from Windsor to London. From Queen Alexandra.' When he entered the White City for the presentation, the other competitors raised their hats to him and some lifted him shoulder high. Even the gymnasts who had been giving a display in the middle of the arena abandoned their routine and sprinted across the grass to catch a better glimpse of the unlikely hero. As Pietri acknowledged the crowd by waving his cloth cap, their cheers drowned out the megaphone announcer. The only hint of disquiet came from the Americans, who were concerned that the feting of Pietri would detract from Hayes's achievement.

Their fears were by no means misplaced. Hayes, the winner, was quickly forgotten outside the United States. He had done much of his Olympic training by running on a cinder path on the roof of Bloomingdale's Department Store in New York, where he worked. His reward for victory was promotion to manager of the sports goods department. Meanwhile Dorando Pietri, the gallant loser, became a household name throughout the sporting world. He was given a special reception on his return to Turin the following month and a Tin Pan Alley songwriter, Izzy Baline, penned a ditty in his honour, entitled simply 'Dorando'. The composer later went on to achieve fame as Irving Berlin. The 1908 Olympics were good for both men.

Pietri turned professional soon afterwards, as indeed did Hayes. They met in two marathon matches around Madison Square Garden, New York, Pietri emerging triumphant on both occasions to gain revenge for London. Less than a month after the first of these victories, he took on Tom Longboat in another Madison Square Garden match but, with alarming echoes of the Olympic marathon, the Italian collapsed during the 26th mile and was carried unconscious from the indoor track. He received $3,750 for his pains.

Upon retirement from running, Dorando Pietri ran a café and worked as a taxi driver. Britain's Harold Abrahams, the 1924 Olympic 100-metres champion, subsequently described him in *World Sports* magazine as 'the most famous name in all the history of the modern Olympic Games'. Reflecting on the race that turned Pietri into a celebrity, Abrahams concluded: 'All the runners who set off at such a fast pace paid the penalty. The winner, Hayes, was not near the front until more than three-quarters of the total distance had been covered. If only Dorando had run more slowly, he might have been the Olympic marathon winner of 1908, and in all probability no one today would ever have heard of him.'

THE ENDLESS BOUT

STOCKHOLM, 14 JULY 1912

The 1912 Olympics are chiefly remembered for something that happened six months after the Games, when American Jim Thorpe, winner of both the decathlon and pentathlon, was sensationally stripped of his medals on the grounds that he was a professional (he had previously played minor league baseball). Yet few people recall that an even more famous American was also competing in Stockholm. Finishing fifth in the modern pentathlon was Lieutenant George S Patton, who later became one of his country's leading generals during the Second World War.

Sweden did not allow boxing contests to be staged but there was no bar on Greco-Roman wrestling, a modern variation on the ancient sport, which had been created in France in the early nineteenth century and by 1912 was popular throughout Scandinavia. The principal difference between Greco-Roman and freestyle wrestling was that in the former the legs could not be used in any way to obtain a fall and no holds could be taken below the waist.

The light-heavyweight final between Anders Ahlgren of Sweden and Ivar Böhling of Finland achieved notoriety for lasting nine hours without a decision being reached. En route to the final the impressive Ahlgren had pinned six opponents, each inside 35 minutes, but he was unable to break down the resistance of the dogged Finn. After nine hours with no sign of a breakthrough and both wrestlers suffering in the heat, the judges declared it a draw. Since Olympic rules stipulated that

41

the first place winner actually had to defeat his opponent, neither man was able to claim gold and they both had to settle for silver medals instead. It had been a lot of effort for very little reward.

Curiously this was not the longest Greco-Roman bout in Stockholm. In comparison the middleweight semi-final between Martin Klein of Russia and Alfred 'Alpo' Asikainen of Finland made the Ahlgren–Böhling final look like a sprint. It took place in such intense heat that the wrestlers had to stop every half-hour for a refreshment break until finally, after eleven hours and forty minutes, Klein won by pinning his opponent. Sadly the exertions proved too much for the Russian and exhaustion prevented him fighting in the final. The gold medal therefore went to Sweden's Claes Johanson by default!

THE PICNIC CASE

STOCKHOLM, 14 JULY 1912

The 1912 Olympic marathon more than lived up to the reputation for drama set by its predecessors. Run in unusually hot conditions for Scandinavia, it witnessed the first Olympic death, a victory marred by accusations of broken promises and, most bizarrely of all, a runner who dropped out halfway to join a family picnic!

Athletes converged on Stockholm from far and wide to take part in the marathon, which was to be run on a course to Sollentuna and back. The South African pair of Christian Gitsham and Kenneth McArthur represented a considerable threat to the traditionally strong American team. Thirty-year-old McArthur, a sturdily built farmer's son from County Antrim, used to work as a postman in Ireland, where he often ran his entire fifteen-mile daily round. Upon emigrating to South Africa in 1905 he became a policeman and probably proved a match for any fleeing burglar, particularly over long distances. He won a major marathon in Cape Town in 1910 and was considered a serious rival to the lithe Gitsham who finished second to Canada's James Corkery in the 1912 Polytechnic Harriers Marathon in Britain. Corkery may well have broken the world record but for being sent the wrong way on entering the stadium, as a result of which he completed only 480 yards on the track instead of the required 840. Meanwhile Tatu Kolehmainen was setting new standards for marathon running in Finland and Shizo Kanaguri, one of the first Asian competitors at the Olympics, carried Japanese hopes.

43

On the day before the Olympic race, Gitsham set out to run the complete marathon distance as part of his training. On hearing of Gitsham's plan, his horrified coach set off in hot pursuit, caught up with him after he had run twelve miles and angrily returned him to the hotel.

When Kolehmainen lined up for the start of the Stockholm marathon at 1.45 p.m. the following afternoon with 67 other runners, he was looking for a family hat-trick, his brother Hannes having already completed the 5,000 metres and 10,000 metres double within the previous week. Tatu set off strongly and led the field in the early stages from Sweden's Alex Ahlgren and Italy's Carlo Speroni, with the South African pair in close contention. By the second control point at Tureberg, Kolehmainen held a thirteen-second lead over the South Africans, but by the halfway point and turn at Sollentuna, Gitsham had forced his way to the front. He was fifteen seconds ahead of the ailing Finn, with McArthur another twenty seconds back in third.

Further down the field Kanaguri was struggling to cope with the heat. In a state of near collapse he stumbled into the garden of a Swedish family who were enjoying a picnic on that glorious summer afternoon. Invited to join the gathering, he needed no second invitation and, after being refreshed with drinks of raspberry juice, he accepted their generous offer of a bed on which to lay his weary head. When he awoke, it was far too late to rejoin the race and so the family gave him clothing and put him on a train back to Stockholm. Embarrassed at having failed to complete the marathon, he decided not to tell anyone and quietly caught a boat home to Japan.

Back at the race, Kolehmainen had gained a second wind and by the time they reached Tureberg again (the seventeen-mile mark) he had caught up with Gitsham. Just a second behind in third was the menacing figure of McArthur, looking full of running. But the energy expended in chasing Gitsham now left Kolehmainen drained and he dropped out a couple of miles later, leaving the two South Africans in control. As is often the case with two equally talented sportsmen from the same country, there was a fierce rivalry between them. One only has to think of Britain's Sebastian Coe and Steve Ovett in the 1980s. Gitsham and McArthur were said to be barely on speaking terms, each apparently resenting the other's success, and now it looked like a straight fight between the two to the finish with neither prepared to yield an inch.

In view of the animosity between the two it seems incredible that they should strike a pact to stay together until the finish, but H B Keartland, manager of the South African team, insisted afterwards that such an agreement had been reached. So as the pair approached a long hill two miles from the stadium and Gitsham stopped at a refreshment stand to take a drink, he expected McArthur to wait for him. Instead McArthur seized the opportunity to push on and open up a decisive gap on his great rival. His rhythm destroyed by the stop, Gitsham was unable to respond and McArthur steadily stretched his advantage, his only blip occurring inside the stadium when a well-wisher placed a laurel wreath in the colours of South Africa over his shoulders, the greeting momentarily throwing him off-stride. Although visibly tiring, McArthur battled on to the finish and breasted the tape in a time of 2hr 36min 54.8sec. Gitsham followed on almost a minute behind to complete a one-two for South Africa, with Gaston Strobino of the United States taking bronze.

After the race harsh words were said to have been exchanged between McArthur and Gitsham as a result of the broken promise. McArthur's camp maintained that their man had paused to wait but ran on when Gitsham developed cramp at the refreshment post.

However, this squabble paled into insignificance the following day when the Portuguese record holder, 21-year-old Francisco Lazaro, died in hospital after collapsing during the marathon. Ironically Lazaro, who passed a pre-race medical, claimed beforehand that the Stockholm course was much easier than the one to which he was accustomed in the mountains of his homeland, but a combination of sun stroke and heart failure caused him to keel over in the closing stages of the race. He was given first aid on the spot and rushed to hospital, but all attempts to revive him proved in vain. Although in the wake of the tragedy it was proposed that the marathon be dropped from future Olympics, the event continued to be a mainstay of the Games.

While the Olympic fraternity mourned the loss of Lazaro, officials were trying to locate the other 33 runners who had failed to finish because of the extreme heat. All were accounted for except one – Shizo Kanaguri. Unaware that he had fled the country, the officials called in the Swedish police in a bid to find him and when the search proved fruitless, he was officially declared a missing person. Kanaguri's whereabouts became something of a joke in Sweden – akin to sightings of Lord Lucan in Britain in the 1970s – and some claimed he was still running around the streets trying to find his way back to the stadium. Other 'sightings' revealed that he had last been seen with a beautiful Swedish girl on each arm.

In 1962, on the fiftieth anniversary of the race, a Stockholm journalist was despatched to Japan to track down the elusive runner and found him teaching geography in the town of Tamana. Kanaguri had no idea that he had achieved cult status in Sweden. Five years later, at the age of 76, he returned to Stockholm to open a new department store. From there he was taken to the Olympic Stadium where, to the delight of the Swedes, he finally jogged across the finish line . . . to complete a marathon that he had begun 55 years earlier.

LOST IN THE TRANSLATION

ANTWERP, 16 AUGUST 1920

With war looming, the IOC hoped that by awarding the 1916 Olympics to Berlin conflict could somehow be averted, but when it became clear that – surprisingly – Germany placed territorial gains and European domination ahead of the prospect of a bronze medal in the triple jump, the Games were cancelled. For 1920 they were awarded to Antwerp in honour of the terrible suffering experienced by the Belgian people during the First World War. Germany, Austria and their allies Bulgaria and Hungary were not invited to participate.

Recognising that the country was still in turmoil after serving as one huge battlefield for four years, visiting athletes made allowances for the standard of Belgian accommodation. All except the Americans, that is. US triple jumper Dan Ahearn was so horrified by the state of the derelict schoolhouse that was designated as his living quarters that he refused to stay there and found somewhere else, whereupon he was thrown off the team. His 200 team-mates promptly signed a petition demanding that unless the accommodation was improved and Ahearn reinstated they would withdraw from competition. Faced with revolt, American Olympic officials allowed Hearn to rejoin the team, although there is no indication that any significant changes were made to the accommodation.

Among the American party was rower John B Kelly, father of future Hollywood star Grace Kelly. Earlier in the year he had been refused entry to the Henley Regatta on the grounds that, as a bricklayer, he had an unfair advantage over 'gentlemen'.

Kelly proved himself in Antwerp by collecting two golds. Another controversial American Olympian was swimmer Ethelda Bleibtrey who, in 1919, had been charged under local decency laws with swimming 'nude' at a public beach. All she had actually done to incur the wrath of the authorities was to remove her stockings on Manhattan Beach in full view of the lifeguards, but in those days society dictated that American women wear swimsuits that covered all their skin. Outrage at her arrest forced New York's city council to amend their indecency laws. Bleibtrey cemented her popularity with the American public by winning three gold medals in Antwerp.

Ethelda Bleibtrey's misdemeanours were negligible compared to those of US shooter James Howard Snook, winner of two golds at the 1920 Olympics. Eight years later Snook, by then a professor of veterinary medicine at Ohio State University, was executed in the electric chair after being convicted of bludgeoning his mistress to death with a hammer.

The American team at Antwerp fielded a particularly strong line-up in the sprints, with no fewer than four men – Charley Paddock, Morris Kirksey, Jackson Scholz and Loren Murchison – making it through to the final of the 100 metres. The Texan Paddock had a running style all of his own, his arms and legs flailing like a drowning man, culminating in a flying leap for the tape that frequently snatched victory from the jaws of defeat at the expense of startled opponents. He also went through a laboured ritual at the start, first insisting on finding a piece of wood to touch for good luck and then, when called to his mark, putting his hands way across the line and drawing them slowly back before the call of 'Get set'. Murchison, for one, was not overawed by Paddock. Unhindered by the slightest lack of confidence, the self-styled golden boy of American athletics spent the hours in the build-up to the final repeating to his team-mates over and over again, 'I'm going to win it.' Although they tried to ignore him, Murchison's mantra must have been wearing pretty thin by the time of the race.

As the runners lined up at the start, Paddock was the last to stoop to his mark. Spotting that Paddock's hands were well over the line but being unaware of the athlete's ritual, the assistant starter ordered him in French to pull back his hands, which he was in the process of doing anyway. The starter then called out *prêt*, meaning 'Get set'. However, Murchison's powers of motivation clearly exceeded his command of French, for he misunderstood the exchange and thought the runners had been instructed to stand up in readiness for another start. So he was just beginning to relax his body when, to his horror, the gun went off. Hopelessly stranded ten yards behind the other runners, Murchison could only watch his dreams of an Olympic gold medal disappear into the distance.

At the business end of the race Kirksey and Paddock fought out a tremendous finish, Paddock snatching the verdict by virtue of his familiar flying leap. Britain's Harry Edward took bronze, while Murchison trailed in last.

Four days later, in the final of the 200 metres, it was Edward's turn to miss the break. Running with a strapped leg after pulling a muscle in his semi-final, Edward lost five yards at the start but, his face contorted in pain, powered through to take third place, just a yard and a half behind the winner, Allen Woodring of the United States.

As for Murchison, he gained some compensation by helping the American quartet to gold in the 4×100 metres relay. His team-mates were probably not sure what he needed most – lessons in humility or lessons in French.

SICK AS A GUILLEMOT

ANTWERP, 20 AUGUST 1920

Between 1920 and 1928 Paavo Nurmi – the Flying Finn – won nine gold and three silver medals to establish himself as one of the all-time Olympic greats. His feats were particularly impressive because they were achieved in endurance events and invariably involved a punishing schedule, not only in training but also on the track itself.

Few people were better groomed to cope with adversity than Nurmi, who was born into hardship in Turku in 1897. His father, a humble carpenter, died of haemoptysis in 1910 and, with the family unable to survive on the mother's meagre income as a cleaner, the twelve-year-old Paavo was forced to give up school and find a job. Working as an errand boy for a bakery, he spent his days pushing heavy goods carts up and down steep hills, thereby strengthening the leg muscles that would carry him to glory later in life. He began running alone through the woods and when, at the 1912 Olympics, Hannes Kolehmainen put Finland on the athletics map of the world by winning three distance races – 5,000 metres, 10,000 metres and individual cross-country – Nurmi resolved to follow in his illustrious footsteps. Armed with his first pair of running shoes, Nurmi started serious training and in 1914 joined the Turku Sports Association, soon winning a 3,000 metres race. In 1919 he was drafted into military service, where he attracted attention for his remarkable performances on twenty-kilometre marches, which he won by such wide margins that he was suspected of having taken short cuts. But whereas his fellow soldiers marched under the weight of the obligatory rifle and 11lb sack of sand, Nurmi ran the whole way! His selection for Finland's 1920 Olympic team was a mere formality.

Nurmi's opening race in Antwerp was a qualifying heat of the 5,000 metres on Monday 16 August. With the first four runners going through to the final, he paced himself perfectly, sprinting effortlessly in the final stretch to move into second spot, five seconds behind Italy's Carlo Speroni. The following day's final was run at 3.15 p.m., on one of the hottest days of the year. Nurmi devised a bold front-running strategy to draw the sting out of the dangerous Swedes Eric Backman and Runar Falk but had reckoned without the twenty-year-old Frenchman, Joseph Guillemot. Born with his heart on the right side of his chest, the diminutive Guillemot trained on a packet of cigarettes a day. Before the 5,000 metres final his trainer handed him a mysterious liquid and told him: 'Swallow this and you will be unbeatable.' The concoction turned out to be nothing more than a mixture of water, sugar and rum, but, as Nurmi was to discover to his cost, it produced the desired effect.

At first everything went according to plan for the Finn. He took the lead from Speroni at the end of the third lap and tried to burn off the Swedes. The 3,000-metre mark was passed two seconds inside Kolehmainen's time when breaking the world record at Stockholm in the 1912 Games, but try as he might, Nurmi could not shake off the doughty Guillemot. Entering the last lap, the Frenchman was poised waiting to pounce and sure enough he swooped past on the final bend. Nurmi, with nothing left to give, jogged dejectedly across the line, twenty yards adrift. It was to be the only distance race Nurmi would lose for eight years.

Nurmi had no time to lick his wounds. Two days later he was back in action for a qualifying heat of the 10,000 metres, finishing a comfortable second behind Scotland's James Wilson. The final took place the next day – Friday 20 August – and was brought forward from 5.30 p.m. to 2.15 p.m. at the request of the King of Belgium, who wanted to attend an art exhibition. Unfortunately the change of schedule was not relayed to Guillemot until just *after* he had eaten a substantial pre-race lunch . . .

The defeat in the 5,000 metres still gnawing away at him, Nurmi opted for a new game plan, stalking the fastest man in the qualifying heats, fellow Finn Heikki Liimatainen. As the race developed Guillemot and Wilson set the pace with Nurmi back in the pack, but it soon became apparent that Liimatainen was struggling. So Nurmi abandoned the plan and, in company with Italy's Augusto Maccario, set about reining in the leaders. With one kilometre remaining, Nurmi had made up the ground and as they began the last lap his only rival was the replete Guillemot. This time Nurmi had the measure of him. Easing off along the back stretch, he allowed the Frenchman to take the lead but with the crowd sensing that Nurmi would have to settle for a second silver, he gave Guillemot a taste of his own medicine by surging past on the final bend and going on to win by eight yards. Nurmi's time of 31min 45.8 sec – over a minute faster than his personal best – ensured him of a warm welcome, not least from Guillemot who, feeling decidedly queasy, brought up his lunch all over the Finn's shoes! Nurmi remained unfazed and unsmiling. His tragic childhood had left him incapable of showing much emotion.

Nurmi and Guillemot met again three days later in the individual cross-country, run over a course of around 8,000 metres. It developed into a battle between Nurmi, Guillemot and Backman until, three kilometres from the finish, the unlucky Guillemot stepped in a hole and had to drop out with an ankle injury. Although Backman led into the stadium, Nurmi produced a devastating sprint finish to collect his second individual gold and help Finland to the cross-country team championship (for which he also picked up a gold medal). He would be back four years later, ready to rewrite the Olympic record books.

THE ABANDONED SOCCER FINAL

ANTWERP, 2 SEPTEMBER 1920

Of all the events at the 1920 Games, the most eagerly anticipated by the host nation was the soccer final in which Belgium
came face to face with Czechoslovakia. Although the Belgians
were quietly confident of taking gold, they had no intention of
underestimating a Czech team, which, in three matches en
route to the final, had scored fifteen goals, conceding just one.
The 40,000-capacity stadium was full two hours before kick-
off while hundreds of ticketless Belgian fans dug a tunnel
under a perimeter fence and crept in without paying. The
resultant overcrowding forced spectators perilously close to
the pitch, as a result of which dozens of Belgian soldiers were
recruited to surround the playing surface and prevent any
attempt at crowd invasion.

The Czech delegation already had their misgivings about the
match. They had unsuccessfully objected to the appointment
of English referee John Lewis who, in a pre-Olympic game in
Prague, had been physically attacked by irate Czech fans. Not
unreasonably, the Czechs feared that, in view of his unpleasant
experience, he would have difficulty in remaining impartial.
Now when the Czech players stepped on to the pitch and found
it guarded by a ring of soldiers, they became convinced that the
odds were stacked against them, later describing the military
presence as 'provocative and menacing'.

Their worst fears were soon realised when, with just ten
minutes played, referee Lewis awarded Belgium a penalty,
which was duly converted by Robert Coppée. In the 28th

minute Rik Larnoe of the host club Antwerp made it 2–0 and the crowd erupted. With order struggling to be maintained both on and off the pitch, the Czechs started to lose their discipline and six minutes before half-time their star man, Karel Steiner, was penalised for kicking one of the Belgian players in the chest. It was a vicious assault and one that left referee Lewis with little option but to send off Steiner. His dismissal proved the last straw for the Czechs and the rest of the team promptly marched off in protest. As the puzzled Belgians waited to see whether their opponents would return, the referee abandoned the match and the Czechs were disqualified.

Czechoslovakia's elimination left the silver medal up for grabs and at the end of a mini-tournament, during which Sweden also threatened to pull out because of poor refereeing, Spain defeated Holland in the match for second and third place. So Belgium were crowned Olympic soccer champions but it was a thoroughly unsatisfactory climax to the Games' showpiece occasion. Indeed, in the aftermath of Antwerp there were calls for Britain to withdraw from the 1924 Games on the basis that the Olympics were no longer conducted in a sporting manner and that they led to bad feeling between competing nations. The Paris Olympics would merely serve to confirm those forebodings.

THE AMERICAN RUGBY CHAMPIONS

PARIS, 18 MAY 1924

Among the choice items of sporting trivia so beloved by compilers of pub quizzes is the little-known fact that the United States are the reigning Olympic rugby champions by virtue of having taken gold on the last occasion that rugby was contested at the Olympics, back in 1924. Although this snippet of information may appear startling enough in itself, the story behind the American victory is even more remarkable and, unfortunately, encapsulates all that was bad about the Paris Games.

The Americans had actually won gold in rugby at the 1920 Olympics, shocking France 8–0, but now, on home soil, the French were thirsting for revenge. Their only opponents, Romania and the USA, were considered nothing more than cannon fodder. As Norman Cleaveland, a member of the American team, recalled: 'They were looking for a punching bag. We were told to go to Paris and take our beatings like gentlemen.'

The 22-man American rugby party was something of a ramshackle affair, comprising seven players from the successful 1920 team along with an assortment of hefty American footballers, none of whom had even so much as touched a rugby ball until a few months before the Games. The coach, Charlie Austin, hoped that sheer brute force would compensate for lack of technical ability.

At the end of a 6,000-mile journey by train, bus, ship and ferry, the US rugby team arrived in Paris, via England, on

27 April. By the time they reached the French capital, their reputation had already gone before them. Angry scenes had broken out in Boulogne where immigration officials mistakenly refused the team entry, at which the players, many of whom had been seasick during the turbulent sea crossing, reacted by barging their way off the ship and on to dry land. The Americans' behaviour saw them labelled 'street fighters and saloon brawlers' by the French press. Things got worse. When the Paris authorities cancelled previously arranged games against local clubs and restricted American workouts to a patch of scrub land next to the team hotel, the US players promptly marched down to the Stade Colombes, climbed over the fence and went through their paces on the hallowed turf. The French were not amused.

The 1924 Olympic Games opened on 4 May with a rugby match between France and Romania, which the hosts won comprehensively 61–3. A similar outcome was expected against the upstart Americans. But first there were further controversies. When US team manager Sam Goodman objected to the appointment of British Admiral Percy Royds as referee for the match, the French responded by refusing to provide any practice pitches for the American players, who were thus reduced to using a nearby park. Fanning the flames, the French press then published an article questioning the amateur status of the US players. Next an argument broke out over the French Olympic Committee's ruling that the Americans could not film their forthcoming match against Romania, a French company having been awarded sole rights to film the Olympics. Goodman was so incensed that he threatened to withdraw his team from the competition.

By now anti-American sentiment in Paris was running so high that the players were insulted and spat upon whenever they ventured out on to the streets. Even the American expatriate community in the capital was giving them a wide berth. To make matters worse, the US team lost around $4,000 in cash and valuables when their clothes were rifled during a training session on the eve of the Romania game . . . despite a French sentry supposedly standing guard.

The threat of a mass walkout was averted by the French finally allowing the Romanian match to be filmed – purely for historical and educational purposes. On Sunday 11 May the US took the field against Romania before a crowd of 6,000 hostile Frenchmen at the Stade Colombes. Every American touch was greeted with boos and jeers; every Romanian attack – and there were precious few – received wild applause. After the Americans had effortlessly triumphed 37–0, even certain sections of the French press delivered grudging praise, but the general public remained openly aggressive. The US team's boisterous behaviour also led to them being kicked out of their hotel and moved into the newly built Olympic accommodation.

The match that was effectively the Olympic final took place on 18 May on a glorious spring day. Some 40,000 spectators were packed into the Stade Colombes, baying in unison for a French win. A high wire fence had been erected around the perimeter to restrain the crowd. Even in the build-up the Americans had enjoyed two significant victories – their own choice of referee, Sam Freethy of Wales, and his agreement that they would play two halves of 45 minutes, instead of 40 minutes. The Americans proposed the extended game to capitalise on their undisputed strength and stamina, all French protests being in vain. Nevertheless the crowd were convinced that even if the Americans played for six hours they would still never beat the French.

France's danger man was fleet-footed winger Adolphe Jaureguy, who quickly became the victim of a succession of bone-crunching, but legitimate, tackles. When yet another assault left Jaureguy lying motionless on the ground, the crowd vented their fury at the aggressors as their hero was carried off unconscious and bleeding. France's hopes disappeared with Jaureguy. Although trailing only 3–0 at half-time, they could not withstand the ferocious American tackles. As one French journalist wrote: 'Our men were too frail and hesitant, too fragile.' With France falling further behind in the second half and defeat appearing inevitable, the crowd turned ugly. French rugby crowds of the 1920s had a reputation for violence and this one was no exception. Any American supporters in the stands were beaten up and their bodies passed down to the pitch side to be taken away by ambulance. 'I thought they were dead,' said Norman Cleaveland. 'We were sure it was only a matter of time before they got their hands on us.' Then, in the closing stages, one of the reserves, Illinois art student Gideon Nelson, was struck in the face with a walking stick. When the final whistle blew to herald a 17–3 victory for the United States, all hell broke loose. 'They were throwing bottles and rocks and clawing at us through the fence,' said Cleaveland. 'We had no idea what was going to happen.'

Team-mate Charlie Doe saw the band pick up their instruments but could not hear a single note above the crescendo of booing. 'Then we saw the Stars and Stripes being raised and realised they were playing "The Star-Spangled Banner". We had completely forgotten about the medal ceremony which took place in front of tens of thousands of people who wanted to rip us to shreds.' At the end of the ceremony the Americans were given a police escort to the changing-rooms.

Although the quality of the American performance was subsequently acknowledged in some quarters, the behaviour of the French fans had set the tone for the rest of the Paris Olympics.

NO GOLD FOR A WORLD RECORD

PARIS, 7 JULY 1924

The name of Robert LeGendre made only a minor impact on the Olympic roll of honour. A fourth place in 1920, followed by a bronze medal in 1924, hardly warrants a place alongside the all-time greats. But he does have the consolation of being the answer to another trivia question: which Olympic long jumper leaped further than anyone else but failed to win a gold medal? For LeGendre not only outjumped every other competitor in Paris by a considerable margin, he also set a new world record. So why didn't his achievements earn him the ultimate Olympic prize? Because at the time he was competing in the pentathlon.

The 26-year-old graduate from Georgetown University, Washington, DC, was very much an all-round sportsman, excelling in ball games as well as track and field. To maximise his versatility, he entered the pentathlon at the 1920 Olympics and finished a creditable fourth. His best event of the ten disciplines was invariably the long jump in which he was one of the first competitors to introduce the 'hitch kick', whereby he would attempt to achieve extra distance by 'running' with his legs while suspended in mid-air. Although this technique proved highly effective, it surprisingly failed to win him a place in the United States long jump team for the 1924 Olympics. Instead the jack-of-all-trades was again left to take part in the pentathlon.

The long jump competition in the pentathlon was held on 7 July – the day before the Olympic long jump proper – and LeGendre, with a point to prove, promptly shattered the world record with a leap of 25ft 5½in (7.76m). This broke fellow countryman Edward Gourdin's mark, set back in 1921, by nearly three inches. When the specialist long jumpers turned out the following day, they were unable to get anywhere near LeGendre's standard, the gold medal eventually going to America's William DeHart Hubbard with a leap of 24ft 5in (7.44m) – a whole foot behind LeGendre's jump.

To add insult to injury, the jump that would have been good enough to have won gold in the individual competition only earned LeGendre a bronze in the pentathlon. For some of his other events let him down and his overall points tally saw him trail in behind Finland's Eero Lehtonen (who took gold) and Hungary's Elemer Somfay (silver). He thus returned home with the unique combination of third prize and a world record.

NURMI'S HISTORIC DOUBLE

PARIS, 10 JULY 1924

Amid all the mayhem of the rugby and, as we shall see, the boxing competitions, there was no shortage of heroes at the Paris Olympics. The British pair of Harold Abrahams and Eric Liddell won gold medals in the 100 metres and 400 metres respectively, their achievements inspiring the 1981 film *Chariots of Fire*; Johnny Weissmuller of the United States collected three golds in freestyle swimming plus a bronze in the men's water polo – feats that helped him to earn a lucrative Hollywood career as Tarzan; and then there was Paavo Nurmi.

Following his three gold medals in Antwerp, Nurmi was determined to do even better in Paris. His eagerly awaited Olympic reappearance began on 8 July in a qualifying heat of the 5,000 metres. Such was his confidence that he spent the early part of the race chatting to fellow countryman Eino Seppala, only picking up the pace when the crowd started to whistle at him. Nurmi went on to win comfortably although his time was a whole minute outside the new world record that he had set the previous month. The following day he cruised through to the final of the 1,500 metres.

The finals of both the 1,500 metres and the 5,000 metres were held on the same day – Thursday 10 July – with just an hour between them. To run in both races would be inconceivable to the vast majority of athletes, but Nurmi scarcely fitted into that category and had actually prepared for such an eventuality back in Helsinki by setting world records at both distances with just an hour's gap between the two runs.

But it still remained a daunting task, his cause not helped by the fact that Paris was in the grip of a heatwave at the time. The 1,500 metres came first and Nurmi's principal aim was to win without overly exerting himself. Taking the lead at 200 metres and running with a stopwatch on his wrist, he produced an immediate injection of blistering pace so that by the halfway point he was almost three seconds inside his own world record schedule. Only Ray Watson of the United States was able to keep within striking distance but he, too, soon realised that Nurmi was on a different plane and dropped back, leaving the Finn to romp home unchallenged. He took the opportunity to ease off over the final 300 metres, but his winning time of 3min 53.6sec was still only a second slower than his world record. The question now on everybody's lips was: had Nurmi saved enough for the 5,000?

The start of the 5,000 metres was delayed marginally, but it hardly provided Nurmi with a significant amount of additional breathing space. Here he faced much tougher opposition in the form of team-mate Ville Ritola, who had already won two gold medals at the Games – in the 10,000 metres (setting a new world record) and in the 3,000 metres steeplechase. The Finnish team officials had deliberately divided up the distance races between their two stars, preventing Nurmi from entering the 10,000 metres. This would be their first meeting. The early pace was set by Finnish-born Swede Edvin Wide but he began to fade after 2,000 metres and at the midway point Nurmi had taken the lead, closely pursued by Ritola. The race developed into a titanic battle between the two Finns. At one stage Nurmi opened up a gap of seven yards but Ritola fought back and presented a real threat going into the last lap. The two men were virtually inseparable over that final circuit until, coming into the home stretch, Ritola made his move on the outside. He must have thought he had timed it to perfection, but Nurmi simply changed gear and accelerated away to win by a yard in 14min 31.2sec. Not only had he won two gold medals in little more than an hour, but he had set Olympic records in both events.

Nurmi was by no means finished yet. The day after his epic double he was back in action for a qualifying heat of the 3,000 metres team race, which he won easily ahead of fellow Finns Ritola and Sameli Tala. His next target was the individual cross-country race, run on the afternoon of Saturday 12 July. It was another sweltering day in Paris, with temperatures touching 45 degrees Celsius (113 degrees Fahrenheit) in the sun. The 10,650-metre course took the runners along the shade-free bank of the Seine through dense weeds and passed uncomfortably close to an energy plant. The combination of the scorching heat and the poisonous fumes that belched out from the plant wreaked havoc among the runners. Of the 38 starters, only fifteen made it to the finish . . . and eight of those were taken away on stretchers. Yet Nurmi seemed impervious to the conditions, crossing the finish line a minute and a half ahead of Ritola to collect yet another gold. He also picked up the team gold when the crucial third member of the Finnish squad, Heikki Liimatainen, staggered home semi-conscious in eighth place. It took Liimatainen two minutes to cover the last thirty metres. Another athlete, Aguilar of Spain, was rushed to hospital after collapsing and hitting his head on a marker. Medics had to work overtime to tend to the sick and wounded. It was like a scene from a disaster movie.

The following day, while most of the cross-country competitors were recovering from their ordeal either in bed or in hospital, Nurmi and Ritola turned out for the final of the 3,000 metres team race. Taking the lead after the first kilometre, Nurmi never looked back and won by 8.6 seconds from Ritola to help Finland to another gold.

That completed Nurmi's Paris Olympics. In six days he had run seven races, winning them all and gathering five gold medals. The French magazine *Miroir des Sports* eulogised: 'Paavo Nurmi goes beyond the limits of humanity.' Ritola was scarcely less impressive, eight races in eight days bringing him four gold medals and two silver.

Nurmi received a hero's welcome on his return to Finland and the government initiated a project to immortalise him in bronze . . . a metal with which eight-time winner Nurmi was not exactly familiar. However, he was still smarting over the decision not to allow him to run the 10,000 metres in Paris and responded by setting a new world record for that distance that would last for nearly thirteen years. At the 1928 Games he collected a ninth Olympic gold – in the 10,000 metres – but had to settle for silver in the 5,000 metres and the steeplechase. He wanted to crown his glorious career with a gold medal in the Olympic marathon, as Hannes Kolehmainen had done in 1920, but was prevented from competing at Los Angeles in the 1932 Games after being suspended by the International Amateur Athletic Federation over accusations of professionalism. He still travelled to Los Angeles but despite pleas from the other marathon runners, the organisers would not relent. Unaccustomed to inactivity, Nurmi could not bring himself to watch the race but claimed afterwards that he would have won by five minutes. Few could argue.

He did make one last Olympic appearance, however, in 1952 when the Games were staged in Helsinki. The identity of the torch bearer had been kept a closely guarded secret but when the 70,000-strong crowd learned that it was Paavo Nurmi, a momentary silence gave way to a deafening roar. Hundreds sobbed openly as 55-year-old Nurmi strode majestically into the stadium past his own bronze statue. His popularity in his homeland never diminished and he was accorded the honour of a state funeral following his death in 1973.

THE BROUSSE–MALLIN AFFAIR

PARIS, 18 JULY 1924

A degree of partisanship in favour of home competitors is only to be expected from Olympic crowds but the French frequently exceeded the bounds of fairness and decency during the Paris Games, often resorting to booing other countries' national anthems. The furore over the rugby final had barely died down before the Parisian fans again showed themselves in their true tricolours – this time at the boxing venue, the Vélodrome d'Hiver.

The local hero in the middleweight class was 23-year-old Roger Brousse, a burly brawler who might have been more gamefully employed against the Americans on the rugby pitch. His opponent in the quarter-finals was 32-year-old London policeman Harry Mallin, the defending Olympic champion. Although he was nearing the veteran stage in boxing terms, Mallin was expected to have too much experience and skill for his eager opponent but Brousse hung in there and the fight went the full three rounds. At the final bell, an angry Mallin marched over to the Belgian referee and pointed to several clear bite marks on his chest, but the referee waved him away contemptuously. Then came the verdict. Mallin appeared to have won comfortably, but incredibly the referee and the Italian judge both voted for Brousse with only the South African judge siding with Mallin. For Mallin, who had never before tasted defeat, it was a bitter pill to swallow.

Reeling from the perceived injustice, the British team hurriedly lodged an objection. A medical examination confirmed the presence of bite marks on Mallin's body and it emerged that in an earlier bout with Argentina's Manolo Gallardo, Brousse had again been accused of biting. The Frenchman's supporters claimed that he had a peculiar tendency to snap his jaw whenever he threw a punch and theorised that Mallin must have ducked one of Brousse's punches and, on rising, bumped his chest against Brousse's snapping mouth. Implausible though this explanation sounded, it must have struck some form of chord with the Jury of Appeal, who ruled that Brousse's biting had not been deliberate. Nevertheless, they disqualified him.

The entire boxing programme had been halted for a day while a decision was reached and when Brousse's disqualification was duly relayed to the Vélodrome crowd the following evening, it was not exactly rapturously received. The boxer himself burst into tears and was carried shoulder-high around the ring by his supporters. Scuffles broke out among the crowd and the police were called in to restore order. Meanwhile Mallin and his semi-final opponent, Belgium's Joseph Beecken, sat quietly in the sanctuary of the ring, observing the commotion. When the fuss had died down temporarily, Mallin outpointed Beechen to meet Britain's Jack Elliot in the final the following night.

Twenty-four hours had done little to calm the Parisian crowd. As Mallin entered the ring, he was loudly booed but he overcame the hostile atmosphere to retain his Olympic title on points. And with that he retired from boxing.

The British press pulled no punches over the Brousse–Mallin affair. The *Daily Sketch* complained: 'It was found necessary to substitute for a mere boxer a man-eating expert named Brousse, whose passion for raw meat led him to attempt to bite off portions of his opponents' anatomies.'

Sadly the boxing fans of other nations took their cue from the French. When English referee T H Walker disqualified Italy's Giuseppe Oldani for persistent holding, Italian supporters pelted the official with sticks, coins and even walking stick knobs. Walker was trapped in the arena for almost an hour until a group of burly British, American and South African boxers escorted him to safety. And the welterweight final ended in uproar after Belgium's Jean Delarge had been awarded a controversial points decision over Argentina's Hector Méndez. Angry Argentine fans howled their protests for fifteen minutes until a vestige of sanity returned.

So when word reached England that a major row had resulted in an Italian fencer challenging one of the Hungarian judges to a duel, *The Times* called for an end to the Olympics. Under the headline 'NO MORE OLYMPIC GAMES', its editorial thundered: 'Miscellaneous turbulence, shameful disorder, storms of abuse, free fights and the drowning of national anthems of friendly nations by shouting and booing are not conducive to an atmosphere of Olympic calm. Disturbances of this kind, culminating in open expressions of national hostility, might conceivably end in worse trouble than the duel which, it is feared, may take place as a result of the personal quarrel in which a Hungarian and Italian fencer have allowed themselves to become involved. The peace of the world is too precious to justify any risk, however wild the idea may seem, of its being sacrificed on the altar of international sport.'

THE TITANIC SURVIVOR

PARIS, 21 JULY 1924

Two Americans defied overwhelming odds to earn gold medals in Paris. Lieutenant Sidney Hinds won gold in the free rifle team event, shooting a perfect fifty – an amazing achievement in view of the fact that he had been accidentally shot in the foot part-way through the competition when the Belgian rifleman positioned next to him threw his loaded weapon to the ground during a heated argument with an official. Then, in the final of the tennis mixed doubles, Richard Norris Williams partnered Hazel Wightman to victory over fellow Americans Vincent Richards and Marion Jessup. For Williams the hope of winning an Olympic gold medal must have seemed an impossibly distant dream back on the night of 14 April 1912 as he floundered in the icy waters of the North Atlantic, trying desperately to stay alive while over 1,500 around him perished following the sinking of the world's largest liner, the *Titanic*.

Born in Geneva in 1891, Williams was educated in France and Switzerland until his promise as a tennis player led to him being offered a place at Harvard University. Thus Williams and his father Charles joined the *Titanic* on her maiden voyage at Cherbourg bound for the United States, where the young man planned to play a few tournaments before commencing his studies. When the ship struck an iceberg shortly before midnight, Williams and his father left their first-class stateroom – for which each had paid £61 7s 7d – and began to investigate. On seeing a steward trying in vain to open a cabin door behind which a panicking passenger was trapped, Richard Williams put his shoulder to the door and broke in. The steward promptly threatened to report him for damaging company property. They then headed for the bar in search of a fortifying drink but found it closed. They asked a steward if he could open it, only to be told that it was against regulations. As the *Titanic* began to list and the first lifeboats started to leave, they wandered down to the gymnasium and sat on the exercise bicycles, chatting to others who had congregated there. When the ship finally foundered, Richard and Charles found themselves swimming for their lives in the sea, Richard still wearing a heavy fur coat. Moments later he saw his father and many others crushed to death when one of the liner's funnels collapsed into the water. Narrowly avoiding being crushed himself, Richard swam sixty feet towards a collapsible boat, clinging to it for six hours until another lifeboat picked up the survivors. He later described his ordeal: 'I was not under water very long, and as soon as I came to the top I threw off the big fur coat. I also threw off my shoes. About twenty yards away I saw something floating. I swam to it and found it to be a collapsible boat. I hung on to it and after a while got aboard and stood up in the middle of it. The water was up to my waist. About thirty of us clung to it. When Officer Lowe's boat picked us up, eleven of us were still alive; all the rest were dead from cold.'

Williams was lucky to survive. He had spent so long up to his waist in the freezing cold water that when he was taken aboard the rescue ship *Carpathia* the following morning, the doctor recommended the amputation of both legs. Williams refused and, by exercising daily, steadily regained the strength in his legs. He took his place at Harvard and crowned his heroic recovery by winning the US Open mixed doubles later that year with Mary Browne. In 1913 he was beaten finalist in the US singles and gained selection for the US Davis Cup team, which he would go on to captain regularly over the ensuing thirteen years. In 1914 and 1916 he gained consolation for his earlier defeat by winning the US singles and in 1920 he joined forces with Chuck Garland to lift the men's doubles title at Wimbledon.

Then came his Olympic adventure and even there he was obliged to overcome adversity after spraining an ankle in the semi-finals. The injury was so bad that Williams wanted to withdraw from the final but his partner Hazel Wightman refused. 'She told me to stay at the net,' said Williams, 'and she'd cover everything else. I didn't move much.' The plan worked better than either could have hoped, Williams and Wightman running out the 6–2, 6–3 winners to take the coveted gold medal. Williams was particularly relieved not to have to play a third set.

In later years Richard Williams – the survivor extraordinary – became a successful investment banker in Philadelphia. He died in 1968 at the age of 77.

THE FIRST WOMAN TRACK CHAMPION

AMSTERDAM, 31 JULY 1928

The 1928 Games saw the readmission of Germany and her allies to the Olympic fold for the first time since the First World War. More significantly, it also heralded the expansion of the women's programme to incorporate track and field, as a result of which the number of women participants rose from 136 to 290. The honour of being the first woman to win an Olympic track event went to an unknown sixteen-year-old American who was so nervous in the build-up to the final that she was all set to run in two left shoes!

Betty Robinson was just another student at Thornton High School, Chicago, until her biology teacher, Charles B Price, saw her running to catch a train. He was so impressed by her burst of speed that he arranged for her to be timed sprinting along the college corridor and when these timed sprints confirmed that he had unearthed a special talent, she was invited to work out with the Thornton boys' track and field team. She took part in her first-ever track race on 30 March 1928 and astounded everyone by finishing second to the American record holder. In her second race she did even better, equalling the world record although her time was not recognised. On the strength of these performances she was sent to the Olympic trials at Newark, New Jersey, where second place was sufficient to earn the novice a trip to Holland that summer.

So, barely four months after her first competitive race, Robinson found herself lining up alongside the cream of the world's women sprinters. The Olympic Games was only her fourth meeting, and the women's 100 metres final itself was just the fifth race of her life.

The final turned out to be a nerve-racking affair. The youthful exuberance and confidence that had carried Robinson so far so quickly began to evaporate as her situation hit home. Flustered, she arrived at the track with two left shoes. Fortunately she realised her error before too long and was able to retrieve a right shoe in time to line up at the start. There, it was her more experienced opponents who felt the tension of the occasion as two runners, Germany's Leni Schmidt and the Canadian favourite Myrtle Cook, were disqualified for false starts. Few could have blamed Robinson if she, too, had cracked under the pressure, but she now remained commendably cool.

The four remaining finalists eventually got away at the fourth attempt. Robinson was quickly into her stride and held a clear lead at halfway but then the Canadian Fanny 'Bobbie' Rosenfeld rallied strongly. At the finishing tape there was hardly a hair's breadth between them, with all four runners separated by just 0.2sec. The first-place judge opted for Robinson, although two other officials thought she had broken the tape with her arms rather than her body – such was her rawness that she had yet to perfect the art of breaking the tape. Robinson was duly awarded first place, equalling the world record time of 12.2sec, and, despite an official protest from the Canadians, the result was confirmed. The historic gold medal went to Robinson with Rosenfeld having to settle for silver and Canada's Ethel Smith taking bronze. A few days later the young American collected another medal when helping her team-mates to second place behind Canada in the 4×100 metres relay.

On returning home, Robinson was given a rousing welcome with a parade through the suburbs of Chicago. Soon her thoughts turned to the next Olympics, but in 1931 she was seriously injured in a plane crash. The man who found her actually thought she was dead, put her in the boot of his car and drove her to a mortician. Instead, an examination revealed her to be clinging to life by a thread. She lay unconscious for seven weeks, having sustained multiple injuries to her arms and legs, and even when she came round, she had to spend six months in a wheelchair, followed by several more months on crutches. In total it was two years before she could walk normally. Having survived against the odds, she was determined to defy doctors' advice and run again. Since she was no longer able to bend her leg fully at the knee, she could not assume the crouched starting position for sprints, but this did not prevent her competing in relays. Sure enough, at the 1936 Olympics – Hitler's Games – Betty Robinson won a second gold medal as a member of the United States 4×100 metres team.

On that note she retired to become a housewife and athletics official. The woman who blazed a trail for all other female track athletes died in 1999, aged 87.

THE FAIRER SEX

AMSTERDAM, 2 AUGUST 1928

It is not clear whether Baron de Coubertin's definition of the Olympic ideal was intended to extend to birds, but Australian rower Henry Pearce endeared himself to naturalists the world over by his selfless deeds at the Amsterdam Games. Rowing in a quarter-final of the single sculls at Sloten against Victor Saurin of France, Pearce had reached the midway point when he spotted a family of ducks swimming dangerously towards his boat. Realising that he and the birds were on collision course, he momentarily abandoned his quest for Olympic glory and stopped rowing in order to allow the mother duck and her ducklings to pass unmolested in single file in front of his boat. Following the near-miss, it took the man from Sydney a while to regain his rhythm but he recovered to win through to the last four and ultimately to become a popular recipient of the gold medal.

There was more drama in the water in the final of the women's 200 metres breaststroke. The sensation of the event was the 18-year-old German swimmer Hildegard Schrader, whose opening heat time of 3min 11.6sec eclipsed the existing Olympic record by an astonishing sixteen seconds. Then, in her semi-final, she equalled the world record of fellow German Lotte Mühe. It came as little surprise therefore when she went on take gold in the final, although her time was a shade slower . . . because the straps of her bathing suit broke in the closing stages. She managed to swim to the finish but felt it advisable to remain in the water at the end of the race until the strap was repaired!

All in all, women created quite a stir at the Games – nowhere more so than in the first-ever 800 metres. There had been misgivings beforehand among the chauvinist sector that to ask women to run such an extreme distance would prove too great an exertion for their frail little bodies. The race itself would only further fuel this argument.

Japan's Kinue Hitomi, the world record holder in the 200 metres and the long jump, led early on but the three-strong German contingent employed team tactics with Marie Dollinger and Elfriede Wever setting a punishing pace for Lina Radke, who pulled away in the final 300 metres to win by almost a second. Hitomi rallied to take silver and Inga Gentzel of Sweden took bronze. Radke's winning time of 2min 16.8sec set a world record that would stand for the next sixteen years. After the race several runners collapsed from exhaustion and had to receive medical attention, prompting renewed calls from both the press and the International Amateur Athletic Federation for women's distance races to be scrapped.

The *Daily Telegraph* correspondent wrote: 'The final of the 800 metres for women as a demonstration of what girls may do and suffer to win renown as athletes made a deep impression on me. But it left me firmly convinced that it would have been better if it had not been done. If it served any purpose at all, it showed that the modern young woman is apt to attempt too much in the name of sport . . . To run roughly half a mile at breakneck speed is surely too much for any girl.'

The *Daily Mail* went further, quoting doctors who said that women competing in races of 800 metres and other such 'feats of endurance' would 'become old too soon'.

As the campaign for a wholesale ban on women's distance races gathered momentum, it was pointed out that men, too, suffered from exhaustion immediately after events. Female athletes found a champion in 1924 Olympic 100 metres winner Harold Abrahams, who approved of women competing and believed that their breakdowns in races were more psychological than physical. The *Daily Express* took Abrahams' views on board. It wrote: 'Women, as he quite truly notes, are apt to break down for reasons not instantly clear to the masculine understanding. They will cry when they win, and they will cry when they are beaten.' The newspaper suggested that the reason for this irrational behaviour was because women hurl themselves into competition 'with a ferocity of self-devotion and because unlike men they haven't been conditioned to accept victory or defeat. With women, their extra intensity and their over-exaggeration of the importance of the occasion combine to produce a condition of mind and nerves that somewhat throws them off their balance.'

With many women athletes unsure as to whether it was preferable to be patronised or banned, Belgium's Henri de Baillet-Latour, the new president of the IOC, tried to make up their minds for them by advocating that all women's sports be dropped from the Olympics. This enlightened soul favoured a return to the all-male competition of the ancient Olympics. In 1929 the IOC did indeed announce a ban on all women's track and field events, but it was lifted when the United States, who boasted a powerful women's team, threatened to boycott the 1932 Games. Nevertheless, no women's races beyond 200 metres were run again at the Olympics until 1960.

A CASE OF INTERFERENCE

LOS ANGELES, 5 AUGUST 1932

The focal point of the 1932 Olympics was the Los Angeles Coliseum, which, with its 100,000 capacity, was at that time the largest stadium in the world. This grand setting witnessed moments of high drama, notably in the 5,000 metres final where, to the disgust of the intensely patriotic crowd, an American fell foul of a flailing Finn.

Whereas its immediate predecessors had spanned anything up to six months, the Los Angeles Olympics were condensed into a sixteen-day period from 30 July to 14 August, thereby setting the trend for future Games. For the first time the concept of an Olympic Village was introduced, with the construction of 550 specially designed small houses for male competitors only. The women were accommodated in a luxury hotel. Despite the strictures of Prohibition, which was still in force in the United States, the French and Italian teams were allowed to bring in wine for their own consumption. China made its debut at the 1932 Olympics, although it sent just one athlete (sprinter Liu Chang Chun) from a population of 400 million.

Another innovation was the use of a photo-finish camera – the Kirby Two-Eyed Camera – to determine the outcome of track events. Jack Keller of the United States might have wished that its introduction could have been delayed for, after being placed third in the 110 metre hurdles, he was obliged to hand his bronze medal over to Britain's Donald Finley when the photo-finish evidence revealed that Finley had pipped him on the line.

Chaos reigned in the 3,000-metre steeplechase after the regular lap-checker was taken ill at the last minute and his inexperienced replacement omitted to change the lap count at the end of the first circuit. So when Finland's Volmari Iso-Hollo reached what should have been the end of the race, he found instead that there was still one more lap to go. Undaunted, he retained his lead to take gold but behind him Britain's Thomas Evenson overtook Joseph McCluskey of the US on the extra lap to finish second. When the blunder came to light, McCluskey was offered a re-run the following day but he declined the offer on the grounds of exhaustion.

In the pool the Brazilian water polo team were disqualified for insulting the referee following a 7–3 defeat to Germany. And a German sports journalist caused uproar during the springboard diving competition by jumping into the pool fully clothed. While the crowd roared with laughter, Olympic officials prepared to hand the offender over to the police but relented on learning that he had gone through with the stunt purely to win a $100 bet.

One of the great heroes of the 1932 Olympics was Britain's Tommy Green, gold medallist in the 50-kilometre walk. Unable to walk until he was five because of rickets, Green then lied about his age in order to join the army, only to be invalided out when a horse fell on him. But when the First World War broke out, he was called up by the reserves and sailed to France with the British Expeditionary Force. Serving with the King's Own Hussars, he was wounded on three separate occasions and also badly gassed, as a result of which he was sent home and warned not to undertake any sporting activity. Instead he took up walking as a form of exercise and helped a blind friend train for the London to Brighton Walk. The friend suggested that Green might consider race walking, which he did with great success, culminating in his triumph in Los Angeles at the age of 38.

Aside from Joseph Guillemot's shock defeat of Paavo Nurmi in the 1920 5,000 metres final, both that event and the 10,000 metres had been monopolised in previous Olympics by Finnish athletes. Although Nurmi was ruled out of the 1932 Games, the Finns sent worthy successors in the shape of Lauri Lehtinen, the new world record holder at 5,000 metres, and Lauri Virtanen. It was expected to become a race between the two but the Finns had reckoned without a home runner, long-legged Oregon graduate Ralph Hill. So instead the Olympic final developed into a scene more reminiscent of the slow lane of the M1 – two Lauris battling against a Hill.

It was Hill who led from the off, but he had been overhauled by the end of the first lap as the two Finns set out to impose their authority. Hill seemed happy to remain at the back of the field until, with ten laps to go, he moved up to sixth. Continuing his steady progress, he eased into third place behind Lehtinen and Virtanen with four laps left, and two circuits later passed Virtanen, who quickly dropped back 35 yards. With one Finn now out of contention, it boiled down to a straight fight between Lehtinen and Hill.

In the course of the penultimate lap Lehtinen desperately tried to shake off the dogged Hill but to no avail, and at the sound of the bell the American was still sitting on his shoulder with Virtanen seventy yards adrift in third. In another attempt to rid himself of his tormentor, Lehtinen sprinted around the first bend of the last lap but Hill responded. Saving himself for a sprint finish, the Finn eased off down the back stretch before accelerating once more on the final bend. Coming off the bend, Lehtinen, who was hugging the inside lane, led by a stride, but fifty yards from the finish the crowd rose in expectation as Hill made his move on the outside. With the shadow of Hill looming up to his right, Lehtinen veered over into lane two, forcing Hill out wider. Before Hill could draw alongside, Lehtinen edged into the third lane. His path impeded, Hill dropped back and tried to pass on the inside. Looking over his shoulder, Lehtinen saw what the American was trying to do and moved back into the second lane. Again Hill tried to pass on the right and again Lehtinen, running a zig-zag path and turning to keep an eye on his opponent, ran out into lane three.

By now bedlam had broken loose. The crowd were yelling encouragement at Hill and imploring the Finn to get out of the way. Fifteen yards from the tape, Hill renewed his challenge on the inside, whereupon Lehtinen swerved back into lane two. The *Track & Field News* correspondent takes up the story: 'Again Lehtinen moved over toward the pole but before he could quite close the gap Hill was there with what one might figuratively call a foot in the door. Only it was a torso, and Lehtinen could not quite gain lane one again without forcing Hill clear off the track. At this precise moment the tape loomed up. Both men lunged for it, and the Finn managed to stumble over the line first, a winner by less than a foot.'

As the two men stepped off the track, the crowd booed the Finn in unison until public address announcer Bill Henry begged: 'Ladies and gentlemen, please remember that these people are our guests.' With that, the booing stopped and was replaced by a smattering of polite applause.

Lehtinen's time of 14min 30sec had won him gold and a new Olympic record but few friends. Charges of unsportsmanlike conduct were lodged but after more than an hour's deliberation the judges ruled that the Finn had not wilfully interfered with Hill. In an ambiguous statement the IAAF declared: 'Although the authorities of the Amateur Athletic Union [of the United States] consider the race NOT fairly run, there will be no official protest from either Mr Hill or the United States.'

Hill himself was prepared to give Lehtinen the benefit of the doubt. He told reporters: 'I do not think that Lauri deliberately tried to keep me from the tape. He was turning around to see where I was and I know from experience that when an exhausted man does that, he loses his sense of direction. Lehtinen certainly got in my way, but I think that he had too much left and could have beaten me anyway. I plan no protest, because I believe that Lehtinen was merely steering a blind course. I have done the same thing myself.'

At the victory ceremony, a distraught Lehtinen tried to haul Hill up on to the first-place platform, but the American declined. Instead, Lehtinen pinned a badge of the Finnish flag on Hill's sweater. The announcement of Lehtinen as the winner was received with quiet applause; when Hill was named as the silver medallist, the crowd cheered and roared.

Afterwards Lehtinen formally apologised while maintaining his innocence. 'I never took Hill for that good a runner,' he admitted. 'I swung wide on the last turn, then saw the American try to get around and went the other way to let him pass. But at the same time he changed his mind. It was unfortunate.'

Seventy thousand Americans in the Coliseum that day might have selected a rather different adjective.

THE ILLEGAL JUMP

LOS ANGELES, 7 AUGUST 1932

As with any Olympics there were plenty of hard-luck stories at Los Angeles. Ralph Hill was not the only American Ralph to suffer the hand of misfortune. In the 200 metres final Ralph Metcalfe was inadvertently placed at the wrong start mark, as a result of which he had to run a metre and a half further than the other athletes. Although he finished third, he could well have taken gold but for the error. However, he sportingly refused the offer of a re-run since the first two places had also gone to Americans.

Then there was the puzzling case of Sweden's Bertil Sandstrom, who was placed second in the dressage competition before being relegated to last for allegedly encouraging his horse by making clicking noises. Sandstrom insisted that the noises were made by a creaking saddle, but the Jury of Appeal was not convinced.

Irishman Bob Tisdall's infringement was wholly unintentional. He took gold in the 400 metres hurdles in a world record time of 51.7sec, but while he was allowed to keep his medal, the record was given to the runner-up, Glenn Hardin of the United States, who had finished 0.2sec behind, because Tisdall had knocked down the last hurdle.

Another who had reason to feel aggrieved was Mildred 'Babe' Didrikson, the Wonder Woman of American sport, who was denied a high jump gold medal by a bizarre judging decision. The controversial ruling also cost Didrikson a third gold at the Games, which would have been a fitting reward for a truly remarkable athlete.

Mildred Ella Didrikson was born in Texas in 1914 to Norwegian immigrant parents. As a teenager she competed in track and field, basketball, baseball, billiards, tennis, diving and swimming. Once, when asked if there was anything she didn't play, she quickly replied: 'Yeah, dolls.' She was given the nickname 'Babe' in honour of her Babe Ruth-like home runs in baseball. Few greater accolades could be bestowed upon an American athlete.

On 16 July 1932 – a couple of weeks before the start of the Olympics – the slim but powerful 5ft 6in girl with the bobbed, boyish black hair entered track and field legend with an incredible solo display in the American Athletic Union Championships at Dyche Stadium, Evanston, Illinois. The championships also served as the American Olympic trials and Didrikson, never one for hiding her light under a bushel, had entered no fewer than eight of the ten events . . . all of which took place on the same day. Some of the competing clubs had as many as twenty athletes participating that day; the Employers Casualty Company of Dallas had just one – Babe Didrikson. It would prove more than enough.

When the PA announcer called out her name as the sole representative, Didrikson waved her arms, grinning from ear to ear. 'You never heard such a roar,' she said later. 'It brought out goose bumps all over me.'

Over the next two and a half hours she dashed from one event to another with no breathing space in between. She won five events outright – the 80 metres hurdles, shot put, javelin, long jump and baseball throw – and tied for first place in the high jump with Jean Shiley of the Meadowbrook Club, Philadelphia. In the course of these events, Didrikson set four world records! She only missed out on the 100 metres (finishing third in her semi-final) and the discus, an event with which she was unfamiliar and came fourth. Her overall total of thirty points – eight more than the entire 22-woman University of Illinois team – won the championships single-handedly for her club. No wonder that one reporter described it as 'the most amazing series of performances ever accomplished by any individual, male or female, in track and field history.'

Didrikson had reached the Olympic qualifying standard in five events and was disappointed that Olympic rules restricted her to taking part in only three. Nevertheless she was super-confident and, on arriving in Los Angeles, told reporters: 'I came out here to beat everybody in sight, and that is exactly what I am going to do.'

She made her first appearance on the afternoon of Sunday 31 July in the javelin – an event viewed with some trepidation, as two men had recently been speared and killed by wayward javelins. This was the inaugural women's Olympic javelin competition and Didrikson faced stiff opposition in the form of the German pair Ellen Braumuller (the world record holder) and Tilly Fleisher, but her opening throw effectively ended it as a contest. As she ran up, all she could see in the distance was the little German flag marking Braumuller's record throw. Didrikson remembered: 'As I let the spear go, my hand slipped off the cord on the handle. Instead of arching the way it usually did, that javelin went out there like a catcher's peg from home plate to second base. It looked like it was going to go right through the flag. But it kept on about fourteen feet past for a new Olympic and world's record of 143ft 4in. Nobody knew it, but I tore a cartilage in my right shoulder when my hand slipped making that throw. On my last two turns, people thought I wasn't trying, because the throws weren't much good. But they didn't have to be.'

Next up was the 80 metres hurdles, the final of which took place on 4 August. Her chief rival was fellow American Evelyn Hall of Chicago, and so keen was Didrikson to get off to a flyer that she false started. A second false start and she would be out of the race, so she held back momentarily just to be on the safe side. However, this left her with a considerable leeway to make up and by halfway she trailed Hall by at least a yard. It was not until the fifth hurdle that Didrikson drew level and the pair then battled side by side to the tape, Didrikson gaining the verdict by an inch in a world record time of 11.7sec. Hall later claimed that she had received a sharp jab in the ribs as the pair took the final hurdle. An impressed Damon Runyan, then plying his trade as a sports journalist, wrote: 'Didrikson leaps the hurdles like a gay gazelle and runs on the flat like a scared coyote.'

With two gold medals already under her belt, Didrikson went for the hat-trick on the final day of track and field – 7 August – in the high jump, an event in which she renewed her rivalry with the tall, attractive Jean Shiley. As all opposition fell by the wayside, the competition developed into the expected head-to-head between the two Americans. The bar was raised to 5ft 5¼in (1.65m). Both girls cleared it, Didrikson at the second attempt. So the bar was raised to 5ft 6in (1.67m), but both failed. Now for a jump-off between the two, the bar was lowered to 5ft 5¾in (1.66m). Shiley cleared it with her first leap to set a new world record, leaving Didrikson painfully aware that failure would mean instant elimination. However, 'failure' wasn't part of the Didrikson vocabulary and she duly sailed over the bar to equal the record.

But just when it seemed that the jump-off would continue, the judges stepped in and declared Didrikson's last jump illegal on the grounds that her western-roll style had caused her head to clear the bar before her body. She was therefore deemed guilty of 'diving'. Didrikson protested that her jumping style had never been questioned in the past and that she had been jumping the same way all afternoon. The judges simply replied: 'If you were diving before, we didn't see it. We just saw it this time.' Didrikson was eliminated from the competition. Shiley took gold and 'Babe' had to settle for silver. Ironically, her jumping style was legalised soon after.

Although in the immediate aftermath of the controversy Didrikson moaned, 'I jumped as high as she did or higher,' she bore Shiley no ill will. Indeed, one story (surely apocryphal) has it that the two athletes agreed to saw their medals in half and join the two halves so that each got a blend of gold and silver.

Anyway, track and field was but a small part of Didrikson's sporting armoury, and she was soon moving on to bigger and better things. She took up golf and went on to enjoy tremendous success, first as an amateur (winning seventeen tournaments in a row, including the US Women's Amateur title in 1946 and the British equivalent the following year) and then as a professional, in which capacity she won ten majors and lost only once in seven years of competition. Her incredible career – she was named American Female Athlete of the Half Century in 1950 – was ended only by her death from cancer in 1956.

PERU PULL OUT

BERLIN, 8 AUGUST 1936

The decision to award the 1936 Olympics to Berlin had been taken five years earlier – before Adolf Hitler came to power. The rise of the Nazi regime prompted grave disquiet outside Germany and there were moves, particularly in the United States with its influential Jewish population, to organise a boycott of the Games. However in 1935 Avery Brundage, the new president of the American Athletic Union, conducted an inspection tour to Berlin and pronounced everything to be just fine.

Hitler and his cronies intended the Olympics to be one vast propaganda exercise, a monument of self-glorification. In the circumstances it was ironic that, having warded off international criticism by selecting a few token Jewish members for the German team, his greatest embarrassment was caused not by the Jews but by a Negro, Jesse Owens. When the host nation's Hans Woelke won the shot put on the opening day, Hitler had the champion paraded before him as a symbol of Aryan supremacy but so irritated were the Nazis by Owens' four gold medals that Hitler was persuaded not to appear publicly with the winners. For his part, propaganda minister Josef Goebbels dubbed Owens and the other black American athletes 'black mercenaries' and when Hitler was unable to avoid Owens at an official reception, he pointedly refused to shake the athlete's hand.

For all the concerns about withdrawals over anti-Semitic issues, the major walkout at the 1936 Olympics followed an everyday case of incompetent refereeing and spectator unrest in the soccer tournament.

Although the advent of the World Cup in 1930 had reduced the importance of the Olympic soccer tournament, the competing nations still wanted to win at all costs. This was illustrated in an early match between Italy and the USA, when German referee Weingartner tried unsuccessfully to send off Italy's Achille Piccini. With Piccini standing his ground and refusing to leave the field, several Italian players surrounded the hapless official, pinned his arms to his sides and put their hands over his mouth. Hopelessly intimidated, Mr Weingartner allowed Piccini to play on and help Italy to a 1–0 victory.

Five days later – on 8 August – Austria met Peru before a crowd of 14,000 in Berlin. Austria led 2–0 at half-time and seemed to be coasting to a place in the last four but Peru rallied strongly with two late goals to force extra-time. The additional period remained evenly balanced until, with tension mounting, a small group of Peruvian fans ran on to the pitch and attacked one of the Austrian players. With the referee and security chiefs losing control, the game descended into chaos and Peru capitalised on the mayhem, scoring twice in quick succession to win 4–2.

As soon as the match had finished, Austria launched a protest. The International Football Federation jury, taking into account the attack on the Austrian player and the weak refereeing, upheld the protest and ordered a replay behind closed doors, the match to take place two days later.

The decision did not go down well in the Peruvian capital, Lima. Whistling, jeering mobs took to the streets, tearing down the Olympic flag and stoning the windows of the German Consulate. Newspaper editorials in Peru attacked the IFF ruling. 'It lacks basis as a reason,' wrote one, 'the Austrians' only pretext was to eliminate the team which had a good chance to win and thereby see its national flag wave from the scene of operations.' The nation's president, Oscar Benavides, was so incensed at the football team's treatment that he ordered the entire Peruvian Olympic squad to return home and urged other South American countries to follow suit.

On 10 August Austria turned up for the replay, the pitch surrounded by guards, but predictably there was no sign of Peru. The referee waited the prescribed fifteen minutes and when Peru still hadn't appeared, he awarded the tie to Austria. By then the Peru players, joined by the rest of the Olympic party and by Colombia in a display of South American solidarity, were on their way home. For the record, Austria went on to reach the final, where they lost 2–1 to Italy after extra time.

A FATAL SLIP

BERLIN, 9 AUGUST 1936

Dropping the baton is an everyday hazard in relay races. There is no good time or place to do it, but some scenarios are markedly worse than others. So if you were a member of the crack German women's sprint team, strongly fancied to take gold in front of a passionate home crowd and your beloved Führer, the ultimate nightmare would be to throw away a commanding lead by spilling the baton at the final changeover . . .

Hitler and the 100,000-strong crowd were fully entitled to have great expectations from the German quartet of Emmy Albus, Ilse Dörffeldt, Marie Dollinger and Kathe Krauss. Only the previous day – in the opening round of the women's 4×100 metres relay – they had set a new world record of 46.4sec, a time that would not be beaten for another sixteen years. Their chief rivals in the final were the Americans, whose line-up contained the 1928 Olympic 100 metres champion Betty Robinson, following her miraculous recovery from a near-fatal plane crash, and Helen Stephens, winner of the individual 100 metres in Berlin. Krauss, Dollinger and Albus all finished behind Stephens in that final, placed third, fourth and sixth respectively.

For the relay final, the Americans decided to allocate the third leg to Robinson with Stephens running the anchor leg. To combat this, the Germans surprisingly chose to change their successful running order at the last minute, Dörffeldt and Krauss swapping places. The German plan was to build up a big lead over the first three legs in order to enable Dörffeldt to hold off the formidable Stephens. Much of the responsibility would rest with the experienced Dollinger, who had run in the previous two Olympiads.

As the first leg runners settled down on their marks, the entire stadium, from paying spectators to visiting dignitaries such as King Boris of Bulgaria, watched in silent anticipation. Hitler could barely contain himself at the prospect of another German triumph. The German girls were drawn in lane four, next to the US team in lane three and therefore just ahead of them in the staggered start. At the sound of the gun, Albus got off to a flyer and produced a perfect handover to Krauss, who returned the favour to Dollinger. It seemed that nothing could stop the Germans. Dollinger had an apparently unassailable lead of ten metres as she prepared to hand over to Dörffeldt for the final leg. Hitler was on his feet screaming with excitement. But Dörffeldt, no doubt mindful of the threat posed by Stephens, accelerated to full speed before she had a firm grip on the baton and merely succeeded in fumbling it on to the track. As Dörffeldt pulled up in alarm, Stephens roared past on her way to victory. The German dream was shattered. Hitler slumped despondently in his seat. The hapless Dörffeldt shed floods of tears. To add insult to injury, the American winning time was 46.9sec, half a second outside the German record.

It was very much a self-inflicted wound, the late switch in the order having disrupted the customary German efficiency. But at least Hitler was in a forgiving mood. Taking pity on the sobbing Dörffeldt, he invited the German team to his booth and offered words of consolation.

Fast forward to the Rome Olympics of 1960 and Marie Dollinger must have dreaded the thought of history repeating itself as she sat in the stands watching her daughter, Brunhilde Hendrix, run the third leg of the women's 4×100 relay final. Happily, Hendrix's handover to Jutta Heine passed without incident and helped the German girls to silver behind the United States.

THE MISSING BOAT

BERLIN, 14 AUGUST 1936

Jack Beresford was the Steve Redgrave of his day. Between 1920 and 1936 the British master oarsman won medals – three gold and two silver – in five consecutive Olympics, his crowning glory coming in Berlin, where he and Dick Southwood gave the Germans a bloody nose.

Beresford was born into a rowing family, his father Julius, a Polish furniture-maker, having been a member of the British four that won a silver medal at the 1912 Games. Young Jack was thirteen at the time, his ambitions torn between his father's love of rowing and his own fondness for rugby. But any hopes he had of pursuing a rugby career were destroyed a few weeks before the end of the First World War when he was shot in the leg while serving with the Liverpool Scottish Regiment. He recuperated by rowing a dinghy off the Cornish coast and reached such a standard that he was selected for the single sculls at the 1920 Antwerp Olympics. He was narrowly beaten by the American Jack Kelly, father of Grace Kelly, after an epic battle that left both men too exhausted to shake hands. Four years later Beresford won his first gold medal in a single sculls final rowed through the heady scents wafting from a perfume factory on the banks of the Seine.

Combining work in the family furniture business with rowing, he trained vigorously for the next two Olympics, collecting a silver in the eights in 1928 and gold in the coxless fours in 1932. At the age of 37, he prepared for his swansong in Berlin.

Beresford was thought to be past his best, as indeed was his partner in the double sculls, 30-year-old Dick Southwood, a studious-looking London jeweller. Furthermore, their boat was obsolete and appeared ill equipped to challenge the might of the Germans and all their modern wizardry. It was like expecting a tug to challenge a speedboat.

But Beresford hadn't won four Olympic medals without being a fearsome competitor. Although his racing weight was only marginally over eleven stone (Redgrave weighed in excess of sixteen stone at Atlanta in 1996), what he lacked in physical bulk he made up for in steely determination. He knew every trick in the book and was damned if he was going to let the Germans have everything their own way.

The British pair had one ace up their sleeve. Germany had relied heavily on the expertise of English coaches and one of these, Eric Phelps, tipped off the British that they needed a lighter boat. Without one, he said, they would be sunk. Accordingly, a new lightweight boat was built within a week. After rapid testing, it was shipped off to Germany in time for the Olympics. Then, mysteriously, it disappeared.

It seemed that all the British efforts would be in vain, particularly as the Germans flatly refused to lend them another craft in which to practise. Then, two days before the Games, the missing boat was tracked down to a railway siding near Hamburg. Suspecting skulduggery, Beresford and Southwood were now hell-bent on defeating their arch rivals, their sense of injustice further fuelled when the Germans appeared to get away with a false start in the heats. The British duo reached the final by winning the repechage . . . by some 300 metres over a 2,000-metre course.

Finals day, in the inevitable presence of the Führer, was turning into a German procession. The home crowd had just celebrated a fifth consecutive gold medal when Beresford and Southwood stepped out to take on the hot favourites, Willy Kaidel and Joachim Pirsch. Beresford was not above resorting to gamesmanship and ruffled the Germans by delaying the start to remove his sweater. Meanwhile, Southwood had noticed that the Belgian umpire could not see the crews beyond the huge megaphone he was using to start the race and so, to combat the Germans' likely false start, he vowed to begin rowing at the same time as them. Thus the British successfully negated the Germans' dubious tactics and were able to retain parity for the first 500 metres. Then the Germans' awesome strength appeared to tell as they eased steadily ahead to lead by a length, but the British weren't finished yet and at 1,500 metres – three-quarter distance – they started to reduce the deficit. At 1,800 metres the crews were level and with 100 metres to go, Pirsch was a spent force and virtually stopped rowing. Beresford and Southwood crossed the line two lengths ahead to take gold. Beresford later described it as 'the sweetest race I ever rowed in'.

On his retirement, Beresford served as a steward and umpire at the Henley Regatta and was awarded the CBE for his services to rowing. At the age of 70, he tried to rescue a young boy who had fallen into the River Thames at Pangbourne in Berkshire. Sadly, Beresford's heroism was to no avail and the boy drowned. It is believed that the trauma of the incident brought about a deterioration in Beresford's health. He lost the sight in one eye and died at his Thames-side home in 1977.

COURAGE BEYOND THE CALL OF DUTY

BERLIN, 16 AUGUST 1936

Aside from the unfortunate Ilse Dörffeldt, German athletes generally excelled in front of their home crowd, particularly in field events, gymnastics and rowing. And Hitler's quest to find a true German hero at the Berlin Olympics bore further fruit on the very last day of competition when 26-year-old Lieutenant Konrad Freiherr von Wangenheim displayed exceptional bravery to steer his team to a gold medal in the three-day equestrian event.

With their customary attention to detail, the German riders had been practising diligently on a specially built replica of the Olympic cross-country course, the second of the three disciplines following the opening day dressage competition. One obstacle that demanded particular attention was the fourth on the course, the water jump, a hurdle and pond where the ground was extremely uneven, combining shallow areas with alarmingly deep holes. Many a rider would come to grief there, including von Wangenheim.

Riding Kurfürst, von Wangenheim approached the hurdle and pond confidently but the horse stumbled, throwing von Wangenheim to the ground with a sickening thud. The rider had dislocated his left arm on landing. However, he knew that if he failed to finish the German team would be disqualified and so, defying the pain, he gallantly remounted and, amazingly, negotiated the remaining 32 obstacles without incurring a single fault. His heroics, coupled with his comrades' prior knowledge of the course, enabled Germany to lead the event going into the following day's climax – the *Prix des Nations* showjumping section in front of a packed stadium. Naturally, Hitler was present.

Von Wangenheim was clearly not fit to ride so soon after his fall, but insisted on competing rather than see the team eliminated. He entered the stadium with his left arm in a sling, but just before he mounted his horse the sling was removed to reveal a tightly bound arm. The spectators held their breath but hopes of a smooth round were shattered early on when Kurfürst went too fast approaching a double, forcing von Wangenheim to pull sharply on the reins with both hands. The rider's left arm being ineffective, the horse reared up, fell backwards and landed on the stricken von Wangenheim. To the relief of the crowd, moments later he crawled out from beneath the horse. It was feared that Kurfürst was dead but suddenly the horse sprang back to life. To the disbelief of even the most fervent Germans, von Wangenheim remounted and once again completed the remainder of the course without another fault. Germany won the gold medal, and the 100,000 spectators gave him a standing ovation. Rarely has such an accolade been more richly deserved.

ONE LAP SHORT

LONDON, 30 JULY 1948

The 1940 Olympics were earmarked for Tokyo but by mid-1938 Japan was at war with China and withdrew as host. The IOC immediately transferred the Games to Helsinki and the Finns eagerly began preparations, only to be invaded by Russia in 1939. The advent of the Second World War meant that the Games were cancelled anyway, as they were again in 1944 when they were due to have been staged in London. On the restoration of peace, the IOC offered the 1948 Olympics to London. Wembley Stadium had survived the Blitz and, after the addition of a temporary running track, it was used as the main venue. Without the finances to build new stadiums, the organisers opted for traditional venues: rowing took place at Henley, shooting at Bisley, yachting at Cowes. As London was still rebuilding in the aftermath of the war, athletes were housed in schools, government buildings and army camps, and because food was rationed, competitors were asked to bring their own meals, any leftovers being donated to hospitals. Not surprisingly, Germany and Japan were excluded from the Games, while the Soviet Union declined the invitation.

Starting blocks were used for the first time in sprints, the chief beneficiary being a 30-year-old Dutch housewife and mother, Fanny Blankers-Koen, who equalled Jesse Owens' 1936 tally of four golds by winning the women's 100 metres, 200 metres, 80 metres hurdles and anchoring the 4×100 metres relay. At the time she was also the world record holder in the high jump and long jump but was prevented from entering

97

those events by the rule limiting women to three individual events in track and field.

For the most part the Games ran smoothly, although there was a right royal mix-up in the boxing competition concerning the names of two Argentine pugilists. At the weigh-in for his first bout, Argentine bantamweight Arnoldo Pares was found to be marginally overweight. For almost twenty minutes the distraught Pares stood on the scales while his entourage gave him a drastic haircut of the kind normally reserved for victims of the Sioux in John Wayne movies. Pares's aides scrubbed the soles of his feet, blew dust off the scales and generally tried everything to make him shed a few ounces. He even shed a few tears, but they could not put him below the weight limit either. The Argentine officials were puzzled by his failure to make the weight and dug deep to raise the £1 required to lodge a protest with the Jury of Appeal. Weights and measures experts were sent for and, after thoroughly testing the equipment, they admitted that the scales were inaccurate. So Pares weighed in again and, having undergone an unnecessary scalping, fought Vic Toweel of South Africa. He won that on a disputed decision but then lost out to Jimmy Carruthers of Australia. Meanwhile, a second Argentine boxer – 22-year-old flyweight Pascual Perez – was also disqualified before his first bout for being overweight. However, when the Argentine camp again expressed disquiet, Olympic officials realised that they had confused him with Pares and reinstated him. Perez went on to take the gold medal.

Another chaotic moment was largely the result of the sheer brilliance of a man who would go on to become one of the all-time great Olympians, Czech army lieutenant Emil Zátopek.

Born in the Northern Moravian village of Koprivnice in September 1922, miner's son Zátopek was a comparative latecomer to running. He worked in the Bata shoe factory and one day in 1940 the factory director persuaded him to take part in a sponsored 1,500 metres race. Without any training or prior experience, Zátopek finished second in a field of 100 youths and was encouraged to take the sport seriously. With his country occupied by Nazi Germany, athletics provided a welcome outlet for the young man.

Zátopek took his new hobby very seriously indeed, embarking on a punishing training regime designed to push back the frontiers of distance running. Until then the practice among athletes competing in races of 5,000 metres or beyond had been to run a steady pace, keeping a little in reserve for a sprint finish. Zátopek changed all that. He trained like a sprinter so that he could inject a sudden electrifying burst of pace into a race when his rivals were least expecting it. 'When I was young,' he said, 'I was too slow. I thought I must learn to run fast by practising to run fast.' So instead of training over race-length distances, he subjected himself to a series of 400-metre sprints, interspersed with 250-metre jogs. Each day he would run up to sixty sprint laps of the track – a distance of fifteen miles – and if the wartime curfew forced him indoors he ran on the spot in a spare room. He experimented relentlessly, often training in heavy army boots so that his feet felt lighter on race days and was even known to carry his wife on his shoulders during practice runs. He also took to running in a gas mask to see whether it helped control his breathing. It didn't, which was probably just as well as the IOC would surely never have allowed him to race in a gas mask at the Olympics!

When war ended, Zátopek upped his training programme, running alone well into the night after completing his day's work as a soldier. Already the Czech record holder at 2,000, 3,000 and 5,000 metres, he finished fifth in the 5,000 metres at the 1946 European Championships in Oslo with that soon-to-be-familiar trait of head rolling from side to side and face contorted in a grimace which, in comparison, makes Paula Radcliffe appear to be positively enjoying herself. At first glance that red face and lolling tongue and those audible wheezings suggested a man in danger of collapse, but in fact the opposite was the case, as opponents left toiling in his wake would testify only too readily.

In 1948 Zátopek was bidding to become the first runner since Finland's Hannes Kolehmainen in 1912 to take gold in the 5,000 and 10,000 metres at the same Olympics. It was an audacious bid, not least because he had run his first 10,000 metres race only two months previously. Indeed, the Olympics marked just his third-ever race over that distance.

Twenty-seven runners lined up inside Wembley Stadium on the opening day of the athletics programme for the start of the 10,000 metres. It was a glorious summer's day. Zátopek's chief rival, Viljo Heino of Finland, led from the outset and at 3,000 metres, the Czech champion was back in seventeenth, but over the next two laps he made his way steadily through the field and moved up to fourth. Maintaining his momentum, he took the lead during the next kilometre, only for Heino to snatch it back by halfway. Zátopek was intent on taking charge and, using the bursts of acceleration that he had perfected in training, proceeded to run the Finn ragged. Heino, who was also paying the price for setting a blistering early pace in such heat, began to lose heart and dropped out after sixteen laps. It was now simply a question of Zátopek's winning margin. Circuit after circuit, he extended his advantage so that by the finish he had lapped all but two of the runners. The second man home, Alain Mimoun of France, was over 300 metres adrift.

Unfortunately, the race officials had become so disorientated by Zátopek's virtuoso performance that they had lost count of the number of laps and called the final circuit a lap too soon. Zátopek was alive to the situation and ran the full distance, but many others didn't and finished a lap early. Severt Dennolf of Sweden was originally awarded fourth place with Norway's Martin Stokken fifth, but the Norwegians protested, their case supported by Dennolf himself, and the positions were reversed. Meanwhile, sixth place had been given to Robert Everaert of Belgium until the runner himself pointed out that he had actually dropped out of the race five laps from the finish. In the end the red-faced organisers admitted that they were unable to record any times beyond eighth place and any positions beyond eleventh . . . except that a Frenchman by the name of Paris was last.

There was no respite for the winner. The heats of the 5,000 metres took place the next day, followed by the final on 2 August. But Zátopek's hopes of the double ended in despair when, despite a flying finish, he just failed to catch Belgium's Gaston Reiff and was pipped at the post by 0.2sec. Zátopek soon forgot his disappointment and spoke warmly of the London Olympics: 'After all those dark days of the war, the bombing, the killing, the starvation, the revival of the Olympics was as if the sun had come out. I went into the Olympic Village and suddenly there were no frontiers, no more barriers. Just the people meeting together. It was wonderfully warm. Men and women who had just lost five years of life were back again.'

Between October 1948 and June 1952 Zátopek remained unbeaten over 5,000 metres and 10,000 metres – a total of 72 races. At the Helsinki Olympics he completed an unprecedented treble, winning the 5,000 metres, 10,000 metres and marathon (his first), all in the space of eight days and all in new Olympic record times. Afterwards, asked what the marathon had been like, he replied, 'Boring.' One commentator compared the treble to scaling mounts Everest, McKinley and Kilimanjaro all in one summer. Furthermore, Zátopek's wife Dana set a new Olympic record in taking gold in the javelin. Curiously Zátopek and his wife were born on the same day in 1922 and won Olympic gold on the same day in 1952.

Zátopek retired from competition after the 1956 Melbourne Olympics, having come sixth in the marathon, his performance impaired by a hernia operation. He rose to the rank of colonel in the Czech army and performed an ambassadorial role for sport, but following the Soviet occupation of his country in 1968, he was stripped of his rank and his Communist Party membership for supporting Alexander Dubcek's reforms. He spent the next twenty years in comparative obscurity, kept away from western journalists, until the overthrow of the Communist regime in 1989 allowed him to emerge from hiding. On his death in 2000 he received a state funeral with thousands of people lining the streets of Prague to pay their respects to the country's greatest-ever athlete.

CHANGING HANDS

LONDON, 4 AUGUST 1948

Among the medallists at London in 1948 was Harold Sakata, who collected a silver for the United States in weightlifting. Sakata went on to play the villainous Oddjob in the James Bond movie *Goldfinger*. Danish swimmer Greta Andersen had mixed memories of the Games. After winning gold in the 100 metres freestyle, the twenty-year-old dramatically collapsed and sank below the surface of the Empire Pool during a heat of the women's 400 metres freestyle. America's Nancy Lees, who had swum in the previous heat, and Hungary's Elemer Szathmarry dived in to hold Andersen's head above water until the race ended. Although unconscious when carried to her dressing-room, she soon recovered.

Perhaps the unlikeliest medal winner in 1948 was Hungarian shooter Károly Takács, who won the rapid-fire pistol event. Born in Budapest in 1910, he made a name for himself in the world of shooting and won a European title in the 1930s. Then in 1938, while serving as a sergeant in the army, he was taking part in a training session when a defective grenade that he was holding exploded in his right hand – his pistol hand – and shattered it completely.

Although he was allowed to remain in the army despite his disability, it seemed that his shooting days were over and he plunged into the depths of despair. But after a month in hospital, his drive returned and he resolved to take up shooting again, this time with his left hand. Despite never having used that hand for shooting prior to the accident, Takács secretly

102

and painstakingly taught himself to shoot with his left, proving so successful that the following year he won the Hungarian pistol shooting championship and was a member of the national team that won the automatic pistol event at the world championships. It was a remarkable transformation.

With no wartime Games, he had to wait until 1948, by which time he was 38, to show off his newly acquired skills on the Olympic stage and duly qualified for the rapid-fire pistol event. Before the competition began, the favourite – world champion and world record holder Carlos Enrique Diaz Saenz Valiente of Argentina – asked Takács why he was in London, to which the Hungarian replied: 'I'm here to learn.' Shooting left-handed, Takács beat the Argentinean by nine points and the world record by ten to capture gold. During the medal ceremony, Diaz Saenz Valiente turned to Takács and said: 'You have learned enough.'

Four years later in Helsinki, Takács successfully defended his title to become the first repeat winner of the rapid-fire pistol event – a fitting end to the career of the man who reinvented himself following such an horrific accident.

TWO UNSUNG HEROES

HELSINKI, 26 JULY 1952

The book of Luxembourg sporting heroes is one of publishing's less substantial tomes. So their contribution to the 1952 Helsinki Olympics was expected to begin and end with the opening ceremony, yet they shocked the athletics world with a surprise gold medal in the men's 1,500 metres.

The joint world record holder, Werner Lueg of Germany, was the pre-race favourite, although the line-up also included a promising young Englishman by the name of Roger Bannister. Nobody paid much attention to little Josef Barthel of Luxembourg, even though he had won his semi-final in impressive style. Coming off the last bend in the final, Lueg looked set to collect gold but he folded badly in the last fifty yards and Barthel sprinted through from the back of the field to hold off Robert McMillen of the United States in an Olympic record time of 3min 45.1sec. Lueg finished third, with Bannister fourth.

Barthel, who had broken his personal best by more than three seconds, could hardly take it all in. 'Afterwards,' he said, 'I didn't appreciate right away that I had won. For me, as for the public, it was a surprise.'

It was also a surprise for the organisers who, not anticipating a Luxembourg medal, had omitted to provide the band with the score for the country's national anthem. So at the medal ceremony the musicians hurriedly improvised a tune that bore little resemblance to the Luxembourg anthem. Nobody was any the wiser.

Five days later – on 31 July – Pakistan swimmer Mohammed Ramzan staked his claim to Olympic fame by swimming two extra lengths in his heat of the 1,500 metres freestyle. The other five competitors had already completed the thirty-length course, but Ramzan kept going after mistakenly interpreting a sign number put up for the swimmers to mean that he still had two more lengths. Cheered on by a crowd of 5,000, he swam the 31st length at such a crawl that an anxious official appeared at the top of his lane, urging him to stop. But Ramzan ignored him and insisted on completing a 32nd leg, coming home in 23min 14.3sec – over four minutes behind the heat winner, America's defending champion Jimmy McClane.

Ramzan was mystified by his sudden elevation to cult status. 'I thought I had another two lengths to go,' he told reporters. 'It doesn't matter really. I thoroughly enjoyed the swim.'

WALK DON'T RUN

HELSINKI, 27 JULY 1952

Race walking is arguably the most unnatural act that remains legal. To see a male Olympic walker in full cry is to be reminded of Barbara Windsor in a *Carry On* film, wiggling down the road in a tight skirt hoping to catch Sid James's eye. Whoever devised the sport must have had either a leg impediment or a strange upbringing. It is also a sport where the rules are notoriously difficult to enforce, with trackside scrutinisers waiting to pounce on what they consider the slightest misdemeanour. Three hints that a competitor has been guilty of running instead of walking and a metaphorical giant crook is produced to yank them out of the race. From the very start a race walker is an accident waiting to happen.

The rules of international race walking state that 'walking is a progression by steps so taken that unbroken contact with the ground is maintained.' In other words, the toe of the rear foot must not be lifted from the ground until the heel of the front foot has touched down. Competitors must not become airborne. However, interpretation of precisely what constitutes a running step is always open to debate; one judge's walk is another's run. Consequently, inconsistency and confusion are an everyday part of the event, as was very much the case in the men's 10-kilometre walk at the 1952 Helsinki Olympics.

No fewer than seven men were disqualified in the course of the heats and the final for running (or 'lifting', to give it the technical term), among them two-thirds of the British team. Roland Hardy, a 26-year-old Chesterfield engineer, was pulled out on lap twenty of the first heat when lying third. Afterwards he complained: 'I'm not only surprised, I'm absolutely fed up after all these months of training.' Then, in the second heat, Britain's Lol Allen was pulled out with five laps remaining when handily placed in fifth. Britain's third string, George Coleman, a thirty-year-old Luton car mechanic, won that heat to reach the final but he, too, was nearly disqualified for 'lifting'. The Finnish judges were prevented from disqualifying him by the intervention of the chief judge, George Obergweger, who overruled them, saying: 'If the third Englishman is to be disqualified, I might myself disqualify the whole field and declare it no race!' British team manager Jack Crump expressed himself 'disappointed and dissatisfied' with the Finnish judges, adding: 'We were astounded that the methods of Coleman, a great stylist who has not before been queried, should have been in doubt.'

In the face of such over-zealous judging, the final descended into a farce. Amid suspicions that the judges were determined to secure a Scandinavian victory, Sweden's John Mikaelsson led into the closing stages from Switzerland's Fritz Schwab (whose father Arthur won silver in the 50-kilometre walk at the 1936 Olympics) and Bruno Junk of the Soviet Union. Then, on the final lap, Schwab and Junk were both informed that they were about to be disqualified. In a bizarre scene, the pair blatantly ran the last thirty metres to outsprint the judge who was scurrying along in hot pursuit, trying desperately to disqualify them before they reached the finish as all eliminations had to take place during the actual race. Since he failed to catch them in time, their second and third places were allowed to stand!

SOVIET STORM

HELSINKI, 27 JULY 1952

During the 1950s relations between the United States and the Soviet Union were, at best, strained. Mutual distrust was the order of the day in the wake of Senator Joe McCarthy's Communist witch-hunt, with Americans living in constant fear of Reds under the beds. Sadly, the Cold War spilled over on to the field of sport when the two nations contested the medals in the light-heavyweight division of the weightlifting at the 1952 Olympics. The three principals were Stanley Stanczyk of the United States, six times world champion and the gold medallist in London four years earlier, and the Russian pair Trofim Lomakin and Arkady Vorobyev.

The simmering unrest came to a head during the press segment. After Stanczyk was allowed a lift of 127.5kg, the Russians complained that he had leaned back too far for it to be considered a legal press. However, the judges voted 2–1 in Stanczyk's favour. The Americans continued the war of words when Vorobyev suddenly lost consciousness in the process of making his last press attempt, voicing the opinion that the Soviet lifters were on drugs. The snatch passed without incident and going into the final section – the jerk – Stanczyk led Lomakin by 2.5kg, with Vorobyev close behind in third. All three lifters managed 160kg, but then Stanczyk lost count. He thought he had another lift in which to raise the stakes but discovered to his horror that he had just made his third and final attempt. So when Lomakin lifted 165kg to take the lead, Stanczyk was unable to fight back. The best the American could hope for now was silver.

The only man who could deprive Lomakin of gold was Vorobyev. With one more chance, he decided to go for broke and attempt a world record 170kg. Approaching the bar cautiously, he grabbed it, raised it a matter of inches off the ground and then dropped it, causing an immediate row as to whether or not it was a proper attempt. Steeling himself again, he seized the bar and pulled the weight to his chest before straining every muscle to thrust it into the air at arm's length. The crowd roared in approval, but just as the referee called out 'Release!' at the end of the stipulated two seconds, Vorobyev staggered wildly and dropped the bar. Now everyone started arguing about whether or not it was a valid lift. One judge said yes; the other two disagreed. At that, a distraught Vorobyev, convinced that he would have to settle for bronze, retired to his dressing-room and started to get changed. Outside, the arguments raged on, with Vorobyev's camp protesting that the lift was fair and that anyway he had been made to hold it for longer than two seconds. Suddenly, some forty minutes after the competition had apparently ended, Vorobyev's coach burst into his dressing-room and told him breathlessly that the judges had decided to award him one more attempt. Since the officials had already started the clock, Vorobyev had no time to compose himself. Hurriedly changing back into his lifting gear and with the clock ticking down, he rushed across to the platform. It was no way to prepare for a world record and inevitably he toppled backwards under the burden. The gold medal was confirmed as going to Lomakin, with Stanczyk taking silver and Vorobyev bronze.

While Vorobyev's supporters continued in vain to press their man's case, Stanczyk was left to reflect on the fatal miscalculation that had denied him the opportunity of toppling Lomakin after leading for most of the competition. 'It was a mistake on my part,' said the American ruefully. 'I could have beaten him with one more lift.'

ATTACK ON THE REFEREE

HELSINKI, 28 JULY 1952

The Uruguayan basketball team took fewer prisoners than the Keystone Cops. They played hard but not fair, their rough-house approach meaning that a half-nelson was as much a part of their vocabulary as a dunk shot. In a tempestuous Olympic semi-final round match with France at Helsinki's Trade Fair Hall Arena, the five-man Uruguayan starting line-up had already been reduced to three because of persistent personal fouls when their anger boiled over in disgraceful scenes that left the American referee, Vincent Farrell, nursing a black eye.

France led 66–64 going into the final minute before Uruguay managed to level the scores. However, their joy was cut short when referee Farrell whistled for a foul against them. Angry Uruguayans leaped from the bench and hurled abuse at Farrell for five minutes until he explained that because the foul had occurred after the basket, their two points would stand. But any hopes of peace being restored were shattered when, on being awarded possession, France switched the ball to Jacques Dessemme, who scored the basket to give his country a 68–66 lead. Almost immediately the final whistle went, whereupon the volatile Uruguayans charged at the unsuspecting Farrell. One player, Wilfredo Pelaez, hit the referee in the eye while another, Carlos Rossello, grabbed Farrell by the throat from behind. Farrell, who was also kicked in the groin, hit his head on the floor as he went down under the weight of the assault and was carried off with a black eye and head injuries. Meanwhile a lone Chilean, Hector Garcia Otero, waded into the crowd, viciously attacking anyone who had been seen applauding the French victory, before he was overpowered by the combined efforts of four police officers. Although the arena's head of security had his right elbow smashed, Finnish police later played down the mass brawl as 'trifling'. 'We are faced by tougher propositions every week,' said the chief of police, 'especially on Saturday nights when the boys get a bit too frisky after having soaked their pay envelopes.'

Pelaez and Rossello were subsequently banned from the remainder of the competition, but their team-mates carried on their good work. When Uruguay met the USSR three days later, three Soviet players had to receive medical attention during the second half. The following day Uruguay met bitter South American rivals Argentina in the match to determine third place. The Uruguayans emerged victorious in a match containing so many personal fouls that they finished with only four players and Argentina with three. Oh, and there was another 'trifling' 25-man punch-up.

When Uruguay came to receive their ill-deserved bronze medals, Pelaez and Rossello had the effrontery to join the rest of the squad for the presentation. However, when their presence was spotted, the pair were forced to hand back their medals. A sad chapter in Olympic history was closed.

A GREAT DANE

Lis Hartel looked set for an illustrious future in the dressage discipline of equestrian sport until, in 1944, the 23-year-old Dane contracted polio while pregnant. Although almost paralysed, she was determined to pursue her riding career and began her rehabilitation during the latter stages of her pregnancy. Over a period of months she learned to lift her arms and regain the use of her thigh muscles. Her daughter having been born healthy, Hartel stepped up her recuperation. She started by crawling and then, some eight months after being stricken, she was able to take a few tentative steps on crutches. Gradually she built up her strength, but when she finally summoned the energy and courage to climb back on a horse, it proved so exhausting that she had to rest for two weeks before trying again. Although still paralysed below the knees, she had learned to do without those muscles and in 1947 entered the women's dressage event at the Scandinavian Riding Championships, finishing a creditable second. Not content with resting on her laurels, she then set her heart on winning a place in Denmark's team for the 1952 Olympics and put up such outstanding performances that she was duly selected for the trip to Helsinki.

There were only four women competitors in the individual dressage competition and Hartel, unable to use her legs, had to be helped on and off her horse. Nevertheless, she impressed everyone with her skill and concentration, eventually finishing a close second behind Henri Saint Cyr of Sweden. In a touching scene at the medal ceremony, Saint Cyr lifted Hartel up on to the victory rostrum – in recognition of the woman whose courage would serve as an inspiration to others. Four years later in Stockholm (where the equestrian events at the Melbourne Games were held because of Australian quarantine regulations), the remarkable Lis Hartel repeated her achievement with a second Olympic silver medal, again finishing second to Saint Cyr in the individual dressage.

Another equestrian competitor who was undoubtedly deserving of a medal at Helsinki was British rider Major Laurence Rook. But fate was to deny him in the cruellest way.

As a boy the Nottinghamshire-born Rook wanted to join the navy but was turned down because of poor eyesight. He served in the army during the Second World War and was awarded the Military Cross for single-handedly capturing a German observation post and marching his prisoner back to British lines through a German minefield. After the war he took up show-jumping and was selected for the British three-day event team at the 1952 Olympics. A gold medal appeared a distinct possibility until his horse Starlight put a foot in a hidden drainage ditch and threw the galloping Major. Despite suffering concussion, 31-year-old Rook managed to complete the course but was unaware that he had briefly ridden the wrong side of a marker flag. Consequently he was disqualified, thus denying him or his team the chance of gold.

However, this story too had a happy ending. Four years later Rook's sixth place in the individual competition on Wild Venture was sufficient to steer the British three-day event team to an Olympic gold medal.

THE NON-TRIER

HELSINKI, 2 AUGUST 1952

Ingemar Johansson is probably the most famous boxer in Swedish history. In June 1959 he became the first non-American to win the world heavyweight title since Italy's Primo Carnera 25 years earlier when he sensationally knocked out Floyd Patterson in the third round of their fight at New York's Yankee Stadium. Although Patterson regained his world title the following year – the first boxer ever to do so – Johansson's exploits had assured him of a place in Scandinavian folklore. Yet how much different it had been at the start of his career, when Johansson returned home from the Helsinki Olympics in disgrace after being disqualified for not trying during the fight for the gold medal.

The nineteen-year-old Swede had a relatively uneventful path to the super-heavyweight final in 1952, his progress being steady rather than spectacular. Following a walkover against Uruguay's Luis Sosa, he won decisions against Harymir Netyka of Czechoslovakia, Tomislav Krizmanic of Yugoslavia and Ikka Koski of Finland. Standing between Johansson and the gold medal was an American called Ed Sanders.

At 6ft 4in and weighing 220lb, Sanders had a fearsome reputation. He once lifted a fellow heavyweight clean off the canvas with a brutal left uppercut and won his place on the US Olympic team by knocking out an opponent despite having a broken hand. Whereas Johansson's route to the final had been smooth and serene, Sanders's was littered with bloody victims. Three of his opponents had suffered severe punishment and the man he had beaten in the semi-final, South Africa's Andries

Nieman, was still in hospital with concussion and a suspected fractured arm. Johansson was scarcely relishing the meeting.

The Swede would become famous for the knockout punch in his right hand, affectionately dubbed 'Ingo's Bingo' or the 'Hammer of Thor'. But the hammer stayed in his toolbox that night as he tried to keep as far away from Sanders as possible. Sanders's son later said of Johansson: 'The guy got freaked out. He was so nervous. He just didn't want to compete.' Johansson spent the whole time back-pedalling without throwing a single punch. He was running scared. The French referee Roger Vaisberg issued the Swede with several warnings until finally, at the end of round two, he lost his patience and pushed Johansson angrily towards his corner before announcing that he was disqualifying him for not 'giving of his best'. Jeered and whistled at by the crowd, Johansson suffered further humiliation when informed that he would not be awarded the silver medal. He slunk back to Sweden in shame.

Both men turned professional later that year but ironically it was Sanders's career that was short-lived: in 1954 he died of a brain haemorrhage after being knocked out in only his ninth professional bout by Willy James. Sanders was just 24. Five years on, the man whom Sanders had reduced to a quivering wreck that night in Helsinki was acclaimed world champion. For Johansson, victory over Patterson brought an end to his personal nightmare. He later recalled: 'I could think of only one thing: it's over. Now I am able to go home with my head held high.' And in 1966 he was awarded his silver medal.

A BOXING MATCH UNDERWATER

MELBOURNE, 6 DECEMBER 1956

They were meant to be the friendly Games – the first time the Olympics had ever been held in the southern hemisphere. But the single event that most people remember from the 1956 Melbourne Olympics is the brutal bloodbath between the water polo teams of Hungary and the Soviet Union.

Although Australia's strict quarantine laws meant that the equestrian events had already taken place in Sweden in June, the country eagerly anticipated the start of the Games proper on 22 November. And even before the opening ceremony, traditional Aussie irreverence left its mark with a hoax involving the cherished Olympic torch. For despite the fact that most of Australia was gripped with Olympic fever, a group of Sydney University students couldn't see what all the fuss was about. To them, the elongated build-up to the Games was proving a monumental bore. What particularly irritated them was all the hype surrounding the traditional carrying of the Olympic torch – a journey that was to wend its way right down the east coast to Sydney before heading south-west towards Melbourne. So the student pranksters decided to register their protest by staging their very own torch ceremony at Sydney Town Hall with the help of a sawn-off broom handle, a used jam tin and a pair of old Y-fronts!

The fake Olympic torch was the brainchild of twenty-year-old veterinary student Barry Larkin. Along with Peter Gralton and other colleagues from St John's College, Larkin painted the broom handle and jam tin silver, stuffed some underpants

116

soaked in kerosene into the tin and lit the hoax Olympic flame. With the real torch-bearer some way behind, Larkin, Gralton and a third associate (all dressed in official whites) made their way into the city's York Street en route for the Town Hall and an appointment with the Lord Mayor, Pat Hills. However, in York Street their bogus runner lost his nerve, dropped the flame and ran off. With their plan facing ruin, the co-conspirators quickly scooped up the torch and the burning Y-fronts and, against the backdrop of a cheering crowd, Larkin set off to carry out a joke that he had intended watching from a safe distance. On and on he ran through the city streets, proudly holding the torch aloft. All the while he was flanked by an escort of half a dozen police motorcycles, since officials and spectators alike were convinced that he was the authentic torch-bearer. Finally, reaching the Town Hall, he ran up the steps and handed the torch to the Lord Mayor, who then embarked on his ceremonial speech.

Interviewed in 2000, Larkin remembered: 'All I could think of at the time was, "Shit, what am I going to do now?" I thought if I play it cool, everything will be OK, so I just walked back down the steps and jumped on a tram back to the old Astoria coffee house in Newtown.'

The real torch turned up shortly afterwards, but by then most of the crowd had gone. All that remained were a few stragglers and a bewildered Lord Mayor.

Sadly, this sense of fun did not spill over into the water polo pool for a match that was a victim of bad timing. On 4 November 1956, 200,000 Soviet troops invaded Hungary to crush a revolution against Communist rule. A month later the two countries met in the Olympic water polo tournament. The nature of the sport was irrelevant. There was no particular animosity between the two sets of players. It could have been cycling, showjumping, or the egg and spoon race – in whatever circumstances those two nations had met at that particular time, there would have been the potential for violence.

Hungary were water polo champions in three of the previous four Olympics but, in view of the recent political events, the 5,500 crowd saw them as very much the underdogs, the good guys. One member of the Hungarian team, Gyorgy Karpati, admitted recently: 'I'm convinced even the referee was pulling for us. We were from a small country battling the huge Soviet Goliath.'

Hungary's Dezso Gyarmati set the tone for the match by hitting his Soviet marker while scoring the opening goal. Soon sly punches were being thrown and kicks were being aimed as, in the words of Harry Carpenter in the *Daily Mail*, the Olympic pool 'became a bubbling cauldron of spite'. Swedish referee Sam Zuckerman tried to control play but was unable to see what was going on behind his back. As scratches and fouls became the order of the day, Hungarian players complained of being kicked in the stomach; the Soviet mood was not helped by the fact that they were on the receiving end of a hammering.

With Hungary leading 4–0 and time ebbing away, the simmering hostility finally erupted. Russia's Valentine Prokobov climaxed a series of ugly fouls by smashing his right fist into the face of Ervin Zador, scorer of two of Hungary's goals. As Zador climbed gingerly out of the pool with blood pouring from his right eye, scores of angry Hungarian fans screamed 'Murderers!' and rushed forward, shaking their fists at the Russians. The Russian players responded by hissing 'Fascists!' at the Hungarians. With the fans still baying for Russian blood, the police were called in to prevent a full-scale riot. Meanwhile, the referee, who had sent off three Russians and one Hungarian, decided to end the match prematurely and Hungary's 4–0 winning margin was allowed to stand as the result.

Among the impartial supporters at the match was Hawaiian swimmer Sonny Tanabe, who watched from near the top of the arena. Recalling that blood was clearly visible in the water, he added: 'There was a lot of fighting in the water, kicking, grabbing and stuff like that. I'd never seen anything like it.'

Both sets of players were given police escorts to their dressing-rooms. While Zador was taken to hospital, two Russians were accused of playing 'like Chicago gangsters'. One Hungarian player said: 'It is always like this when we play Russia.' And Zador, pictures of whose bloody face would be splashed across newspapers around the world, sighed: 'It wasn't water polo. It was a boxing match underwater.'

Even without Zador, who was forced to miss the final against Yugoslavia, Hungary went on to take gold. But the repercussions of the water polo battle would be felt elsewhere in the Games. When Hungarian and Soviet fencers met in the final of the individual sabre, Russian army sergeant Lev Kouznetsov was loudly barracked by the crowd. And there was a fresh row after Mexico's Joaquin Capilla had won the men's high-diving competition by less than half a mark from two Americans – the first time since 1912 that the US had not taken gold in that event. Outraged US diving coach Karl Michaels promptly accused Russian judge Eva Bozd-Morskaya and Hungarian judge Bela Bapp of colluding to deny victory to America's Gary Tobian. He claimed the pair had not shown their marking cards simultaneously but had waited to see what the other had scored before deliberately disagreeing. Michaels added that the two judges had undermarked American divers and overmarked their rivals. In short, they had 'ganged up' on the Americans. Michaels also accused another Hungarian judge of illegally coaching his divers while judging. Even the victorious Capilla confessed: 'The marking was disgusting. It made the competition ridiculous. The judges let their national feelings get the better of them.'

At the end of the Games, 45 members of the Hungarian Olympic delegation refused to return to their Soviet-occupied homeland.

PHOTOGRAPHIC EVIDENCE

MELBOURNE, 7 DECEMBER 1956

Gaining an Olympic gold medal should be reason for scenes of unbridled joy, yet two winners at the 1956 Games were left with mixed emotions. Canadian shooter Gerald Ouellette shot sixty consecutive bull's-eyes in the small-bore rifle event to record a perfect score of 600 points, one point ahead of the USSR's Vassily Borissov. Ouellette's outstanding achievement ought to have brought him a new world record in addition to his gold medal, but then it was discovered that the targets on the rifle range had been set one and a half metres short of the standard distance for Olympic competition. So although he was able to keep his gold, his world record was not recognised. Meanwhile, eighteen-year-old Soviet rower Vyacheslav Ivanov was so delighted at winning the single sculls that he jumped up and down for joy and threw his gold medal into the air in jubilation. Unfortunately, he failed to catch it on the way down and the precious medal sank into the depths of Lake Wendouree. Although he dived in to try and retrieve it, the search proved in vain. He was subsequently given a replacement and was less reckless when winning the same event at the next two Games.

A third gold medallist, American weightlifter Charles Vinci, was simply relieved at having been allowed to compete. Approaching the weigh-in time, Vinci was 1½lb over the 123lb limit for the bantamweight division. He was sent away to run it off for an hour, but when he returned to the scales he was still seven ounces over. Now there were just fifteen minutes left. In a last desperate attempt to remove the excess weight, his advisers gave him a brutal haircut. The plan worked. Vinci passed the weigh-in and went on to win the gold medal, setting a new world record in the process.

However, the British cycling team were less fortunate, being denied victory in the road race by a foolhardy photographer. The event was dogged with controversy from the outset. The start was delayed for fifteen minutes when it became apparent that three unauthorised Irish riders – 23-year-old carpenter Paul Fitzgerald, the Irish road cycling champion from Kerry, 21-year-old butcher Tom Gerrard from County Meath, but who had been living in Melbourne for the past nine months, and 22-year-old furniture machinist Tom Flanagan – had managed to sneak in among the 88 riders. All three were members of the National Cycling Association of Ireland, a body not recognised by the International Cycling Union, the organisation responsible for the Olympic event. The Irish body affiliated with the ICU was the Eireann Cycling Association, which had declined to send any cyclists to the Games. In a protest orchestrated by Irish nationalists, the trio, all wearing singlets bearing the word 'Ireland', travelled to the road circuit by van before unloading their bicycles and infiltrating the line-up. When their presence was discovered, the police were called in to remove them. 'We demand justice,' shouted the three protestors. 'We came 10,000 miles to compete and now we cannot start.' They then joined 200 supporters in handing out Irish nationalist pamphlets that posed the question: 'Must we beg crumbs from England's table so that we may eat on Mount Olympus?'

The 117-mile race itself was equally eventful. The individual race was won by Italy's Ercole Baldini from France's Arnaud Geyre and Britain's Alan Jackson. Although Baldini literally won by a mile, France and Britain complained that the Italian had ridden the closing stages sandwiched between two film trucks and had thus been shielded from the wind. The protest was dismissed. Britain had even more cause to feel that they were robbed of victory in the team event, the outcome of which was determined by the results of the individual race. The team of Jackson, Arthur Brittain and twenty-year-old Yorkshireman

Billy Holmes were very much in contention until a freak accident destroyed their chances. At the end of the seventh lap – the 75-mile point – and with temperatures in the high 20s Celsius (high 80s Fahrenheit), Holmes cycled slowly to the side of the road to grab a wet sponge from his helpers. Just then an amateur photographer jumped into the road to take a picture. Neither seeing nor expecting the trespasser, Holmes crashed into him and suffered a nasty fall, sustaining cuts to his arms and legs. Moreover, his front wheel was badly buckled and Holmes was delayed two and a half minutes while it was replaced. Having lost a mile as a result of the incident, he set off in pursuit and although he managed to catch up with the leaders ten miles later, the exertion took its toll and he faded to finish fourteenth. With Jackson third and Brittain sixth, a twelfth-place finish for Holmes would have given Britain the team gold at the expense of France.

To round off a day to forget for the race organisers, the tape recorder containing the various national anthems broke down during the victory ceremony. The crowd were asked to applaud politely instead.

DEATH ON THE TRACK

ROME, 26 AUGUST 1960

Assessing the sweltering weather before the cyclists took part in the 100-kilometre team race, an official muttered ominously: 'I've never known such conditions. The heat is pumping up from the road. Dozens of the competitors won't make it.' His prediction was to prove chillingly accurate, as the first Olympics with worldwide television coverage had the painful duty of reporting the first death in the Games since the marathon of 1912.

From the moment that Rome was awarded the Olympics, questions were asked concerning the wisdom of staging them during what was traditionally the city's hottest period of the year. But the warnings were ignored, with the result that the cyclists were left at the mercy of temperatures that reached 34 degrees Celsius (93 degrees Fahrenheit).

At previous Olympics the results of the individual road race had been used to decide the team event, but in Rome there was a separate team race, held over 62 miles of the Cristoforo Colombo circuit. Four cyclists from each team raced against the clock, riding together in a line and changing positions as in a team pursuit, the official time being that of the third rider home. Denmark were lying in fourth place when one of their quartet, Jorgen Jorgensen, collapsed with mild sunstroke. His exit left the Danes a man short and put extra pressure on the remaining three, among them 23-year-old Knut Jensen, the Scandinavian road racing champion. In the unrelenting heat the depleted Danes were making a big effort to snatch the bronze medal position when, thirteen miles from the finish,

Jensen, too, collapsed and was sent sprawling from his machine. Although treated by a doctor on the spot, Jensen had suffered a fractured skull in the fall and later died in hospital.

News of Jensen's death was withheld from members of the Danish Olympic soccer team before their match with Argentina and the rest of the country's cyclists pulled out of the Games as a mark of respect. While his fellow competitors queued up to criticise the 'torturous' conditions, there was a further shock when it emerged that the heat was only partly to blame for the tragedy. For tests revealed that prior to the race Jensen had taken Ronicol, a banned blood circulation stimulant. The combination of heat and performance-enhancing drugs had proved fatal.

On a lighter note the heat obviously got to a man who tried to enter the Olympic Village with a colander on his head, claiming that he was the cook for the Lunar Olympic delegation from outer space!

LARSON TIMED OUT

ROME, 26 AUGUST 1960

America's big hope for the men's 100 metres freestyle at the Rome Olympics was 23-year-old Jeff Farrell. However, six days before the start of the US Olympic trials in Detroit, he awoke with a pain in his side. Despite undergoing an emergency appendectomy, he seemed certain to withdraw, much to the consternation of the US swimming officials who, all too aware of his value to the team, offered him the opportunity of qualifying a week after everyone else in the hope that he would have returned to something near full fitness. To his credit, Farrell rejected the offer, insisting that he did not want preferential treatment, and took his chances at the official trials. Although his recovery had been quicker than anticipated, he was still forced to swim with his abdomen tightly taped and missed out on qualification for the 100-metre freestyle by 0.1 of a second. Consolation of sorts came with a fourth-place finish in the 200 freestyle, which earned him an Olympic place on two relay teams – the medley and the 4×200 freestyle.

With Farrell out of the 100-metre freestyle, US medal hopes in that event now rested with Lance Larson, a twenty-year-old student at the University of Southern California. Despite being the first American high school swimmer to break the fifty-second barrier in the 100 yards freestyle, Larson specialised in the 100 metres butterfly, a race not included at the 1960 Games. Furthermore, he faced stiff opposition in the freestyle from the world record holder, John Devitt of Australia, who naturally enough started as clear favourite.

As expected, both men reached the final, where they lined up in adjacent lanes: Devitt in lane three and Larson in lane four. With twenty yards to go, Devitt was a yard ahead and the result looked likely to follow the form book but Larson launched a grandstand finish, pegging the Australian back with every stroke. Two strokes from the finish, Larson was inches ahead and, to most poolside observers, appeared to touch fractionally ahead of Devitt. The latter certainly thought so and, after congratulating Larson, climbed from the pool in disappointment. Awaiting official confirmation of his victory, Larson remained in the water, swimming a casual, celebratory backstroke length of the pool before metamorphosing into his favoured butterfly at the turn while the photographers gathered around ready to capture his reaction to the announcement of gold.

For ten long minutes they waited. These were the last Olympics before the introduction of automatic timing, the results being decided instead by handheld stopwatches and the accuracy of the judges' eyesight. And therein lay the problem. Of the three judges designated to determine first place, two voted for Devitt. However the three judges charged with naming second place also voted 2–1 for Devitt to be second. Thus the six judges were split straight down the middle – three thought Larson had won; the other three thought Devitt was the winner. With the judges undecided, the chief judge, German Hans Runströmer, was called in for the casting vote. He opted for Devitt and the delayed result was duly announced over the tannoy to a disbelieving Larson, who was still in the perfect place for drowning his sorrows. The photographers immediately rushed off to find the Australian gold medallist.

Larson was baffled. 'Everybody down there told me I had won,' he said. 'I can't understand it.' Devitt, too, could offer no explanation other than: 'On my last stroke I touched under water and maybe that's why I won.'

Both swimmers had been given an Olympic record time of 55.2sec but as the increasingly disgruntled American camp began voicing their feelings, it emerged that of the three official watches, one timed Larson at 55.0sec and the other two at 55.1sec. All three watches on Devitt timed the Australian at

55.2 sec. Not unreasonably, the Americans asked why Larson's time was given as 55.2 and not 55.1, to which they were informed that under international rules the runner-up could not have a faster time than the winner!

It was not only the official handheld stopwatches that named Larson as the victor – the unofficial electronic timer also showed Larson winning by 0.06sec, in 55.10sec to Devitt's 55.16. In the circumstances it was hardly surprising that the Americans launched a protest, which, in turn, was overruled by the International Amateur Swimming Federation (FINA). Max Ritter, treasurer of the US Olympic Committee, was particularly angry at the intervention of Herr Runströmer who, despite technically being ineligible to vote, had ordered Larson's time to be amended to 55.2 before declaring Devitt the winner. Maintaining that recording machines on three different tapes showed Larson as the winner, Ritter stormed: 'The appeal jury claimed that the judges were not indecisive. I asked how it was possible when the judges were split to say that it was a decision. They said the chief judge voted for lane number three as the winner and this made it 4–3 to Devitt. The chief judge has never voted in any previous Olympics in swimming. He simply collects the cards and correlates the votes. Also, anyone who judges a race must be put on an elevated stand and have a printed card on which to vote. The chief judge in this race was not on an elevated stand and he did not have a printed card. When I pointed this out, the secretary said that the chief judge wrote his vote on a slip of paper. To have their way, they resort to trickery like this. It was against all the rules and regulations.'

As the row festered, Ritter went on to brand the Olympic swimming judges 'a bunch of timid, unemployed pussy-footers', adding: 'It's high time we threw these people out and trusted to the machines.' In that respect at least, he would get his way.

His view his supported by Sammy Lee, coach of the US diving team, who claimed that American competitors were being victimised by the officials in Rome. Lee said that the diving judges had two standards. 'They expect one kind of performance from the Americans but they will settle for something less from all the rest. If an American makes a mistake in the diving, they come down heavily. But if a European makes a mistake, they are quick to close their eyes.'

The FINA appeal jury countered that it had viewed a CBS TV tape of the contentious finish on no fewer than twelve occasions . . . and still reached the same conclusion. FINA's Dutch president Jan de Vries confessed: 'I looked and I looked and I do not know. I have said that only if I am 200 per cent convinced will I change and I am not 200 per cent convinced.'

While FINA thought there was insufficient evidence to overturn the original result, New York officials of the US Amateur Athletic Association were viewing fresh footage from United Press International Movietone. They claimed that the UPI pictures definitely showed that Larson had won and, in a last-ditch effort to reverse the decision, arranged for the film to be flown out to Ritter in Rome. However this appeal, too, fell on deaf ears. The result stood.

Larson accepted his fate graciously and gained a degree of consolation by picking up a gold medal in the medley relay where he swam his speciality, the butterfly, the fully recovered Jeff Farrell sealing the US triumph on the anchor freestyle leg. In second place – fifteen metres behind – were the Australians.

THE BIG FIX

ROME, 31 AUGUST 1960

One of the great hard luck stories of the Rome Games surrounded Wym Essajas, the first person selected to represent Surinam in Olympic competition. Sadly, a breakdown in communications meant that he was mistakenly informed that the heats of the men's 800 metres were being held in the afternoon instead of the morning. After spending the morning relaxing in bed in preparation for his big moment, he arrived at the stadium only to be told that the heats were over. Thus the despondent Essajas returned to Surinam without even competing.

The Belgian men's hockey team also fell foul of the fates during a match against France. With the game goalless and France on the attack, an Italian traffic policeman, on duty just outside the ground, blew his whistle. The Belgians, thinking it was the umpire's whistle, instinctively stopped playing, allowing France to score the only goal of the game. The same competition saw the end of India's 32-year run of Olympic success, during which time they had won thirty consecutive games, scoring no fewer than 197 goals and conceding just eight. In Rome they met their match in bitter rivals Pakistan, who defeated them 1–0 in the final to take the gold medal.

The wrestling events in Rome were staged in the Basilica of Maxentius, site of similar contests some 2,000 years earlier, where the lightweight division of the Greco-Roman competition ended in acrimony amid allegations that one of the wrestlers had deliberately taken a 'dive'. Avtandil Koridze of the USSR met Bulgaria's Dimitro Stoyanov knowing that he needed to score a fall to have any chance of wrestling the gold medal from Yugoslavia's Branislav Martinovic. Anything less – a draw or even a points win – would hand gold to Martinovic. With just one minute remaining of their twelve-minute contest, Koridze and Stoyanov were locked in stalemate, neither man looking capable of achieving a fall. Martinovic seemed assured of gold. Then Koridze whispered a few words in his opponent's ear, suddenly threw Stoyanov to the ground and pinned him for the winning fall.

The Yugoslavs lodged an immediate protest and the International Amateur Wrestling Federation ordered an investigation by a technical committee on the grounds that there had been a 'suspicion of collusion' in the contest. Ichiro Hatta, Japanese vice-president of the federation, went further, claiming that Stoyanov took a dive because the Communist-world wrestlers wanted to stop the gold medal going to a Yugoslav. Koridze meanwhile insisted that he had won 'correctly and fairly'. He went on: 'At the end the match my opponent was clearly tired. I could have disposed of him any way I wanted. I understand my talking to him during the match could have been mistaken for an arrangement between us. But all I said was, "You have lost and you'd better give up."'

After hearing all the evidence, the committee disqualified Stoyanov yet incredibly Koridze escaped punishment and was allowed to fight on for the gold, which he duly won by defeating the luckless Martinovic. To increase the Yugoslav's sense of injustice, on the orders of the committee the result of the contentious Koridze-Stoyanov match was subsequently amended to a points win for the Russian rather than a fall.

THE BAREFOOT MAESTRO

ROME, 10 SEPTEMBER 1960

The 1960 Games marked the first occasion that the Pope was a spectator at the Olympics. Pope John XXIII watched the semi-finals of the canoeing from a window of his summer residence at Castel Gandolfo, above Lake Albano. And there was a royal champion when Crown Prince Constantine (later King Constantine II) of Greece helped his country win a gold medal in the Dragon class yachting. The then Cassius Clay made his name by winning the light-heavyweight boxing tournament while America's Wilma Rudolph, unable to walk until she was ten because of paralysis in one leg, completed the sprint double. But all of these athletic stars were in danger of being upstaged by an unknown Ethiopian guardsman who took the world of the marathon by storm.

Abebe Bikila was the first of the great East African runners that would come to dominate world distance running. Born in 1932 into a large and poor peasant family, he enlisted in the army at the age of seventeen, becoming a member of the Household Guard of Emperor Haile Selassie. The guardsmen were renowned for their marathon running but Bikila showed little interest until he watched a parade of Ethiopian athletes who had taken part in the Melbourne Olympics. His imagination fired, he came into contact with Swedish trainer Onni Niskansen. Under Niskansen's guidance, Bikila was transformed from rough diamond into a sparkling jewel. One trait that the Swede made no attempt to change, however, was Bikila's fondness for running barefoot. Instead, he simply compared

Bikila's times when running with and without shoes and concluded that his protégé did indeed run faster barefoot.

The 1960 Olympic marathon was the first to be run at night, the organisers having realised, in the wake of the cycling tragedy, that daytime heat could prove fatal over extreme distances. The course, which took in the cobblestones of the Appian Way, was lit by torches held by Italian soldiers. It was only Bikila's third marathon and he arrived in Rome virtually unheard of outside his homeland, the rest of the world unaware that, just a month before Rome, he had recorded a time of 2hr 21min 23sec at the altitude of Addis Ababa – a couple of minutes inside Emil Zátopek's existing Olympic record.

The sight of the barefoot Bikila at the start line beneath Capitol Hill raised a few eyebrows among those who wondered how he would cope with the cobbled streets. Sixty-nine runners set off and Bikila was happy to stay with a pack of more experienced runners in the early stages. He steadily began to take closer order in company with the Moroccan runner Rhadi ben Abdesellem and by the halfway point this pair had opened up a lead of 26 seconds. Nobody else could live with them and within two miles they had increased their advantage to one of nearly three and a half minutes. The Moroccan, winner of the international cross-country title earlier in the year, had already tried once to rid himself of Bikila's presence – briefly pulling sixty metres clear – but now the two were matching stride for stride.

When going over the course with his coach a few days before the race, Bikila had noticed, less than a mile from the finish, the obelisk of Axum, which Italian soldiers had taken from Ethiopia and brought to Rome. There was a slight incline after the runners passed the obelisk and Bikila, confident that he would be in contention, had decided that this would be a symbolic and timely place to make his move. Sure enough, with 500 metres remaining, Bikila sprinted away. The Moroccan had no answer. The only thing that threatened to deny Bikila victory was a wayward motor scooter that suddenly appeared on the course sixty metres from the finish, forcing Bikila to take hasty avoiding action. He crossed the line in 2hr 15min 16.2sec to set a new world record and shatter the Olympic record by an astonishing eight minutes. Indeed, the first fifteen home broke Zátopek's time.

Bikila looked amazingly fresh. Declining the offer of blankets, he limbered down gently, smiling and waving to the crowd. Whereas most marathon runners shed nearly nine pounds during a race in those days, Bikila had lost only three-quarters of a pound. The world's press wanted to know why he ran barefoot. 'I wanted the world to know that my country, Ethiopia, has always won with determination and heroism,' he said. 'We train in shoes, but it's much more comfortable to run without them. If it had been hot, I might have worn shoes.'

Not for the first time Olympic organisers were caught out by a shock winner. When it came to the medal ceremony, the stadium band didn't know the Ethiopian anthem . . . so they played the Italian one instead.

On his return home, Bikila was given a hero's welcome. Following his triumph, he received numerous invitations to run but restricted himself to just five marathons between Rome and the next Olympics in Tokyo. He underwent an appendectomy only forty days before the 1964 Olympic marathon but showed no ill effects and, this time running in shoes, went on to claim a second gold, winning by over four minutes in a world record time of 2hr 12min 11.2sec. The first man to capture two Olympic marathons still had so much energy left at the finish that he was treating the crowd to a display of callisthenics as the second and third men entered the stadium.

The remarkable Bikila returned for his third Olympic marathon, at Mexico City in 1968, nursing a hairline fracture to his right foot. The injury proved insurmountable, however, and he was forced to drop out after eleven miles. The following March he was involved in a terrible car crash that left him paralysed from the waist down. This supreme athlete, the idol of millions of Africans, spent his remaining years in a wheelchair. He died of a cerebral haemorrhage in 1973 at just 41 years of age.

THE YEAR OF THE SEX OLYMPICS

TOKYO, 15 OCTOBER 1964

For nearly thirty years there had been dark mutterings about the true sex of certain supposedly female Olympic athletes. Mildred 'Babe' Didrikson's manly appearance had prompted an ill-informed whispering campaign, while after being beaten into second place in the 1936 women's 100 metres final, Polish sprinter Stanislawa Walasiewicz petulantly accused her conqueror, America's Helen Stephens, of being a man. The Pole (who would subsequently acquire US nationality as Stella Walsh) had herself come under scrutiny for her 'long man-like strides' and 'deep bass voice' – suspicions that would prove well founded. For when Walsh was shot dead in Cleveland, Ohio, in 1980 – innocently caught up in an armed robbery – the autopsy revealed that she was a man.

Fourth in the women's high jump at those 1936 Olympics was eighteen-year-old Dora Ratjen of Germany. Twenty-one years later Dora was revealed to be Hermann Ratjen, who had been forced to bind up his genitals and pose as a woman by officials of the Nazi Youth Movement.

At the 1964 Tokyo Olympics stocky Ewa Klobukowska won bronze in the women's 100 metres before helping the Polish team to gold and a world record in the 4×100 metres relay. But three years later, having just passed a visual inspection, she was banned from international competition after failing a sex chromosome test. She was found to have 'one chromosome too many to be declared a woman for the purposes of athletic competition'. Although her team-mates were allowed to keep their relay gold medals, their world record was scrubbed. Klobukowska said of the test: 'I know what I am and how I feel. It's a dirty and stupid thing to do to me.' Stripped of all her records, she became depressed and underwent a series of operations to correct her 'ambiguous genitalia'. Ironically the condition from which she suffered would not, under current regulations, prevent her from competing.

The Tokyo Olympics also increased the suspicion surrounding the legendary Russian sisters Tamara and Irina Press. Tamara, who was built like the Kremlin, followed up her 1960 gold in the women's shot put by completing the shot and discus double. Younger sister Irina, who had won the 80 metres hurdles in 1960, now triumphed in the pentathlon. Between them the Press sisters set an incredible 23 world records during their career, but their unlikely physiques, which stopped just short of beards, led to rumours that they were either being injected with male hormones by Soviet officials or that they were actually men. And immediately before sex tests were introduced at the Olympics in 1968, the Press sisters – so dominant for years – suddenly vanished from the face of international competition. We were left to draw our own conclusions.

The 1964 Games also saw the first Olympic wedding when two Bulgarian athletes, long jumper Diana Yorgova and gymnast Nikolai Prodanov, exchanged vows at a ceremony in the Olympic Village. Baron de Coubertin would surely have approved . . . particularly as they weren't both men.

BREAKING THE PAIN BARRIER

TOKYO, 15 OCTOBER 1964

When two-time Olympic discus champion Al Oerter turned up for the qualifying round at Tokyo wearing a neck brace, his opponents could have been forgiven for thinking that the king was finally about to be dethroned. But Oerter was not about to surrender his title without a fight. As he remarked after defying obvious pain to clinch a third gold medal in the event: 'These are the Olympics. You die for them.'

Curiously for one whose eventual tally of four Olympic golds would mark him down as the greatest-ever exponent of the discus, Oerter started out his athletics career as a sprinter. His road-to-Damascus moment came on the Sewanhaka High School athletic field, Long Island, New York, in the spring of 1952. Fifteen-year-old Oerter was running on the track when a discus skipped on to it. Instinctively he picked it up and hurled it back . . . considerably further than it had been thrown towards him in the first place. The coaches took note, and young Oerter was earmarked in future for the discus.

His ability soon shone through at college level and by the time of the Melbourne Olympics he was ranked sixth in the world even though he had yet to win an international competition. But raw aggression ably compensated for lack of experience and the nineteen-year-old produced an Olympic record 184ft 10½in (56.35m) with his very first throw. The competition was as good as over. Afterwards he said: 'I don't know how I did it. Everything just went right and this throw came out.' And he added ominously: 'I'm not going to quit until I win five gold medals.'

His dreams appeared shattered when he was involved in a near-fatal car crash the following year, but he made a full recovery to earn selection for the 1960 Olympic team. His great rival was Richard 'Rink' Babka, who had beaten him at the Olympic trials – Oerter's first defeat in over two years. Babka looked set to retain superiority in Rome and led Oerter by fifteen inches with just one round of throws remaining, but then, in a remarkable gesture at the height of Olympic competition, Babka offered Oerter a piece of advice. He said he had noticed that Oerter's left arm was out of position before he threw. Oerter took Babka's comments on board, adjusted his wind-up and promptly pulled out a new Olympic record throw of 194ft 2in (59.15m) to snatch the lead. Returning the spirit of generosity, he then wished Babka luck on his last throw, but Babka came up short. Oerter had won a second gold.

And so to Tokyo. After being in outstanding form all year, his build-up to the Games was wrecked when he dislocated a cervical vertebra and suffered torn cartilage in his lower ribcage while practising. Doctors urged him to wait six weeks before competing in order to avoid the risk of internal bleeding, but he ignored their warnings. He felt he had little choice. After all, the Olympics were only six days away.

Ludvik Danek, a Czech who had won 45 consecutive discus competitions, inherited the mantle of favourite when Oerter arrived at the Games covered with ice packs and bandages and shot full of painkillers. The vultures circling overhead thought Oerter was there for the taking but he set out his stall in the qualifying round, discarding his protective neck brace 'to worry the opposition' and throwing an Olympic record 198ft 8in (60.50m). Nevertheless he knew that, given the lack of mobility and constant pain, it would be difficult – if not impossible – to sustain such a level throughout the entire competition and he confided to reporters: 'If I don't do it on the first throw, I won't be able to do it at all.' Well, he didn't do it on the first throw and was only third behind leader Danek with two throws remaining. Then, spinning more slowly than he had on his first four attempts, Oerter somehow unleashed a massive throw of 200ft 1in (61.0m) for yet another Olympic record. Danek had nothing more to give. It was gold medal number three for Oerter.

He was again the underdog approaching the 1968 Olympics, having been overtaken by a new kid on the block, fellow American Jay Silvester. The latter already held the world record and then he broke Oerter's Olympic record with a throw of 207ft 10in (63.02m) in the qualifying round in Mexico City. However, come the competition proper he knew he would have to cope with Oerter's tremendous psychological presence. Silvester admitted: 'When you throw against Oerter, you don't expect to win. You just hope.' And when it came to the crunch Oerter, despite having pulled a thigh muscle, coped better with the wet conditions and won a fourth gold with another Olympic record – 212ft 6in (64.67m). Silvester trailed in a disappointed fifth.

Oerter announced his retirement the following year but eleven years later, at the age of 43, planned a sensational comeback. He threw a personal best 227ft 10½in (69.28m) and, after finishing fourth in the national trials, was in line for a place at the 1980 Moscow Olympics, only for the United States to boycott the Games. That was as near as he would come to getting that promised fifth gold medal under his ample belt. He did try again in 1984 but an Achilles injury prevented him from competing in the US Olympic trials.

Reflecting on his four Olympic victories, the man who described himself as a 'terrible technician' of discus throwing said: 'The first would be the most surprising, the second the most difficult, the third the most painful, the fourth the most satisfying.'

THE GREAT SIT-IN

TOKYO, 19 OCTOBER 1964

Defeat can be hard to take at the highest level of sport, although we in Britain like to think that practice makes perfect. Fortunately, disappointment rarely manifests itself in the way that Peruvian soccer fans reacted to a 1–0 home defeat by Argentina in an Olympic qualifier in May 1964 – dreadful scenes that left 328 people dead and over 500 injured.

Soviet javelin thrower Elvira Orzolina took drastic action after finishing only fifth in Tokyo. She had come to Japan as reigning Olympic champion and was so appalled at her lacklustre performance that afterwards she went straight to the hairdresser at the Olympic Village and demanded to have her head shaved as a form of punishment. When the puzzled Japanese coiffeur expressed reservations about carrying out such severe pruning, Orzolina snatched the clippers and started doing the job herself, hacking away great chunks of her flowing locks. Sensing that the end result might be bad for business, the hairdresser relented and finished the job professionally, enabling Orzolina to depart with a shiny dome.

There were plenty more sore losers in the boxing competition. Argentine light-middleweight Chirino was banned for three years for hitting the referee and Spanish featherweight Valentin Loren received a life ban for a similar infringement. Disqualified for repeated holding and open-glove hitting in his opening fight, Loren vented his anger on Hungarian referee György Sermer by punching him in the face. But the incident that made all the headlines was the 51-minute sit-in staged by Korean flyweight Choh Dong-kih.

Choh, a 26-year-old shipping clerk, was just one minute and six seconds into his quarter-final bout with Stanislav Sorokin of the USSR when Australian referee Archie Tanner disqualified him for repeatedly boxing with his head too low. When the verdict was announced, Choh angrily returned to his corner, sat on his stool and refused to leave, remaining in the ring after Sorokin and Tanner had departed. As the Korean camp protested loudly about the result, Choh refused to budge. After ten minutes of inactivity the Korean officials discussed the situation but failed to arrive at a decision. By now the International Amateur Boxing Association just wanted the Koreans to get Choh out of the ring and file an official protest later but the Koreans, insisting that their man was not guilty of any infraction of the rules, held out for the matter to be resolved there and then. And so the standoff continued. After 45 minutes of stalemate, Choh's coach demanded a re-match with Sorokin. Then, five minutes later, at 7.40 p.m., with Choh still in the ring, the Korean delegation left the auditorium to hold a meeting in their dressing-room. On their return, although unable to guarantee him the second crack at the Russian that he wanted, they finally persuaded Choh to end his sit-in. He was clearly unhappy at having to leave and before departing he made one last statement, throwing his stool into the middle of the ring and hurling his towel and sweater on to the canvas. If nothing else, it probably made him feel better.

Sam Mossberg, an American gold medallist in 1920, had some sympathy with the Korean. He told *Boxing News*: 'If anybody should have been disqualified, it was the Russian. The officiating here is just terrible. Half of the boxers here don't understand the rules and don't know what the referees want them to do. On top of that, I don't think the referees know what they want!'

Ultimately Sorokin was forced to withdraw before the semi-final as a result of a cut that had failed to heal. The irony was probably not lost on Choh Dong-kih.

BLACK POWER

MEXICO CITY, 16 OCTOBER 1968

Black America was a troubled land in 1968. The April assassination of civil rights leader Dr Martin Luther King led to riots across the United States as black people reacted angrily to what they perceived as white oppression and racial injustice. The bitterness and resentment spilled over into the world of sport and had already brought about the formation of the Olympic Project for Human Rights, an organisation calling for black athletes to boycott the Mexico Olympics. The group, led by sociologist Dr Harry Edwards, aimed to expose how the United States used black athletes to project a lie both at home and internationally. The OPHR's founding statement declared: 'We must no longer allow this country to use a few so-called Negroes to point out to the world how much progress she has made in solving her racial problems when the oppression of Afro-Americans is greater than it ever was. We must no longer allow the sports world to pat itself on the back as a citadel of racial justice when the racial injustices of the sports world are infamously legendary . . . So we ask, why should we run in Mexico only to crawl home?'

The OPHR had three central demands. It wanted the restoration of Muhammad Ali's world title, of which he had been stripped for refusing to be drafted for the Vietnam War. It also sought the removal of the controversial Avery Brundage as head of the US Olympic Committee. Brundage, the man responsible for America's participation in Hitler's Games back in 1936, was despised by black athletes for having supported

141

the admission of South Africa to the Olympic movement. Thirdly it wanted the apartheid-ridden South Africa and Rhodesia banned from the Mexico Olympics. The IOC agreed to the third demand, which was sufficient to prevent a mass boycott by black athletes. However, individual competitors were still determined to make a stand, to plan some form of protest at the Olympics. Vince Matthews, a member of the 400 metres relay team, remembers: 'We had meetings. We all had different opinions on what it would take to do it. It was left up to each individual what to do when he got to the stand. Some felt more militant than others.'

Before the Games, Brundage warned that any athlete who demonstrated would be sent home. His hardline stance antagonised a number of black American athletes – including long jumper Ralph Boston and sprinters Tommie Smith, Jim Hines and Charlie Greene – who responded by announcing that they did not want Brundage in his capacity as IOC president officiating at medal ceremonies. So when two black Americans, Smith and John Carlos, won gold and bronze respectively in the men's 200 metres final, it was decided that, in order to avoid confrontation, Lord Exeter should present the medals.

Having set a world record time of 19.83sec, 24-year-old Smith prepared to mount the podium. First he took out a pair of black gloves and handed one to Carlos. Both men had black scarves draped around their necks and wore long black socks with no shoes. As they climbed on to the podium, they kept their hands hidden behind their backs. The one white athlete on the stadium – silver medallist Peter Norman, from Australia – had dashed into the stands to borrow an OPHR badge from a supporter and now showed his support for the black runners by joining them in wearing the badges. When the United States flag began rising up the flagpole and 'The Star-Spangled Banner' started to play, Smith and Carlos bowed their heads solemnly and brought their hands into view to reveal that Smith's right hand and Carlos's left were each covered by a black glove. The two men then clench their gloved fists and raised them skywards in a black power salute.

Smith later explained the significance of their dress. 'My raised right hand stood for the power in black America. Carlos's raised left hand stood for the unity of black America. Together they formed an arch of unity and power. The black scarf around my neck stood for black pride. The black socks with no shoes stood for black poverty in racist America. The totality of our effort was the regaining of black dignity.'

The ceremony over, the pair marched towards the stand with their arms still raised. Although England's Roger Bannister described the demonstration as 'a gesture conducted with dignity and poise', white Americans in the crowd took exception and started booing. At a press conference Carlos revealed that he and Smith had bowed their heads to emphasise their belief that the words of freedom in the United States anthem only applied to white Americans. 'If I win I am an American,' he said, 'not a black American. But if I did something bad then they'd say I was a Negro. We are black and we are proud of being black. Black America will understand what we did tonight . . . When Tommie and I got on that stand, we weren't alone. We knew that everyone who was watching at home was upon that stand. We wanted to let the world know the problems about black people, and we did our thing and stepped down. We believe we were right. We'd do it again tomorrow.'

Within hours of the protest, the US Olympic Committee suspended Smith and Carlos and threw them out of the Olympic Village. Brundage justified the expulsion by saying: 'They violated one of the basic principles of the Olympic Games: that politics play no part whatsoever in them.'

Sections of the American press followed Brundage's lead. The *Los Angeles Times* accused Smith and Carlos of a 'Nazi-like salute' while *Time* magazine ran a picture of the Olympic logo, replacing the motto 'Faster, Higher, Stronger' with 'Angrier, Nastier, Uglier.'

However, the pair could count on support from fellow athletes. The victorious American women's 4×100 metres relay team dedicated their victory to Smith and Carlos, while even the all-white US rowing team offered their backing. In a statement the Harvard-based rowers declared: 'As members of the US Olympic team, each of us has come to feel a moral commitment to support our black team-mates in their efforts to dramatise the injustices and iniquities which permeate our society.' And when the men's 400 metres final resulted in a clean sweep for black Americans, Lee Evans, Larry James and Ron Freeman mounted the podium wearing black berets but stopped short of donning the infamous black gloves.

On their return home, Smith and Carlos were vilified not only by the press but also by large sections of the public. They and their families were subjected to death threats and when Smith returned to college, he felt it necessary to attend night classes. 'I didn't want to be seen,' he said. 'We had put our lives on the line.' As white-operated doors repeatedly slammed in their faces, Smith and Carlos both struggled to make a living from athletics as coaches. Carlos lamented: 'Doing my thing made me feel the finest I ever felt in my whole life, but I came home to hate.'

Thirty years on, decathlete Bill Toomey, a gold medallist in 1968, still believed that Smith and Carlos acted properly. 'I was moved by it,' he said in a 1998 interview. 'Tommie and John had unique personalities. I respected what they did. It was an act of courage. We needed that to happen. We needed more peaceful demonstrations to make people aware.'

ONE GIANT LEAP FOR MANKIND

MEXICO CITY, 18 OCTOBER 1968

World records are meant to be broken in stages – in the case of the long jump, by fractions of an inch at a time. When Jesse Owens leaped 26ft 8¼in (8.13m) in 1935, his record stood for 25 years. Between 1960 and 1967, the record was either broken or equalled on eight separate occasions by America's Ralph Boston and the Russian Igor Ter-Ovanesyan, yet in all that period it only extended by eight and a half inches. So at the start of the Mexico Olympics, Boston and Ter-Ovanesyan jointly held the world record at 27ft 4¾in (8.34m). Then along came Bob Beamon. He didn't just break the record, he blew it away. In just six seconds he wrote himself into the record books for the next 23 years with a colossal leap of 29ft 2½in (8.90m), shattering the world best by an incredible 1ft 9¾in. Not only did he become the first jumper to exceed 29ft, he became the first to pass 28ft too! To paraphrase Captain Kirk, he had boldly leaped where no man had gone before. And that's why nobody who ever saw Beamon's jump will ever forget it. With total justification, it has gone down as one of the most remarkable moments in Olympic history – a once-in-a-lifetime achievement.

Bob Beamon was born in Jamaica, New York, in 1946. His mother died from tuberculosis when he was young, leaving an irreplaceable gap in his life. It was the sort of neighbourhood where a young man either turned to crime or sport. In a recent interview Beamon admitted: 'My high school was a jungle. You had to be constantly alert – ready to fight or run. If you joined

145

one of the gangs, you might escape harm but you also might be in trouble the rest of your life. If you stayed decent, you stood a good chance of being clobbered every day. So I went hot and heavy for basketball – and I feel it saved me from being cut up. Basketball is big stuff in New York. If you're good in it, everybody respects you. Nobody would want to ruin your shooting eye or your shooting arm.'

At 6ft 3in tall, the slender Beamon was a natural athlete and was encouraged to take up the long jump. He joined the rising track team at the University of Texas in El Paso, where he worked on his speed and perfected a technique first employed by the likes of Robert LeGendre some forty years earlier in which the jumper does not so much jump as walk in the air.

Beamon went into the Mexico Olympics on the back of 22 wins from 23 meets that year. Yet he was considered inconsistent and prone to fouling and was still effectively the number two American to Boston, who had already proved himself at the highest level with gold at Rome in 1960 and silver at Tokyo in 1964 behind Britain's Lynn Davies. Furthermore, Beamon had been without a recognised coach since June after being suspended by the Texas-El Paso track team for refusing to compete against the Mormon Brigham Young University in protest at the racial policies of the Mormon Church. In the absence of a coach, Ralph Boston filled the void in an unofficial capacity. For the two men were not only rivals, they were also good friends. And without Boston, Beamon would not even have qualified for the finals in Mexico.

Beamon struggled badly in the qualifying round. He could not get his run-up right and fouled on his first two jumps. One more foul and he would be eliminated from the competition. Before his final try, he received a piece of invaluable advice from Boston, echoing the events of the 1936 Olympics when Jesse Owens, having fouled in his first two qualifying attempts, was told by Germany's Luz Long how to avoid another foul. 'Ralph Boston did the same for me,' said Beamon afterwards. 'He told me, "Bob, you won't foul if you take off a foot behind the foul line. You can't miss." Basically, that's what Luz Long told Jesse [the German placed a towel

146

at the spot for Owens to use as a takeoff marker] and I took Ralph's advice. I qualified.'

Beamon faced stiff opposition in the final, including all three medallists from Tokyo – Davies, Boston and Ter-Ovanesyan. The night before, Beamon, who was experiencing marital problems and was still reeling from the loss of his Texas scholarship, found his mind in a turmoil. 'Everything was wrong,' he said. 'So I went into town and had a shot of tequila. Man, did I feel loose. I got a good sleep.' He also had sex that night – the first time he had ever done so before a major competition. He was worried that the physical exertion would diminish his performance the next day, but as it turned out, it clearly had the opposite effect.

Beamon was the fourth of the seventeen finalists to jump on an overcast day. The first three had all fouled, and as Beamon waited to begin his run-up, he kept repeating to himself, 'Don't foul, don't foul.' Then he was away. In nineteen huge strides he sped down the runway, stretched out his last step to the board and soared into Mexico City's thin air. The Wright Brothers scarcely managed further on their maiden flight. He reached a height of six feet (photographs show him hanging in the air way above the heads of the seated judges) and when he finally came to ground, he was nearly out of the pit. Indeed the sheer momentum, created by his run-up pace and that technique of walking through the air, propelled him forward out of the pit.

'He's jumped right out of the pit!' exclaimed a TV commentator, scarcely able to believe his eyes. Beamon ran around excitedly, waiting for the official distance. 'I knew I made a great jump,' he said, 'I knew it was more than the world record. I heard some of the guys saying things like 8.9 metres . . . or something. Outside the United States, everything is in metres, so I wasn't sure how far I had jumped. Then Ralph Boston came over and said, "Bob, I think it's over 29ft," which was almost two feet farther than the world record. I said to Ralph, "What happened to 28ft?"'

The electronic scoreboard flashed 8.90 metres and eventually the public-address system announced the conversion – 29ft 2½in. It was only then that the enormity of Beamon's achievement hit home. His legs gave way beneath him and he sank to the ground in what doctors subsequently diagnosed as a 'cataplectic seizure', brought on by sheer excitement. The ever-helpful Boston supported him until the dizziness had passed.

Beamon's other rivals were stunned. Ter-Ovanesyan said: 'Compared to this jump, we are as children.' A dejected Davies said to Boston: 'I can't go on. What is the point? We'll all look silly.' Then the Welshman turned to Beamon and said: 'You have destroyed this event.'

Beamon had indeed ended the competition virtually before it had begun. Boston, Ter-Ovanesyan and Davies were so shocked by Beamon's leap that they were unable to find anything approaching their best form and could only finish third, fourth and ninth respectively. The silver went to Klaus Beer of East Germany.

When he had recovered his composure, Beamon talked reporters through his momentous jump. 'I eased up on my last step before I hit the board, and that makes the difference when I jump well. My mind was blank during the jump. After so much jumping, jumping becomes automatic. I was as surprised as anybody at the distance.' But afterwards when he was up on the podium receiving his gold medal, he remembers thinking: 'Where do I go from here?' At 22, he had attained the pinnacle of his career; the rest, he feared, might become an anti-climax.

While some observers hailed Beamon's jump as the greatest athletic achievement of all time, others drew attention to the thin air and the following wind of two metres per second – the maximum speed permissible for a record. When Viktor Sanayev of the USSR and Brazil's Nelson Prudencio had set new world records for the triple jump the previous day, the wind speed had once again been precisely 2mps, raising suspicion in certain quarters. Indeed, the first five finishers in the triple jump competition all broke the existing world record. Beamon became irritated by insinuations that he had made a 'lucky jump' and quite rightly pointed out that the favourable conditions were the same for his fellow long jumpers, none of whom had come remotely close to matching his feat.

However, as Beamon feared, that one jump became something of a millstone around his neck. The remainder of his career was disrupted by injury and he never again jumped beyond 27ft. Having stood for 23 years, his world record was finally broken in Tokyo in 1991 when the USA's Mike Powell jumped 29ft 4½in (8.95m).

'I've always been a very realistic person,' said Beamon shortly after Powell's jump. 'I knew the day I set it that eventually someone would come along and surpass it. Now that it has finally happened, I don't feel any different. I don't feel as though something's been taken away from me. And don't forget, I still hold the Olympic record.'

Thirty-six years on from Mexico City, Bob Beamon's mark remains the longest-standing current Olympic record.

Of course, for every champion there are hundreds of losers and the saddest tale from Mexico City concerned one athlete who didn't even make it to the Games. In finishing third in the 1964 Olympic marathon before his home crowd, Kokichi Tsuburaya picked up Japan's first track and field medal for 28 years. A member of the Training School of the Japanese Ground Self-Defence Force, he was immediately elevated to the status of national hero and put on a strict regime to prepare for the 1968 Games. This included giving up his fiancée. But in 1967 he suffered two injuries, which required him to spend a period of three months in hospital. Although doctors told him he could resume training, his body had been so weakened by the enforced layoff that it soon became painfully obvious that his hopes of winning Olympic gold were an impossible dream. Feeling that he had let down the Japanese people, he slashed his wrists with a razor blade in January 1968. He was found in his dormitory, clutching the bronze medal. Next to his body lay a note that read simply: 'Cannot run anymore.'

THE FOSBURY FLOP

MEXICO CITY, 20 OCTOBER 1968

Whereas Bob Beamon's phenomenal leap came out of the blue, the sporting public had been warned in advance about the curiosity that was Dick Fosbury. The man who eschewed centuries of tradition by doing the high jump backwards and head first over the bar had captivated audiences in the United States in a manner not seen since Phineas T Barnum unveiled his mermaid and bearded lady. Now the Mexico Olympics offered Fosbury the opportunity to perform his wacky routine on a worldwide stage.

He did not disappoint. The 80,000 spectators inside the stadium were hooked on Fosbury's every move. The high jump had never enjoyed such popularity. All eleven of his opponents employed the familiar straddle method but one by one they dropped out as Fosbury flopped his way over every height up to 7ft 3¼in (2.22m) without so much as a miss. His first two attempts at 7ft 4¼in (2.24m) ended in failure, but he still had one last try. Olympic protocol states that when the marathon leader re-enters the stadium he receives the crowd's undivided attention for his final lap. But when Mamo Wolde of Ethiopia completed his final circuit on the way to the marathon gold, all eyes were instead fixed on Fosbury. And when the 21-year-old from Oregon cleared the bar in his then inimitable style to seal gold, in the process setting a new Olympic record and personal best, the crowd roared in approval. A new Olympic hero was born.

Before Fosbury, jumpers used to take off from the inside foot and swing the outside foot up and over the bar, either by

150

means of the western roll or, from the 1950s, the straddle. The other, more antiquated, method was the scissors, the basic technique that children are usually taught at junior school, whereby the trailing leg follows the front leg over the bar in an upright scissors movement, somewhat akin to hurdling in the 3,000 metres steeplechase. But Fosbury changed everything, approaching the bar in a J-shaped run, taking off from the outside foot and twisting his body at the last minute so that he went over head first with his back to the bar. It revolutionised the sport.

Raised in Medford, Oregon, the son of a truck sales manager and a secretary, Fosbury was a tall, slim boy who, by process of elimination, alighted on the high jump as his preferred athletics event. He started out using the scissors until his high school coach, all too aware of the limitations of the movement, tried to teach him the more elaborate and more efficient straddle. Although Fosbury learned the straddle, he was unable to master it and so, against his better judgement, his coach allowed the sixteen-year-old to revert to the scissors for a meeting in 1963. With the straddle Fosbury had never jumped more than 5ft 4in (1.63m), but scissoring that day he went higher and higher. As the bar was raised two inches at a time, he found that, in order to get over the greater heights, he was instinctively lifting his hips and pushing back his shoulders. 'As the bar got higher,' he recalled, 'I started laying out more and pretty soon I was flat on my back.' This prototype of the Fosbury Flop enabled him to clear 5ft 10in (1.77m).

Over the next two years Fosbury, convinced that he could clear greater heights by lowering his centre of gravity as the bar was crossed, polished his style so that he was crossing the bar at right angles. But nobody paid much interest. Fosbury remembered: 'Everybody just thought, it's good to look at, it's pretty funny and everything, but he'll never do anything.'

By the summer of 1965 Fosbury was able to flop 6ft 7in (2.02m) yet Berny Wagner, his coach at Oregon State University, still encouraged him to adopt the straddle instead. Then one day the following year, Wagner watched Fosbury clear the bar, which was set at 6ft 6in (2.0m), by a good six inches wearing a pair of plaid Bermuda shorts. 'That,' said Wagner, 'was when I first thought he was going to be a high jumper.' Fosbury forsook the straddle for good and cleared 7ft 3in (2.21m) to make the 1968 US Olympic team, although his third place in that competition scarcely suggested that he was likely to win gold in Mexico. But cometh the hour, cometh the Flop.

'Spectators were in awe the first time they saw it,' remembered Fosbury. 'As I went from the warm-ups to the competition, and the bar kept raising higher, there were 80,000 people going silent, watching this kid, this "gringo", take his mark, and rock back and forth preparing to take a jump.'

The Fosbury Flop burst upon the scene during a period when many traditions were being cast aside and, to some, it was every bit as unsettling as Tommie Smith and John Carlos's black power protest. 'Kids imitate champions,' said US Olympic coach Payton Jordan at the time. 'If they try to imitate Fosbury, he will wipe out an entire generation of high jumpers because they will all have broken necks.'

Despite Fosbury's triumph, tradition died hard and it took another decade before the Flop dominated the sport. 'The problem with something revolutionary like that,' said Fosbury in a 1999 interview, 'was that most of the elite athletes had invested so much time in their technique and movements that they didn't want to give it up. So they stuck with what they knew. The revolution came about from the kids who saw it, and had nothing to lose – the kids who saw it on TV and said, "Gosh, that looks fun – let's do that"; grade school kids who didn't have coaches saying, "No, you stick with the straddle."'

By the 1980 Moscow Olympics, thirteen of the sixteen finalists were using the Fosbury Flop. And nobody had broken their neck.

NEVER TOO LATE

MEXICO CITY, 20 OCTOBER 1968

By 7 p.m. the last few spectators were drifting away from the Olympic stadium. Over an hour earlier they had watched the Ethiopian, Mamo Wolde, win the marathon by more than three minutes from Naftali Temu of Kenya, thereby gaining revenge for defeat at the hands of the Kenyan in a thrilling 10,000 metres final the previous week. The marathon, coupled with what was for many in the stadium a first glimpse of the gravity-defying Fosbury Flop, added up to a thoroughly enjoyable day's athletics. But as they headed for the exits, the fans' attention was suddenly drawn to the sound of police sirens. Then the marathon gate to the stadium was thrown open and into the near-empty arena stumbled a lone runner, hobbling painfully on a heavily bandaged leg, his face contorted in agony.

It was John Akhwari of Tanzania, the last finisher in the marathon. Not unreasonably the crowd thought all the marathon runners had long since gone, not realising that there was a solitary straggler. The reason Akhwari was so far behind was because he had suffered a heavy fall in the course of the race, but he insisted on completing the course even though he was hopelessly detached from the rest of the runners. The remaining spectators turned on their heels and lent their wholehearted support to the man with the blood-soaked bandage. As they cheered and applauded, Akhwari responded by breaking into a gentle trot. After eventually crossing the line, he collapsed and was taken away by the Red Cross to a clinic where he recuperated for two weeks before returning to Tanzania. During his convalescence, a reporter asked him why he had kept going. Akhwari replied famously: 'My country did not send me 7,000 miles to start the race. They sent me 7,000 miles to finish it.'

Although he was part of only a three-man Tanzanian Olympic team (along with a boxer and a 400-metres runner), Akhwari was no also-ran. Raised in a mud hut in the Arusha region of Tanzania, the thirty-year-old came to Mexico as a potential champion. He had run, mostly barefoot, in marathons all over Africa and in 1962 had competed in the Commonwealth Games in Perth, Australia. The following year, when running in Athens, he tried to wear shoes to negotiate the rocky surfaces, but they pinched his feet so badly that he had to take them off. Over the next five years he maintained his form and was seen as a live hope for the Mexico Olympics – another distance athlete to roll off the African conveyor belt. However, he did not take participation for granted and was only too aware that the Tanzanian Olympic Committee had barely been able to afford the tickets for the three competitors. 'They had made so many sacrifices,' he later recalled.

A total of 72 runners from 44 countries lined up for the Olympic marathon, including the double champion Abebe Bikila and his Ethiopian team-mate Wolde. But Bikila was still suffering the effects of a badly injured leg and before the race the Ethiopian team trainer, Negussie Roba, told Wolde that the great Bikila might not be able to finish the race and that he (Wolde) was the nation's only hope. The Ethiopians set the early pace, but at eleven miles Bikila's injury proved too much for him and he was forced to retire. As he pulled over to the side of the course, he yelled to Wolde: 'Mamo, make the ultimate sacrifice.' Wolde, who had made his Olympic debut back in 1956, duly passed Bikila for the first time ever and went on to maintain his country's proud tradition in the event.

Akhwari, too, had started well until he began to feel the effects of the altitude. He had been training at sea level but running at altitudes of between 10,000ft and 12,000ft proved a more exacting proposition. 'We all started feeling dizzy,' he

154

said. 'The conditions were causing fatigue and people were starting to collapse.' By the eighteen-mile mark he was suffering extreme cramp and spasms. Disorientated and struggling to keep his balance, he fell awkwardly a mile later and badly gashed his right leg. His coach, Raste Zambi, dutifully bandaged the leg to stem the bleeding and Akhwari moved gingerly on his way, having lost a vast amount of time. However, within a few miles it was clear to the coach that Akhwari was in considerable pain and in no fit state to continue. He was hopelessly tailed off with no hope of finishing in a remotely respectable position. Rambi urged him to give up. 'He said everyone had gone,' remembered Akhwari, 'that I had done enough, that I should drop out now and save myself. My head said, "Give up", but my heart said, "Keep going."'

And so Akhwari limped on towards the stadium and Olympic immortality. Bud Greenspan, the renowned Olympic film-maker, whose footage captured Akhwari's last faltering steps, described the scene as 'the greatest moment in Olympic history'.

In the short term, Akhwari's selfless heroics made him an instant media celebrity and in the long term an inspiration for millions. Back in his homeland he continued to serve in the army for another two years before becoming a government sports officer. During preparations for the 2000 Olympics, Sydney lawyer John McCarthy, who had been greatly moved by Akhwari's courage 32 years earlier, arranged for him to be flown out to Australia to help manage the Tanzanian squad. McCarthy feared that Akhwari's fellow countrymen did not appreciate the hero in their midst, and stated: 'He is a prophet without honour. If there is any country that values courage and persistence, even when you're losing, it's Australia, with all the images of Gallipoli.'

Ironically while John Akhwari was being feted in Australia, the 1968 Olympic champion, Mamo Wolde, was languishing in jail. Wolde should have been a national hero for life but in the 1990s he and thousands of others were thrown into prison on unspecified charges by the coalition government. He spent six years in jail, eventually being released early in 2002. Six months later he died penniless, leaving behind a wife and three children.

TIMED OUT

MUNICH, 31 AUGUST 1972

Missing out on the chance of an Olympic medal because of injury is one of the greatest misfortunes that can befall an athlete. But crack American sprinters Eddie Hart and Rey Robinson found an even more frustrating way of snatching defeat from the jaws of victory when they failed to show up for their 100 metres quarter-finals in Munich following a mix-up over the start times.

Along with the Russian Valery Borzov, twenty-year-old Robinson from Florida and 23-year-old Hart from California were the favourites for the men's 100-metres title. Both Americans had equalled the world record of 9.9sec earlier in the year and were considered to be at the peak of their form going into the Games. The three lead-up races to the final were thought to be mere formalities and so it seemed when they breezed through their first-round heats on the morning of 31 August, both winning comfortably to guarantee their places in the quarter-finals, which, they had been informed by the US sprint coach Stan Wright, were due to begin at 7p.m. that evening.

That afternoon, with time on their hands, they relaxed in the Olympic Village, three-quarters of a mile from the athletics stadium . . . blissfully unaware that their heats had been switched to start at 4.15 p.m. The first signs of disquiet came at the warm-up track near the stadium when, with the start time steadily approaching, American officials became aware that there was no sign of Hart and Robinson or the third US

156

sprinter, Robert Taylor. Mild concern soon turned to outright panic and 400-metres runner Lee Evans was despatched to run to the Olympic Village and search for them.

Evans missed them by two minutes. For moments earlier, Hart, Robinson, Taylor and Wright, thinking they had all the time in the world, had sauntered to the Olympic Village bus stop in preparation for the ride to the stadium. While waiting for the stadium bus, they wandered into the foyer of the ABC television studio and watched the action on the monitor. Seeing the 100 metres runners lining up, Robinson asked whether it was a replay of the first-round heats . . . and was horrified to be told that it was live. Sure enough, when he inspected the screen the graphic listing the competitors had N/A next to his name, denoting Not Available. It dawned on him that he was watching the very race in which he was supposed to be running.

He later recalled: 'It was like being involved in a car accident that's your fault when you have no insurance and everyone on the freeway is stopped to look at you.'

The three athletes and Wright were hastily bundled into a car and driven at speed to the stadium by ABC employee Bill Norris. There was clearly little hope for Robinson, who was running in the first heat, nor indeed for Hart, who should have been in heat two, but at least the emergency dash might pay off for Taylor, who was running in heat three. Whereas his two compatriots were duly eliminated, Taylor arrived in the nick of time and went on to finish second in his race to Borzov. Ironically, Borzov had also been misinformed about the start time and had nearly missed the quarter-final. Luckily for him, his coach had persuaded him to remain in the stadium after the first-round races and, although Borzov had subsequently fallen asleep, he woke up just as his heat was being called. Despite an argument with a German official who had attempted to prevent him entering an unauthorised area, Borzov made the start line just in time. The Russian went on to take gold in the final with Taylor snatching silver. But it was scant consolation for the American sprint team.

The recriminations began as soon as the blunder over the start times came to light. Asked how he had missed the race,

Hart explained that because he did not know any German, he hadn't bothered reading the papers and had relied on the coaches and his fellow athletes for information. The finger was quickly pointed at Wright who, it transpired, had been working from an eighteen-month-old preliminary schedule because he had been unable to find anybody with a new one! Wright was suitably apologetic, blaming a 'breakdown in communications', but while he took the initial flak from the wronged runners and the world's media, it soon became apparent that he was not the only American official at fault.

In a report to the US Olympic Committee from US track and field team manager George Wilson, it was noted that the sport's governing board, the International Amateur Athletic Federation, had held a technical meeting two days before the 100 metres, at which the schedule had been changed so that the 100 metres quarter-finals preceded the 10,000 metres heats. Wilson admitted that he had been aware of the switch but claimed to have been distracted by a controversy regarding the size of poles used by the pole vaulters. As a result he had forgotten to relay the new information to Wright. Wilson said he thought that US coach Bill Bowerman had also known about the change but Bowerman strenuously denied this and instead blamed the IAAF for not effectively communicating its amended schedule.

It was an unsatisfactory episode all round yet Hart (who at least gained some consolation as a member of the victorious United States sprint relay team) and Robinson weren't the only runners to miss a race at Munich in bizarre circumstances. The great Ethiopian distance runner Miruts Yifter (nicknamed 'Yifter the Shifter') missed his 5,000 metres heat because he was stuck in the toilet!

POLES APART

The reigning Olympic pole vault champion, America's Bob Seagren, feared that the greatest threat to the defence of his title in Munich would not emanate from his fellow competitors but from the sport's governing body. For throughout the year the International Amateur Athletic Federation had been working itself into a lather over a revolutionary new fibreglass pole and was still in a dither even after the Games had got underway.

The bone of contention was a piece of equipment called the cata-pole. Manufactured by George Moore of California, the cata-pole was one and a half ounces lighter and fractionally smaller in diameter than conventional fibreglass poles, and had been widely praised by vaulters for its flexibility. So impressive was its reputation that it was adopted by most of the world's leading vaulters in the prolonged build-up to Munich. However, there were dissenting voices, notably from European athletes who complained that the new pole had not been readily made available to them, and in the summer of 1972 they persuaded the IAAF to ban the cata-pole from the forthcoming Games on the grounds that a federation rule stated all poles should be accessible on the open market for a full year before use in the Olympics. Naturally the Americans were none too pleased and George Moore promptly launched an appeal against the ban.

Seagren's preparations were thrown into chaos but at the US Olympic trials he used the cata-pole to vault to a world record height of 18ft 5½in (5.64m). In that sort of form and with that equipment he would clearly take a lot of stopping in Munich.

Then on 27 August – the day after the opening ceremony at Munich – the IAAF suddenly reversed its original decision and came to the conclusion that the cata-pole did fulfil the various regulations relating to the event. Seagren's relief was short-lived, however. Three days later – and just three days before the pole vault final was to take place – the IAAF, following an official protest from East Germany, changed its mind again, reversing its reversal and finally banning the cata-pole from the Olympics!

The ruling played into the hands of East Germany's top vaulter, Wolfgang Nordwig, the bronze medallist behind Seagren in 1968. Although he had been practising with the cata-pole, Nordwig had not adjusted to it as well as his American rival and was apparently only too happy to revert to the old poles. The night before the qualifying competition, officials duly confiscated all the cata-poles and gave the athletes different ones to use the following day. As a result only ten men were able to clear the qualifying height of 16ft 8¾in (5.11m), so a couple more who had only cleared 16ft 4¾in (5.01m) were added to make up the numbers.

Most of the vaulters that had been practising with cata-poles performed well below par in the final. The difference between one fibreglass pole and another might be lost on the layman, but to these men it was like asking Jack Nicklaus to putt with a baseball bat. After Nordwig cleared 17ft 8½in (5.40m) at the first attempt, Seagren failed three times at the same height. The East German went on to seal gold by clearing 18ft 0½in (5.50m) on his second vault, thereby ending US domination in the event. In fact it was the first time that an American had not won the Olympic pole vault since its inception in 1896. Seagren reacted angrily at winning only silver, shunning the traditional handshake with Nordwig and testily presenting his pole to Adrian Paulen, the pole vault judge who was one of the IAAF panel. Convinced that the ban had been instigated by Nordwig, Seagren snapped: 'He had six months to use the new poles.'

Even today Seagren feels cheated. 'We had a pole vaulting controversy and they removed the poles from about seventeen world-class competitors,' he says. 'I had gone over there with nine vaulting poles and they determined that all nine were illegal. It definitely put me at a disadvantage. I was forced to use a pole that I would normally use in a practice session with shorter runs, so I had to make major adjustments in my technique. I was very fortunate to end up winning a silver medal that year. Still to this day I'm confused with the rules and regulations they initiated to enforce the decision.'

The Pakistan men's hockey team also took umbrage at the Munich officialdom. After being beaten 1–0 by West Germany in the final, the Pakistan team were so annoyed by what they thought was biased umpiring during the match that they proceeded to pour water over the president of the International Hockey Federation. Then, during the medal ceremony, several Pakistan players again expressed their disgust by turning their backs on the German flag. The IHF immediately imposed a draconian lifetime ban on Pakistan, but this was later reduced to a more sensible two years.

THE TICKING CLOCK

MUNICH, 10 SEPTEMBER 1972

On 5 September the whole face of the Munich Olympics
changed when eleven Israelis were killed after Arab terrorists
had stormed the Olympic Village. The Games were suspended
for a day and on their resumption sport somehow seemed
inconsequential . . . unless you happened to be an American
basketball player, that is.

The United States had never lost a basketball game in
Olympic competition – a proud record that stretched back
62 encounters. So when they reached yet another final, the
entire country wanted to watch what would surely be another
night of glory at the expense of arch rivals, the Soviet Union.
To accommodate US television, the start time was put back to
the unearthly hour of a quarter to midnight. The Americans
took a young squad to Munich. Top collegians such as Bill
Walton and David Thompson had declined to travel to
Germany, so hopes rested on talented but inexperienced
shoulders – players such as Tom McMillen, Ed Ratleff, Doug
Collins, Jim Brewer and Dwight Jones. The man chosen to
guide these youngsters was 68-year-old Hank Iba, the successful coach in 1964 and 1968, and a conservative campaigner
who liked to employ a slow, passing game. Some within the
squad questioned his tactics . . . in hindsight. By contrast the
Russians were wily veterans who had been around the Eastern
Bloc a few times.

The millions of television viewers who had been expecting a
US landslide in the final were quickly jolted out of their

complacency. The Soviets led from the start and the Americans were weakened when their top scorer, Dwight Jones, was ejected along with a Russian, Mishako Korkia, for fighting. In the bitter exchanges that followed the final whistle, the Americans claimed that Korkia, far less valuable to his team, might have started the scuffle intentionally. With five minutes remaining the USSR still held an eight-point advantage, 44–36. The pressure was mounting on coach Iba to loosen the reins. Apparently Iba had always believed that the Russians would choke at the death and now he finally unleashed the full might of the Americans. Facing pressure all over the court, the Russians began to crumble and with six seconds left their lead had been cut to a single point, 49–48. The odds still favoured the Soviets until the dangerous Aleksandr Belov, trapped on the baseline, threw an ill-advised pass that was intercepted by Collins, who in turn was fouled by Zurab Sakandelidze. Though still dazed, Collins successfully converted the two free throws to put the US ahead for the first time in the game, 50–49, with just three seconds to play.

When the Soviets failed to score in those remaining three seconds, jubilant American fans and players swarmed on to the court in celebration of what they thought was an eighth consecutive basketball gold medal for the United States. But their joy was cut short when it became apparent that through the deafening noise of the crowd, the Soviet coach, Vladimir Kondrashkin, had been frantically trying to call a time out. Head referee Renato Righetto of Brazil went to investigate the commotion at the scorer's table and, on learning that Kondrashkin had tried unsuccessfully to halt play after Collins's first shot, called a time out with one second remaining. To add to the confusion, the time out horn had been sounded as Collins made his second throw and some mistook this for the final horn to signal the end of the game. Both Righetto and timekeeper André Chopard thought one second remained but then Britain's R William Jones, secretary-general of the International Amateur Basketball Federation (FIBA), intervened and ordered the clock to be set back to three seconds, the point at which the Soviet official had originally called a time out.

The players were mystified as to what was going on. One of the US squad, Mike Bantom, said afterwards: 'Nobody explained it to us. They just told us to go out there and replay the time. Our initial reaction was, "No way are we going to do that, why would we do something like that?" And then basically through the threat of forfeiting the game, we went back out to do it, only because they told us if we didn't we would lose.'

The court was cleared and play resumed. Kondrashkin introduced Ivan Edeshko in a last-ditch gamble, but the switch seemed in vain when a Soviet long shot dropped short and the three seconds passed without any further score. Once again the Americans celebrated at the sound of the horn, only to discover that the timekeeper had not been ready when play had restarted. The public address announcer told a startled arena that three seconds was to be put on the clock. More chaos ensued with people shouting in various languages around the scorer's table. One of the American assistant coaches, Don Haskins, was all in favour of pulling the US team off the court but Iba, looking red-faced and bewildered, was worried about a possible appeal. 'I don't want to lose this game later tonight, sitting on my butt,' he confided.

Bantom recalled: 'After the second one, with everyone jumping around, celebrating, happy, and then we're told to do it again, we thought it was getting ridiculous. We thought, "We've won the game twice – why do we have to replay these three seconds?" I think what happened was that the Russians understood early on that they were going to be given another chance, so they were over there preparing, devising a play, setting up what they were going to do. We were still kind of disjointed, arguing. I mean, we were all over the place, totally oblivious to the fact that we're going to have to go back out there and play.'

Once again the court was cleared and the clock reset. With two of the biggest Americans – Jones and the injured Brewer – out of action, the net was patrolled by Kevin Joyce, a comparative midget by basketball standards at 6ft 3in, and James Forbes, a sinewy 6ft 7in. The man they were guarding was the muscular 6ft 8in Belov. The ball was placed in the hands of Edeshko on the end line for the restart. McMillen, who had been told to hound Edeshko by waving his arms in front of him, was inexplicably ordered to back off by one of the referees, Artenik Arabadjian of Bulgaria, thereby allowing the Russian an unimpaired throw. No rule in basketball requires a defender to back away and referee Arabadjian has since denied telling McMillen to do so. However McMillen claims that he drifted back towards the free-throw line after remembering a pre-match warning he received from coach Iba that the entire world was set against the US basketball team. 'We were conscious the game could be won by hook or by crook,' said McMillen recently. 'I was afraid of a technical foul being called on me.' With a clear view and precision accuracy, Edeshko launched the ball the length of the court in the direction of the lurking Belov. The Russian went up for the ball with Joyce and Forbes but the two Americans were knocked to the floor in the battle for possession, leaving Belov to score a simple layup. Immediately the final horn sounded. At the third attempt the Soviets had snatched an improbable victory, 51–50. Bantom remembered: 'We went from complete elation to utter confusion, then the dejection of having them tell us we had lost the game.' It was shortly after one o'clock on the morning of 10 September 1972.

Coach Iba went berserk and had to be restrained by his players as he stormed after the referees and officials. With the Americans insisting that they had won 50–49, Iba petulantly refused to sign the scoresheet and issued a formal protest to FIBA on the grounds that the events of the last three seconds violated international rules. 'I don't think it's possible to have made that play in three seconds,' raged Iba. 'There's no damn way he can get that shot off in time.' The Americans protested about everything and everyone. Apart from the complaints over the timing, they claimed Edeshko had stepped on the baseline while making the fateful full-court pass, an infringement that should have negated the play and given the ball to the Americans. They also moaned that Belov had stationed himself inside the keyhole beneath the basket for five seconds, whereas three seconds is the maximum permitted time, and for good measure had fouled Joyce and Forbes. And above all they argued that R William Jones had no authority to order the clock to be put back to three seconds.

FIBA hastily convened a meeting to study TV footage of the closing moments. Afterwards it was announced that the US protest had been rejected by three votes to two, the Eastern Bloc countries voting for the USSR and the Western nations for the US. Secretary-general Jones explained: 'The whole trouble started when someone at the scorer's table sounded the buzzer too late for a time out requested by the Russians.' And he added tartly: 'The Americans have to learn how to lose, even when they think they are right.' The decision prompted ugly scenes between Herbert Mols, assistant manager of the US squad, and Ferencs Hepp, the Hungarian president of the appeals committee, Mols demanding to know where the extra three seconds had come from. Hans Tenschert, the match scorer, revealed: 'Only the technical delegate at the table could cancel out this signal of three seconds, which came from Dr William Jones. But the delegate kept silent and the referee had, therefore, no choice but to play three seconds.' The Americans were far from appeased and, in what one columnist described as 'a sorry display of poor sportsmanship', they refused to accept their silver medals. US Olympic basketball committee chairman Bill Summers said: 'We do not feel like accepting the silver because we feel we are worth the gold.' Meanwhile Clifford H Buck, president of the US Olympic Committee, recommended that the United States suspend indefinitely any further participation in Olympic basketball 'as a protest to the unconscionable injustice done to the USA basketball team in Munich.' The Americans were taking their ball home.

Over thirty years on, it would be nice to report that the American Olympic basketball squad of 1972 have drawn a line under the whole affair. But the medals remain unclaimed in a Swiss vault and the resentment remains as intense as ever. Every anniversary opens up old wounds. Detailed study of the video footage suggests that the American grievances are unjustified. Impartial observers have detected nothing untoward regarding the timekeeping and assert that Belov did not foul his defenders. They even dismiss the allegation that Korkia was a benchwarmer sent in to the fray to provoke Dwight Jones. In fact Korkia started the game and the videotape appears to show Jones swinging the first elbow as the two players tussled for a rebound.

Yet as recently as 2002 Tom McMillen announced that he was planning a fresh appeal to the IOC, based largely on the actions of the late R William Jones. In an interview a few years before his death, Jones insisted that his decision to put three seconds on the clock was correct but admitted that he had no authority to step in. McMillen claimed Jones's illicit intervention meant that the 1972 final was 'victimised by manipulation'. Former team-mate Ed Ratleff echoed those sentiments. 'We're not militants or anything,' he told the *Los Angeles Times*. 'We feel we got the gold taken away from us. We're not the team that got beat, we're the team that got cheated.' And no video evidence or independent assessment will ever persuade them otherwise.

THE MAN IN ORANGE

MUNICH, 10 SEPTEMBER 1972

A matter of hours after the uproar on the basketball court, the USA gained some consolation with victory in the Olympic marathon. But even then winner Frank Shorter's thunder was stolen by a crafty impostor.

Along with the vast majority of the athletes, Shorter, who was actually born in Munich, had grave reservations about running in the aftermath of the terrorist attack, his feelings hardened by the fact that he had a closer view of the atrocity than most. 'I was literally 100 yards away, direct line, on the same floor,' he said. 'We could see the apartment where the athletes were trapped and saw the terrorists. Afterwards people simply wanted to go home – to be around people they love and be in a secure place and feel that nothing is worth human life, not even an Olympic Games.' But Avery Brundage ordered that the show must go on and so Shorter, who had finished fifth in the 10,000 metres earlier in the Games, found himself lining up with 72 other runners for the start of the marathon.

Shorter's pre-race preparation was decidedly unorthodox. The night before the marathon he enjoyed 'a litre and a half or two of beer' before going to bed. 'That German beer is great,' he said later: 'I don't worry about it; it's good carbohydrates, a few calories and a lot of water. You can rationalise it real well. I like it and it's the way I like to relax.'

Any lethargy following his drinking session was removed early in the race. For no sooner had the runners exited the stadium than Shorter was nearly knocked out of contention in

168

an altercation with a camera truck. The two nearly collided, causing the University of Florida law student to bang furiously on the side of the vehicle and swear loudly at the driver. The incident cost him some thirty yards. He made up the ground, only to feature in another bizarre episode at the first refreshment table. Finding that his drink had taken by one of the Ethiopian runners, he ran after the offender, grabbed the bottle out of his hand and said, 'That's mine!'

Despite suffering from blisters, Shorter made a bold move for the front after only nine miles and steadily pulled away from the field. Behind, fellow American Kenny Moore almost came to grief in the park section, being forced to hurdle an approaching dachshund! With a lead of over two minutes, Shorter began to experience the loneliness of the long-distance runner. 'You just say to yourself, "Oh God, how much further? Please let me finish."'

As the Olympic Stadium finally came into view, the 24-year-old American mentally prepared himself for a hero's welcome. Instead he heard booing from the 80,000 crowd. What had he done wrong? Was this an anti-American protest after the basketball shenanigans? Then he realised that the spectators had been duped by an impostor and were expressing their anger at the man's antics. For with the crowd waiting for Shorter, Norbert Sudhaus, a 22-year-old German student, had joined the race about half a mile from the stadium where there were few people around. Wearing orange shorts and a blue vest bearing the number 72, Sudhaus strode into the stadium, looking every inch a winner. Most people inside thought he was the race leader until, halfway along the back stretch, he was suddenly hustled away by officials, causing the cheers to turns to jeers and whistles. It was at that point that a puzzled Shorter emerged. Sudhaus said afterwards: 'These Games have been far too serious. I thought they needed some cheering up.' The spirit of Fred Lorz lived on.

Shorter eventually crossed the line in 2hr 12min 19.2sec – two minutes and twelve seconds ahead of the runner-up, Belgium's Karel Lismont. Mamo Wolde of Ethiopia collected bronze at the age of forty.

Shorter celebrated his gold medal as only he knew how – by drinking three gins in the bath. That night he went out with family and friends and toasted his victory in champagne. The licensed victuallers of Munich must have been sorry to see him return to Florida.

A RIGGED WEAPON

MONTREAL, 19 JULY 1976

The Montreal Olympics were plunged into chaos before they had even started. Not only had the bill for the Games risen from an original budget of $310 million to a staggering $1.5 billion (this despite the city's mayor, Jean Drapeau, famously promising that 'the Olympics could no more run a deficit than a man could have a baby'), but also Tanzania had urged the African nations to boycott the event if New Zealand were allowed to compete. New Zealand had incurred the wrath of the African nations by sending their rugby team to tour South Africa, who were still pursuing a policy of apartheid, and although rugby was not an Olympic sport, 23 nations supported the boycott.

The star of the Games was fourteen-year-old Romanian gymnast Nadia Comaneci, who followed in the dainty footsteps of Russia's Olga Korbut by captivating the viewing millions with her grace and agility. And despite those early hiccups and the bill facing Canada at the end, the Montreal Olympics passed off smoothly . . . with the exception of one extraordinary incident in the fencing section of the modern pentathlon.

Registering hits or touches in fencing competition required a complex electrical contraption that looked as if it had been devised by a mad scientist. Each weapon was fitted with a spring-loaded point connected by fine wires that ran down a groove in the blade to a plug inside the bell-shaped guard. Before indicating to the judges that he was on guard and ready, the fencer connected his body wire to the plug. The body wire ran up inside the sleeve of the fencer's jacket and emerged at

171

the back, where it was plugged into a wire from a spring-loaded spool. From the spool the wire ran to a light indicator at the scorers' table. When a hit was made, the light came on and a buzzer sounded. The system appeared foolproof, but in Montreal an eminent Russian fencer was determined to make fools of judges and opponents alike.

Red Army Major Boris Onishenko, a 38-year-old teacher from Kiev in the Ukraine, was regarded as one of the world's foremost modern pentathletes. A former individual world champion, he had been an international since 1976 and had won an individual silver medal at the Munich Olympics. Modern pentathlon comprises five disciplines – riding, fencing, shooting, swimming and running – and the second day of competition in the team event was devoted to fencing, arguably Onishenko's strongest suit. Having won team gold in 1972, the Soviets were clear favourites to repeat the feat and Onishenko was already leading the event when he came face to face with Britain's Adrian Parker. Not only was he reaching the veteran stage but Onishenko had also been lined up as a future coach for the Soviet pentathlon team, so Montreal was expected to bring the curtain down on his illustrious career. Yet within days he would be hustled out of Canada in disgrace with headlines around the world denouncing him as 'Disonishenko'.

Whereas in standard men's fencing competitions five touches on an opponent were required to secure a win, fencing in the modern pentathlon was a sudden death affair with the first hit in each bout being sufficient for victory. Theoretically this left the pentathlon open to possible corruption – not that anyone would have expected any cheating from such honourable men, least of all from Onishenko.

An accomplished fencer in his own right, Parker was expected to prove a major obstacle in the Ukrainian's quest for a farewell gold and had every right to feel aggrieved when the light registered the decisive hit for Onishenko even though no touch appeared to have taken place. Watching from the sidelines was British veteran Jim Fox, whose eyes convinced him that Parker had been robbed. Fox was Onishenko's next opponent and when he, too, lost a hit to the Soviet fencer without being touched, he launched an official protest.

As soon as Fox challenged the touch, a contrite Onishenko agreed that there had been no hit and volunteered to change the épée with which he had been fighting. But Fox, believing that it was somehow short-circuiting, demanded that it go to weapon control for detailed inspection. When referee Guido Malacarne ordered Onishenko to surrender his épée, Onishenko pretended not to understand and scurried away to the bosom of his team-mates, where another weapon had already been produced ready for exchange. However, Malacarne was growing increasingly suspicious of Onishenko's evasive tactics and, right from the moment of protest, had made a point of keeping a close watch on the faulty weapon to make sure that it could not be switched. When the referee duly prevented the swap and insisted that the Russians hand him the correct weapon, a heated argument broke out.

While the offending épée was taken away for examination, Onishenko fought on with another sword until, sensationally, word came through that he had been disqualified. In what one official described as an act of 'blatant cheating', the weapon had been wired with a concealed push-button circuit breaker, thereby enabling Onishenko to trigger the electronic scoring system with his hand and register a hit at will. Under the rules of the International Fencing Federation, all competitors' swords were checked on arrival in Montreal and re-inspected prior to each fight. Each team had its own armourer whose job it was to submit the various épées, sabres and foils to an inspecting committee before use in the competition, but Onishenko's illegal device was so sophisticated that it was impossible to detect without actually dismantling the weapon.

Onishenko's immediate reaction to his disqualification was to deny that the rigged sword was his. However, it had been made for a left-hander, and of the entire Soviet team, including the reserve, Onishenko was the only one who was left-handed. Announcing the rejection of Onishenko's appeal against disqualification, Carl Schwende, the appeal jury's chief of discipline, said: 'The weapon definitely had been tampered with. Someone had wired it in such a way that it would score a winning hit even without making contact. The jury of appeal listened very carefully to Onishenko's explanation that the equipment was not his own, but decided that his explanation was not good enough.'

In addition to Onishenko the rest of the Soviet team were also disqualified although the other two members were allowed to compete in the individual section of the team competition. In a bid to avert a repeat of the scandal, the rules of the sport were subsequently amended, with grips that could hide wires or switches being banned.

Although Britain went on to win the modern pentathlon team gold, Jim Fox was saddened by the Onishenko affair. 'Why did he do it, he of all people?' Fox asked reporters. 'He's been such a great sportsman for ten years. The pressure's getting too much, the political pressure. People are so desperate to win now. Onishenko was expecting promotion to lieutenant colonel soon, and this was his last chance to win the gold. Perhaps he needed it too much. Poor old Boris, now his life is ruined.'

In the wake of Onishenko's downfall, speculation grew as to how long he had been cheating, particularly when it was revealed that his fencing scores had improved suddenly around 1970. A Soviet team official remarked: 'It is a very sad matter and he will probably be stripped of all his medals and honours back home.'

The disgraced fencer did not linger long in Canada. Within a matter of hours of his disqualification, he had been spirited out of the country. Taken quietly from his room at the Olympic village, he was driven to the airport in a private car and removed from the line of media fire before too many embarrassing questions could be asked. He was never again seen outside the Soviet Union. Back home he was indeed stripped of his medals and discharged from the army but, thanks to an influential uncle, was able to land a job as manager of a large swimming complex in Kiev. His subsequent life remains shrouded in mystery. Rumours abound that in 1991 he was found drowned in that very pool, the victim of a KGB assassination, but others claim to have spoken to him since by telephone. Whatever his precise fate, the Onishenko affair remains fencing's darkest hour.

THE GYMNAST WITH THE BROKEN KNEE

MONTREAL, 20 JULY 1976

As Japanese gymnast Shun Fujimoto rounded off his floor exercises in the men's team combined competition at the Montreal Forum with one final tumbling run, he felt a strange sensation in his right knee. 'It felt hollow,' he recalled later, 'as if there were air in it.' In fact he had broken his kneecap, an injury that would ordinarily have brought his participation in that year's Olympics crunching to an immediate halt. But the 26-year-old was no ordinary competitor and resolved to battle through the pain in the remaining disciplines in the hope of helping his team pip the Soviet Union to the gold medal.

Furthermore, Fujimoto decided not to tell anyone about his injury, not his team-mates, not even his coach, Yukuji Hayata. 'The competition was so close,' said Fujimoto afterwards, 'and I didn't want them to lose their concentration with worry about me.'

The next event was the pommel horse and, although he was in pain throughout, his determination and courage pulled him through to a score of 9.5. 'I was completely occupied by the thought that I could not afford to make any mistakes,' he said. Whereas the pommel horse was not a discipline that put too much strain on the knee, the upcoming event – the rings – most certainly was, not least because his routine was due to end with a high-flying dismount from eight feet up in the air. 'I knew when I descended from the rings, it would be the most painful

176

moment. I also knew that if my posture was not good when I landed, I would not receive a good score. I knew I must try to forget the pain.'

Shutting out the agony and his very real fear of the landing, he performed magnificently, finishing off with a twisting triple-somersault dismount. The pain when his feet hit the floor 'shot through me like a knife', but he somehow kept his balance, his right leg buckling only slightly. Gritting his teeth and with tears in his eyes, he raised his arms in the traditional finish. The judges awarded him 9.7 – the highest score he had ever achieved on the rings.

It was immediately obvious, however, that something was seriously amiss, for no sooner had he completed his routine than he staggered away from the apparatus before collapsing in agony into the arms of his coach. The spectacular dismount had caused additional damage to his injured knee, dislocating the broken kneecap and tearing ligaments in his right leg. Incredibly, he still wanted to carry on and limped off to the medical centre for some painkilling shots, but the moment they saw his condition, the horrified doctors ordered him to withdraw from the rest of the competition or risk being permanently disabled. One Olympic doctor commented, as much in disbelief as in admiration: 'How he managed to do somersaults and twists and land without collapsing in screams is beyond my comprehension.'

When news of Fujimoto's enforced withdrawal reached his five team-mates, they reacted positively. Far from being discouraged, as he had feared, they used his courage as an inspiration even though they were now a man short for the remaining disciplines. Since the five highest scores on each apparatus counted, there was no room for error. In the end everything rested on the horizontal bars, with Mitsuo Tsukahara needing to score higher than 9.5 to overhaul the Soviets. He excelled himself with a 9.9, thus giving Japan victory in the closest gymnastics competition in Olympic history by 576.85 points to 576.45. At the awards ceremony, Fujimoto insisted on climbing unaided up to the victory podium. 'Now I have a gold medal,' he said, 'the pain is gone.'

Since Nadia Comaneci made nearly all the gymnastics headlines in Montreal, Fujimoto's heroics went largely unnoticed, but he was proud to return home with a gold medal in his hand and a cast on his leg. Asked years later whether, given the same circumstances, he would repeat what he had done in Montreal, he replied emphatically: 'No, I would not.'

And who could blame him?

THE OTHER JIMMY CARTER

MOSCOW, 27 JULY 1980

When US president Jimmy Carter announced that his country would be boycotting the 1980 Moscow Olympics following the Soviet invasion of Afghanistan, many feared that the Games would be something of a nonentity. But sport rose above politics to provide some epic duels, notably between Britain's middle-distance track heroes, Sebastian Coe and Steve Ovett. Most of the publicity emanating from Moscow was positive, although there was almost a fatality in the fencing competition.

Twenty-one-year-old Soviet fencer Vladimir Lapitsky, the 1979 world champion, was taking on Poland's Adam Robak in the men's foil team tournament. When the two men attacked simultaneously, Robak's foil snapped against the side of Lapitsky's face mask. As the Russian turned away to avoid a collision, the broken foil went through the protective leather clothing at the back of his arms and came out through the front of his chest. His white fencing jacket stained with blood, Lapitsky was rushed to hospital unconscious, but happily while the foil had pierced a blood vessel it had missed his heart and he soon made a full recovery. It was the first serious injury in the history of Olympic fencing and did not prevent the Soviet team taking the silver medal behind France.

Of course, it would not be an Olympic Games without the usual accusations of home bias and in Moscow the focus was very much on the men's triple jump competition, where Jaak Uudmae and Viktor Sanayev of the Soviet Union collected gold and silver respectively. The Soviet judges repeatedly called

179

fouls on non-Russian jumpers and were accused of quickly raking the pit before their chicanery could be exposed. Joao Carlos de Oliveira of Brazil took bronze and Australia's Ian Campbell finished fifth even though the judges called fouls on no fewer than nine of their twelve combined jumps!

While the American president had already made his mark on the 1980 Olympics, another Jimmy Carter also became embroiled in controversy. The 23-year-old British backstroke swimmer was sent home from Moscow in disgrace along with team-mate Gary Abraham following a row over a broken door-lock on the night of Sunday 27 July.

Abraham, from Southampton, had good reason to celebrate the end of the swimming competition that night, for he had earlier picked up a bronze medal as part of the 4×100 metres medley relay team. He and Carter said they were invited into the Irish quarters in the Olympic Village by two Irish swimmers but a fracas ensued during which the lock on the door of an Irish boxer's flatlet was smashed. When Russian officials dis-covered the damage, the pair were forced to pay for the repairs although, initially at least, they denied responsibility. News of the incident reached the ears of the British swimming team management and the following morning Abraham and Carter were summoned to a meeting at which they were accused of trying to break into the Irish quarters in order to pick a fight with a boxer. 'It appeared that our sentence had already been decided on,' mused Abraham as he and Carter were ordered home immediately – two days before the rest of the squad.

Speaking from the family home in Greenock, Scotland, Carter's father claimed that a mountain had been made out of a molehill. Carter himself vowed never to swim for Britain again and said that he and Abraham had been made scapegoats for a spot of 'high jinks'. He went on: 'The British officials treat you like a bunch of ten-year-olds. It would have been impossible to break into the quarters. There were three or four soldiers on each door. There was a door bolt broken, but it was just horseplay.'

It was not Carter's first brush with authority. In 1978 he was sent home from the world championships in Berlin for misbehaving. 'I admit I deserved it then,' said Carter, 'but this time it is totally unjust.' He and Abraham were also blamed for a food fight in the Olympic Village cafeteria earlier in the Games. 'I was there,' admitted Carter, 'but I was not throwing any food about. This was just a bunch of highly strung athletes letting off steam after four years of hard work and preparation. The Russians could not seem to understand that.'

Abraham eventually confessed to his involvement in the incident where the door-lock was damaged but denied any punch-up with an Irish boxer. Saying he already felt he had suffered enough for 'a few moments of stupidity', the 21-year-old was stunned when the following month the British Swimming Federation slapped a sixteen-month-ban on himself and Carter, putting them out of international competition until 31 December 1981. Both men appealed against the sentence and in November 1980 Abraham's suspension was reduced by nine months, which conveniently made him available for the European Champion-ships in Yugoslavia. Carter's ban remained intact.

In many countries, the decision as to whether or not to participate in the Moscow Olympics was made by individual sporting organisations. This process left the inaugural women's field hockey tournament in disarray and at one stage it appeared that the USSR would be the only entrants. So in a state of panic, just five weeks before the opening ceremony, a series of late invitations were sent out. Among those invited was Zimbabwe. The squad was selected less than a week before the Games and rushed to Moscow, where Zimbabwe amazed everyone by going on to take gold at the expense of Czechoslovakia and the USSR. On returning home, each member of the triumphant Zimbabwe team was rewarded with a special prize of one live ox! It brought a whole new meaning to the term 'bully-off'.

THE LONG LAST LAP

LOS ANGELES, 5 AUGUST 1984

In tit-for-tat retaliation, the USSR boycotted the 1984 Los Angeles Games, the only country to participate from the Soviet Bloc being Romania. In deciding to stay at home, the Russians missed the introduction to the Olympics of two events that owe more to dance than sport – rhythmic gymnastics and synchronised swimming. Perhaps if Cossack dancing had been an Olympic sport that year, the Russians might have showed up.

Another new event for Los Angeles was the women's marathon, previously forbidden because women were considered too weak to run 26 miles . . . unless, of course, there was a shoe shop at the end. Among the favourites for the inaugural race were Joan Benoit of the United States, Norwegian pair Grete Waitz and Ingrid Kristiansen, and Portugal's Rosa Mota, but instead most of the following morning's headlines were made by Gabriele Andersen-Scheiss, a 39-year-old Idaho ski instructor who, by virtue of dual nationality, was representing her country of birth, Switzerland.

Unbeaten in the marathon since November 1981, Benoit subjected herself to a rigorous training regime of running more than 100 miles a week. Her coach, Bob Sevene, called the 27-year-old from Maine 'the toughest athlete I have ever seen'. She had suffered a bad knee injury shortly before the US Olympic trial but her indomitable spirit helped her through and now in Los Angeles she was determined to prove herself the best in the world. After a cautious start, she took to the front at three miles and gradually imposed her will on her rivals. Waitz and Kristiansen kept in touch for a while, but as Benoit upped the tempo the Norwegians began to drop back. With temperatures touching 32 degrees Celsius (90 degrees Fahrenheit), Benoit's rivals were waiting for her to wilt in the heat and the notorious LA smog that hung over the city, but she never looked like succumbing. She came home in 2hr 24min 52sec – a minute and a half ahead of Waitz, with Mota third and Kristiansen fourth.

Further back in the field, New Zealand runner Anne Audain asked bystanders to direct her to the nearest medical post after being taken ill with dehydration at the eighteen-mile mark. Unfortunately nobody knew where the facilities were, so Audain staggered on until finally collapsing at the feet of two Los Angeles Fire Department paramedics who had stopped to watch the race. They carried her to their ambulance and drove her to hospital, where she quickly recovered after treatment. Meanwhile Leda Diaz de Cano of Honduras was finding the going equally tough. After just three miles she was already six and a half minutes behind the other runners and by twelve miles she was nearly half an hour adrift. At that point race officials, worried about disrupting the day's schedule, managed to convince her that she had little prospect of winning a medal and persuaded her to retire. Her withdrawal also allowed the streets to reopen to traffic.

Twenty minutes after Joan Benoit entered the stadium in triumph, an altogether more pitiful spectacle struggled into view. It was Andersen-Scheiss, reeling from the effects of the heat. Her left arm was hanging limp, she was listing to the left at the waist and her legs buckled as she wobbled from side to side. The *New York Times* wrote: 'She looked like a brave bull after the picadors have done their cruel business.'

The 77,000 spectators inside the Coliseum stadium gasped in horror. Medical officers rushed to her assistance but, mustering what little remaining strength she had, she waved them away. Weaving a slow, erratic path around the track, she paused occasionally and held her head. Doctors hovered, waiting to pounce if she collapsed. On she went in a painful re-enactment of Dorando Pietri at London back in 1908. As her condition fluctuated, the crowd alternated between cheering her on and begging her to stop. Her anxious husband, Dick Andersen, tried to get to her but the officials would not let him near the track. The Swiss team doctor, Bernard Segesser, watched alarmed on TV. Finally she made it to the tape and promptly collapsed in the arms of three attendants. She was placed 37th. That long last lap had taken her 5min 44sec.

While Andersen-Scheiss received medical attention, a row broke out over whether she should have been allowed to complete that painful lap. Dr Richard Greenspun, chief medical officer for track and field at the Games, defended the decision to let her finish. 'As she came through the tunnel,' said Dr Greenspun, 'my first thoughts were, "This is the most courageous thing I've ever seen." If she had fallen, a doctor [there were twelve on duty on the stadium floor] would have asked her about stopping. If her answers were appropriately incoherent, she would have had to be helped.' However, the Canadian team doctor, Doug Clement, thought she should have been removed for fear of suffering brain damage. Dr Clement added: 'She was a helluva mess.' Even race winner Joan Benoit had concerns about allowing Andersen-Scheiss to continue. 'I can understand her feelings,' said Benoit, 'wanting to complete the run, but at the same time, I think she was risking her health and her life – and nothing is more important than life.'

Happily, it was soon confirmed that Andersen-Scheiss's body temperature was only 37.8 degrees Celsius (100 degrees Fahrenheit) and that she was suffering from nothing worse than dehydration in the excessive heat. After two hours of medical attention she was discharged and allowed to return to the Olympic Village.

The debate did not go away, however. Dick Andersen admitted that he had wanted his wife stopped but conceded: 'As long as she continued to go forward and did not fall or start going in the wrong direction, they were going to let her go. It was a very, very, big race. She's kind of embarrassed about finishing a race like that.'

She was indeed. In interviews she stated that she felt fine for the first twenty miles but thought she may have forgotten to take a bottle of water at the last supply stand, resulting in her dehydration. At first when she entered the Coliseum she thought she could finish by just running a few steps then walking a few, but she then realised she had another 400 metres to cover and began zig-zagging. 'I tried to get myself going,' she said. 'I tried to relax more, to gain control over my movements. But I just couldn't do it. I was hurting. I think I had some blackouts. I remember parts of it, and parts of it I don't.' Expressing irritation with those who had questioned her right to participate, she added: 'I'm not an inexperienced runner who goes out and collapses at the finish.'

Over the following weeks Andersen-Scheiss received hundreds of letters from people who saw her as an inspiration. She was touched by the sentiments. 'They think of me as a hero,' she said three months after the event. 'To me, the natural thing was to give my best and finish the marathon. It is an honour for someone to look at me as an inspiration. I hope I can live up to it but as an athlete, you would rather be remembered for a successful race than the one I ended that way.'

In the wake of the controversy over the marathon finish, the IAAF introduced the 'Scheiss rule', which allows athletes to receive a hands-on medical examination without risking disqualification.

AN INNOCENT VICTIM

LOS ANGELES, 9 AUGUST 1984

The light-heavyweight boxing competition in Los Angeles was a unique affair: the bronze medallist, who was disqualified, stopped the silver medallist, and the gold medallist never reached the final! The cause of this confusing scenario was a highly controversial semi-final between American hope Evander Holyfield and Kevin Barry of New Zealand, which saw Holyfield, the tournament favourite, disqualified in decidedly dubious circumstances.

By popular consensus, Holyfield was the outstanding boxer at the 1984 Olympics. He had knocked out all of his opponents on the way to the semi-finals and now only Barry stood between him and the chance to claim an anticipated gold medal. However, complaints about biased US judging had earlier prompted Korea to threaten to withdraw from the boxing, so debatable decisions were not exactly unexpected. As Holyfield himself later remarked: 'I knew somebody was going to get a raw deal down the line, but I didn't think it was going to be me.'

In the first semi-final Yugoslavia's Anton Josipovic comfortably defeated Mustapha Moussa of Algeria and the boisterous 11,000 crowd at the Convention Center sat back and waited for Holyfield and Barry. The referee for the second fight was Gligorije Novicic from Yugoslavia, a location that would soon assume great significance in the eyes of conspiracy theorists.

Barry was outclassed from the start. Clumsy, awkward and slow, he was reduced to hanging round Holyfield's neck in an attempt to negate the superior skills of the nimble American.

186

Holyfield almost finished the job in that opening round and not surprisingly led on the cards of all five judges when the bell went to provide Barry with much-needed respite from the barrage of blows. The second round followed a similar pattern, except that Barry's frustrating tactics became more blatant. Referee Novicic had already cautioned him several times for holding and now finally his patience snapped and he issued the New Zealander with two warnings, resulting in two points being deducted from his score.

With just five seconds of the round remaining, Barry was still hanging on for dear life. The referee ordered the fighters to break and shouted 'Stop!' but Holyfield didn't and sent Barry sprawling to the canvas with a ferocious left hook to the head. As Barry fell, the referee turned immediately to Holyfield and ordered him to the neutral corner before signalling that the fight was over. The crowd went wild, believing that referee Novicic had stopped the fight because Barry, who had got up after a mandatory eight count, was unable to continue. Then came the announcement: Holyfield had been disqualified for hitting after the stop order. Again the arena went wild, but this time in fury. Paper cups, wads of paper and ice cubes rained down on the ring (fortunately no bottled drinks were sold at the arena) and security guards were drafted in to provide an escort for the referee.

Holyfield was stunned and confused by the decision, while even Barry looked sheepish. 'Maybe I ought to go over and apologise,' Barry said to his father, who also acted as his manager. When the referee raised Barry's hand in triumph to a crescendo of booing, the New Zealander plodded after his opponent and sportingly raised Holyfield's arm in the air. He knew who had really won that fight. Still unable to take in the fact that he had lost the chance of going for gold, Holyfield gave his version of events: 'He kept holding me, and in the clinch I hit him with a hook. I heard the referee say to go to the neutral corner. He told me I hit on the break. I'm upset.'

The US Amateur Boxing Federation president, Loring Baker, launched a formal protest, claiming that Holyfield had already thrown the punch when the referee ordered the fighters to break. Baker also said that Holyfield never heard the command, partly because of the noise from the crowd and partly because Barry was holding him around his protective headgear. Anyway, added Baker, Barry should have been disqualified earlier in the round for repeatedly holding and at the same time hitting Holyfield. American protests never like to leave anything to chance.

Having been stopped by a blow to the head, Barry was not allowed to fight again for thirty days, so the gold automatically went to Josipovic, who had been in the shower at the time. And that provided ample ammunition for those who believe that every American defeat is a gross injustice. For by his intervention the Yugoslav referee had assured a Yugoslav boxer of the gold medal. At least Baker refrained from mentioning that fact in his protest. 'We were aware,' he confided, 'but it would have been in bad taste to say it.'

The protest was heard the following day but the panel stood by the referee's decision. Under normal circumstances, a disqualification would have denied Holyfield the bronze medal but, taking into account Barry's 'infringements of the rules', the panel took the unusual step of recommending that Holyfield should receive his medal. It smacked of a compromise. As one American journalist wrote: 'Because he had been disqualified, Holyfield shouldn't have been eligible for any medal. But the behaviour of the Yugoslav referee was so outrageous that the IOC had to find a way out without creating future problems. The decision left Barry with the silver medal and the Yugoslav with the gold. A near perfect scenario.'

As it turned out, Holyfield's lowest point became his zenith. The outrage at his disqualification meant that he was more popular in defeat than he may have been in victory. From then on, of course, he never looked back and developed into one of the greatest heavyweights in the history of boxing. That miserable day in 1984 was swiftly to become but a distant memory.

ENJOY THE TRIP

LOS ANGELES, 10 AUGUST 1984

There was a precedent to the most infamous incident at the 1984 Olympics. A few days before Mary Decker and Zola Budd got in a tangle, Sweden's Svante Rasmuson, competing in the cross-country race, the final event of the modern pentathlon, was denied a certain gold medal when he had the misfortune to trip over a potted plant that had been positioned to brighten up the course. Whether the embittered Swede ever spoke to the plant again is not known, but he certainly didn't milk the mishap in the same way as Decker.

The irony of the Decker/Budd clash is that Decker was Budd's idol. Above her bed in the Afrikaans town of Bloemfontein, young Budd had kept a cut-out picture of the American. And even in the build-up to the Olympics, she had spoken admiringly of Decker, telling American reporters: 'It would be wonderful to be so pretty.'

For Mary Decker was the Golden Girl of US athletics, a fierce competitor blessed with supreme talent and an iron will to win. Nobody was allowed to get in her way. At a 1983 track meeting in New York she had coldly pushed Puerto Rican runner Angelita Lind to the ground when Lind, who was about to be lapped, failed to move to the outside to enable Decker to pass in comfort. Everything was geared towards the 26-year-old winning the Olympic 3,000 metres before her adoring fans in Los Angeles, the city where she had grown up. She had missed out on the 1976 Games through injury and the 1980 Olympics because of the US boycott and was a warm favourite to make it

189

third time lucky, particularly as she was in prime form, having won both the 1,500 metres and 3,000 metres at the 1983 World Championships in Helsinki. An added bonus was that the world record holder at 3,000 metres, Syvetlana Ulmasova of the USSR with 8min 26.78sec, was missing from the Olympic line-up as a result of the Soviet boycott. Decker had high hopes of gold. 'Finally it all seems so perfect,' she trilled at the start of the Games.

Whereas Decker was confident and outgoing – the all-American girl – Budd cut a completely different figure. The shy little South African had been breaking distance records in her homeland since the age of thirteen and in January 1984 had run 5,000 metres in 15min 1.8sec – seven seconds inside Decker's world record. However, her time could not be recognised because South Africa's policy of apartheid meant that the country was banned from international sport. Desperate to compete at that summer's Olympics, she was encouraged by her father to apply for British citizenship on the grounds that she had a British grandfather. With the *Daily Mail* taking up her case, she was granted an instant British passport and fast-tracked into the British Olympic team. To many, it seemed nothing more than a cynical attempt to secure a British medal at any cost and certainly a move not in accordance with the Olympic spirit. Paraded for the inevitable wave of publicity, the eighteen-year-old appeared nervous and awkward, displaying the general disposition of someone about to face a firing squad. She answered questions abruptly in those harsh, clipped tones that were so alien to the plummy accents of the English middle-classes who were supposed to be welcoming her to their collective bosom. It would be fair to say that the British public failed to warm to her.

Both athletes made it through to the final without too much fuss, although Decker complained that in the course of the semi-final Canada's Lynn Williams had stepped on her heel four times. It would turn out to be an omen.

Decker's gameplan was simple. 'She was looking for about an 8:29 pace in the final,' said her coach Dick Brown. 'With a kilometre to go, she would begin picking it up.' This was a similar tactic to the one Decker had used in Helsinki, but on that occasion she started her push from 600 metres out. But now she intended to make her move 1,000 metres from the finish, partly because she was stronger than the previous year but also because the Romanian Maricica Puica, the reigning world cross-country champion and mile-record holder, could produce a dangerous kick if it wasn't run out of her. Budd also had to run from the front a long way from home, as she had no kick finish to speak of. It would set the two on a collision course.

Before the final the athletes were required to show their running spikes to an official to ensure that they conformed to specifications. Budd, in her first major international competition, was placed in something of a dilemma, as she always ran barefoot. She later recalled: 'I just picked up my feet and showed them to him, white plasters on my toes and all. The poor man nearly cracked up laughing, but what else could I have done? Everybody else had spikes and I had to show him something.' It was just about the only occasion that Zola Budd and laughter were mentioned in the same breath.

Decker led the final from the gun, first at world record pace, then slowing a second or so per lap. Budd's plan, as arranged with her coach Peter Labuschagne, was to stay behind Decker for the first part of the race and then take over. Budd's wide arm action had already caused the pair to bump elbows at 500 metres, following which Decker shot her a withering look. Now, approaching 1,700 metres, Budd, running wide, was still glued to Decker's shoulder with the American's chief threat, Puica, close up in third. That final kilometre – when Decker would make the break for home – would begin in just 300 metres on the backstretch. She relaxed the pace a little, gathering herself in preparation for the big push that lay ahead. Feeling the pace drop, Budd became alarmed. All too aware that she did not possess the finishing kick of either Decker or Puica, Budd realised that this was the time to take matters into her own hands and raise the tempo. So she began to edge past Decker on the bend. Coming off the turn, Budd appeared to have enough margin to cut in to the inside lane without interfering with Decker's stride, but instead she hung wide, on the outside of lane one. Decker was tucked right on the inside, a yard behind Budd, whose British team-mate Wendy Sly had moved up into third, just ahead of Puica. At the top of the straight Decker sensed Budd drifting to the inside. 'She tried to cut in without being, basically, ahead,' Decker would later complain. But, in the words of *Sports Illustrated*, 'Decker didn't do what a seasoned middle-distance runner would have done. She didn't reach out to Budd's shoulder to let her know she was there, too close behind for Budd to move to the pole.' Instead Decker shortened her stride for a couple of steps and made contact with Budd's left foot. The bump knocked Budd slightly off balance and caused Decker to lose momentum briefly but five strides later the two were almost level once more, at which point Budd, trying to reassert her position, inched further over towards the inside lane. Again there was a collision. Decker's right foot struck Budd's left calf, the impact forcing Budd to shoot out her left leg for balance, whereupon Decker's right foot spiked Budd's trailing left heel. The American crashed to the ground. As she fell, she ripped the wax paper number from Budd's back.

Budd looked back anxiously to survey the carnage and saw Decker lying in a crumpled heap on the infield. The American later said that her first instinct had been to get up and rejoin the race but when she tried, 'it felt like I was tied to the ground'. She had pulled a muscle in her hip. Decker was still lying there when the field came round a lap later, but by then she was sobbing uncontrollably, having been joined by medical attendants and her fiancé, British discus thrower Richard Slaney. Her face was contorted in a combination of pain and venom.

The object of her hatred, Zola Budd, might just as well have fallen out of the race with her, for she no longer had the stomach for the fight. Already a controversial figure, Budd now faced the full wrath of 85,000 fiercely patriotic Americans who, convinced that she was the villain of the piece, booed her every remaining step of the way. With tears streaming down her face, Budd trailed in a distant seventh, the gold medal going to Puica and the silver to Sly.

Slaney gently escorted the limping Decker across the track before lifting her into his arms as they entered the tunnel. She was still playing the dying swan when Budd caught up with her and tried to apologise. Decker saw her coming and barked: 'Don't bother. Get out of here. Get out. Just go. I won't talk to you.' When other runners tried to console the tearful Budd by telling her that it wasn't her fault, Decker snapped: 'Yes it was. I know it was.' Budd was then led to the medical area to have her bleeding ankle bandaged. On her way back to the Olympic Village, British team manager Nick Whitehead tried to cheer her up. 'I just said that it was her first Olympics and she ought to be proud. All she said was, "How's Mary?"'

The crowd's desire for revenge seemed set to be rewarded when referee Andy Bakjian disqualified Budd for breaking rule 141 of the IAAF rule book, which states: 'Any competitor jostling, running across or obstructing another competitor so as to impede his or her progress shall be liable to disqualification.' The British team protested Budd's innocence, claiming that Decker had tripped herself, so the matter went to the jury of appeals.

Budd received considerable support from her fellow athletes. Gold medallist Puica said unequivocally: 'It was Mary's fault. She was the girl behind and should have seen the way forward.' The fifth-placed finisher, Switzerland's Cornelia Burki, also condemned Decker. 'When you're behind, you're the one to have to watch out,' she said. 'It was Mary's fault.' Ireland's 1,500-metre runner Eamonn Coghlan thought it a tough one to call. 'You're supposed to be one stride ahead before you can cut in,' he commented, 'but this happens all the time. You have to protect yourself out there. Perhaps it was inexperience on Zola's part. Perhaps it was being too ladylike on Mary's part. You can't blame either one.'

The jury of appeal agreed and, after viewing videotape of the race from six angles, overturned the disqualification. Budd was reinstated. 'There was no foul,' explained Mort Tenner, the Olympic competition director for athletics. 'In some races, things happen that are nobody's fault. In this case the jury has ruled that Zola Budd was not responsible.'

Interestingly, the United States team did not file a protest on this occasion.

The jury's verdict cut no ice with Decker. 'I think the rules are, you have to be in front,' she told reporters. 'I don't think there was any question she was in the way. Maybe it was inexperience on her part. You have to be a full stride ahead to cut in. She wasn't anywhere near passing. I hold Budd responsible for what happened. I didn't do anything wrong. She tried to cut in without being in front. I tried not to push her. To keep from pushing her, I fell. Looking back, I probably should have pushed her.'

Budd related her own account to her friends at the *Daily Mail*. She revealed how she had felt Decker slacken her pace and knew that it was time to take up the running. 'Suddenly from behind I felt a bump. I think it was Mary's knee on my left leg. Thrown off balance, I lurched a little and felt pain as spikes raked down the back of my left heel. I fought for balance and suddenly I sensed Mary falling, crashing to the track. I half turned and glimpsed her roll toward the grass. I couldn't believe it. It was terrible.' Budd said she wanted to stop but instinctively carried on, her mind in turmoil. She didn't think it was her fault until she heard the boos. 'The booing came down like a tidal wave of concentrated hostility,' she added. 'It was like being punched in the stomach. I am upset that Mary fell and that the crowd seemed to think it was my fault. I think she ran into the back of me.'

Initially Budd was pilloried in the US press and subjected to death threats by Neanderthal members of the American public, but then the newspapers vindicated her and even the race commentator, Marty Liquori, who had heavily criticised her at the time, admitted he was wrong and apologised on screen. The sight of the frail Budd being bullied across the water had actually endeared her to the British, who began to look upon her in a more sympathetic light.

Decker recovered from her injury to set a new world mile record the following year, but Budd's career was thrown into turmoil in 1988 when she was suspended for attending (but not competing in) a cross-country race in South Africa. Fed up with being a political pawn, she packed her bags and returned to her homeland, thereby finally consigning to the spike a newspaper editor's dream that she might one day achieve Olympic glory for Britain.

Budd and Decker bumped into each other again in the 1990s at a race meeting in Australia. They chatted . . . briefly. Budd said recently: 'She still blames me but has forgiven me. We don't keep in touch – she's not an easy woman to talk to.'

THE DEATH THREAT

LOS ANGELES, 12 AUGUST 1984

Zola Budd was not the only victim of death threats at the Los Angeles Olympics. For Haitian marathon runner Dieudonné Lamothe later revealed that the country's notorious dictator, Baby Doc Duvalier, had threatened to kill him if he failed to finish the race. As incentives go, it was right up there with the best.

Lamothe had first come to prominence at the 1976 Olympics when in a heat of the 5,000 metres he succeeded in finishing a full five minutes behind the other runners. The suspicion both inside and outside Haiti – although naturally it was never voiced to his face – was that Duvalier selected loyal soldiers and family friends for the country's Olympic teams rather than genuine athletes, with the result that they invariably trailed in just as everyone else was packing up to go home.

The 1984 marathon had already lost one runner in tragic circumstances when, during pre-Olympic training in his home-land, Tanzania's Richard Mbewa was shot dead while jogging on a golf course by a police officer who mistook him for a thief trying to make his escape. Then, just fifteen days before the Los Angeles race, one of the favourites, Carlos Lopes of Portugal, was hit by a car. In the impact his elbow smashed through the windscreen and he rolled over the bonnet, but he managed to escape with nothing worse than cuts and bruises and was passed fit to run in the big race.

Lopes chose to break one of the cardinal rules of marathon running by competing in new shoes. He had obviously never heard of his compatriot, Manuel Dias, who elected to try out

196

new footwear at the 1936 Olympics in Berlin. At first Dias appeared comfortable and after ten miles he was lying second, but then the new shoes started to pinch. He gradually dropped back until, with his feet deteriorating by the minute, he decided to throw the shoes aside and ask a spectator to lend him a replacement pair. Unfortunately the only person willing to help Dias was a boy from the Hitler youth movement, who lent him his heavy marching boots! Dias goose-stepped his way home to finish seventeenth. Lopes took the precaution of breaking in his new shoes in advance of the race, but discovered that one of them was too tight. So he was hurriedly fitted for a new pair just five days before the marathon. The shoes were then made in Japan and hand-delivered to Lopes in Los Angeles two days before the race. In fact, there were two pairs but his wife Theresa advised him to wear the ones with the gold trim because it would match the colour of the medal he was going to win.

Theresa Lopes knew her stuff, for her husband went on to demolish a quality field in a new Olympic record time of 2hr 09min 21sec. At 37 years, 176 days, he also became the oldest-ever winner of an Olympic running event. Lopes brushed aside concerns about his age. 'I have followed the same programme for fifteen years,' he said. 'I bet on my youthfulness. The keys are endurance and happiness.' And presumably a new pair of shoes.

Long after Lopes had crossed the line – 43 minutes later, to be precise – Dieudonné Lamothe, Haiti's finest, lurched home, the last of the 78 finishers. Those who wondered why he had kept on going despite being so far adrift received the answer when he eventually revealed the details of Duvalier's death threat. Without the sword of Damocles or Duvalier hanging over him, Lamothe actually went on to record some highly respectable marathon times, even managing to finish twentieth at the 1988 Seoul Olympics. Perhaps the threats weren't really necessary after all.

A HEADACHE FOR GREG

SEOUL, 19 SEPTEMBER 1988

Animal welfare groups had voiced widespread concerns about the award of the 1988 Olympics to South Korea, a country not noted for treating God's creatures with great kindness. Their fears were hardly eased by an accident at the opening ceremony when some of the pigeons released symbolically in the stadium were caught up in the rush of the Olympic flame.

Table tennis was added to the Olympic menu and tennis returned after a 62-year absence. East German cyclist Christa Luding-Rothenburger won a silver in the women's match sprint to add to the gold and silver speed skating medals that she had won at the Winter Olympics in February, thus becoming the first athlete to win medals at both Olympics in the same year. And since the Summer and Winter Games are now held in different years, it is a feat that will never be repeated. On the running track sisters-in-law Florence Griffith 'Flo-Jo' Joyner and Jackie Joyner-Kersee won six medals between them and in the swimming pool East Germany's Kristin Otto collected an astonishing six golds while America's Matt Biondi picked up seven medals, including two gold.

For many Americans, however, the real star of the pool was diver Greg Louganis, who became the first Olympic diver to complete the springboard and platform double for a second time. Yet his participation in either event was thrown into doubt following an horrific accident when, with a sickening thud, he smashed his head on the board during the preliminaries, resulting in a gash that required five

198

stitches. Then again, Louganis's entire life had been one of surmounting obstacles.

He was born in San Diego in 1960 to parents of Samoan and northern European ancestry who, being only fifteen at the time, decided to give up their baby. At nine months he was adopted by Peter and Frances Louganis, but he had a troubled childhood. Taunted at school because he was dyslexic and brownskinned, and also for his love of dance and gymnastics, he found that his tumbling talents came in useful around the family pool, where he enjoyed playing on the diving board. This led to him being enrolled in diving classes at the age of nine and two years later he scored a perfect ten at a national competition in Colorado Springs. Diving became the only release from an otherwise miserable existence, which saw him dabbling in drugs and even attempting suicide. He moved away from his adoptive parents in 1975 and into the home of his coach, Dr Sammy Lee, himself an Olympic diving gold medallist in 1948 and 1952. Lee put Louganis on a strict training schedule for the Montreal Olympics and the youngster responded by collecting a silver medal in the platform diving competition and by finishing sixth in the springboard.

However, Louganis felt that he had failed in Canada and turned to a new coach, Miami-based Ron O'Brien. After winning the springboard and platform at the 1979 Pan-American Games, Louganis was expected to win gold at the Moscow Olympics, only to be deprived of his chance when President Carter called for a US boycott. The year before the Olympics, Louganis hit his head on the board while diving at a meeting in Tbilisi and was knocked unconscious. After being dragged from the water, it was another twenty minutes before he came round. It was a taste of things to come.

In the early 1980s Louganis cleaned up his act and in Los Angeles in 1984 he became the first man to pull off the Olympic springboard and platform double since fellow countryman Pete Desjardins back in 1928.

Four years later in Seoul, Louganis was the favourite for both events. He was leading going into the ninth round of the preliminaries for the three-metre springboard when he attempted a reverse two-and-a-half somersault pike. But without a strong enough jump, he left the board too straight, instead of pushing away, hit his head on the board and fell clumsily into the water. 'I didn't realise I was that close to the board,' he said later. 'When I hit it, it was kind of a shock, but I think my pride was hurt more than anything else.' Even so, the scalp wound required immediate medical treatment by means of temporary sutures and it was with a small bandage on his head that he returned to the pool 35 minutes later to complete the remaining two qualifying dives. As soon as the preliminaries were over, he went to hospital to have the sutures replaced by stitches.

The following day, in the competition proper, Louganis hit all eleven dives and won easily. He admitted afterwards: 'I was a little nervous going into the ninth dive because of what had happened. Hitting my head shook my confidence a lot and the fact that everybody was watching me very closely on my ninth made me nervous. I just kept telling myself: "Do it the way you've done it before. Just go for it."'

A week later, in the finals of the platform competition, Louganis trailed fourteen-year-old Xiong Ni of China by three points going into the last round. With a reverse three-and-a-half somersault facing him, Louganis successfully performed the most difficult dive in his programme to snatch gold by 1.14 points. In doing so, he became only the second person – and the first man – to win double diving golds at two Olympics (America's Patricia McCormick captured the springboard and high diving competitions in 1952 and 1956).

After announcing his retirement from competition in 1989, Louganis became a stage actor and five years later publicly came out as being homosexual. The next year his auto-biography, *Breaking the Surface*, became a best-seller after he confessed on national television that he was suffering from AIDS. The revelation prompted anxious flashbacks to that cut head in Seoul. At the time Louganis had secretly known that he was HIV-positive. If he had bled into the pool – which he did not – could he have spread the AIDS virus to his fellow competitors? Although doctors agreed that the chances of that happening were remote, Louganis acknowledged: 'It must seem irresponsible now, but I hadn't considered the possibility that I could injure myself in that way.'

PLATFORM FOR PROTEST

SEOUL, 19 SEPTEMBER 1988

The United States women's gymnastics team were not given much hope of winning a medal in Seoul, as they faced stiff opposition from the Eastern Bloc countries. Yet the girls surpassed themselves to move into third place behind the Soviet Union and Romania, only for their medal hopes to be snatched away as a result of an obscure protest.

The incident took place as America's Kelly Garrison-Steves began her compulsory round performance on the uneven bars. Like most gymnasts, she used a springboard to mount the apparatus and after she had jumped on to the bars, the team's reserve, Rhonda Faehn, ran over to pull the board out of the way. But instead of stepping off the raised podium on which the bars stood, Faehn remained to watch, thereby violating a little-known rule that forbids anyone except the performing gymnast from being on the competition podium during a routine. Faehn did not assist Garrison-Steves in any way whatsoever – nor had she any intention of doing so. It was a simple momentary aberration, and one that had no effect on her colleague's performance. However, the rules said she should have stepped back down to the floor and the mistake was brought to the attention of East Germany's Ellen Berger, head of the International Gymnastics Federation's technical committee. By pure coincidence, the East German team were lying close up in fourth place, just out of the medals behind the US girls.

As Berger convened a hasty meeting to discuss the infringement, the competition was put on hold. The Americans were furious. Ebullient US coach Bela Karolyi promptly accused Christa Herrmann, the East German judge on the uneven bars, of telling tales to Berger, but Yuri Titov, the Russian president of the IGF, maintained that several people had called attention to Faehn's lapse. After much discussion, the judges voted 3–0 in favour of the rule being upheld with America's Jackie Fie, the head judge for the uneven bars, abstaining. The Americans were deducted 0.50 points – sufficient to move the East Germans up to third.

'That's dirty,' raged Karolyi, 'and that's sick. What does it matter, even if the kid is on the podium? What change is there in the routine? It doesn't disturb anything. I've never seen that before.' Suggesting that the decision to apply the rule was politically motivated, Karolyi continued: 'It's obvious the East German judge wanted to keep the scores down. They're fighting desperately to keep their place.' His sentiments were repeated by Mike Jacki, executive director of the US Gymnastics Federation, who accused Herrmann of only watching for infractions by American gymnasts 'because we were challenging them'. Jacki added sourly: 'It's a Mickey Mouse kind of thing to do.'

That lost half-point was to prove decisive, for in the final reckoning the East Germans finished third, taking the bronze medal by just 0.30 points from the United States.

CHAOS IN THE RING

SEOUL, 21 SEPTEMBER 1988

One of the first indications that the boxing competition at the Seoul Olympics would eventually disintegrate into the kind of anarchy that would prompt *Boxing News* to label them the 'Games of Shame' came with a fracas in the light-middleweight section. Inevitably it involved a South Korean, Park Si-hun, whose victory over Sudan's Abdallah Ramadan was not so much tinged with controversy as plastered with the stuff. Park's speciality was the illegal kidney punch, which he was allowed to deliver with impunity, and by the second round Ramadan was in such pain from the illicit blows that he was unable to continue. At this point the Australian referee, Ronald Gregor, realised that something was amiss and consulted the five judges, only to be informed that because he had failed to caution Park after any of the low blows, disqualification was not an option. So Gregor ruled that Ramadan had 'retired' and duly declared Park the winner.

The verdict infuriated the Sudanese squad who, lacking the clout of some of the bigger nations, registered their dissatisfaction in a subtler manner than the usual bellicose protests. As soon as Sudan's super-heavyweight Mohamed Hammad stepped forward to begin his fight with Kim Yoo-hyun of South Korea, his coach Abdellatif Mohamed threw in the towel . . . before either boxer had even thrown a punch.

The Sudanese had made their point about Park's outrageous victory, but it did not prevent him going on to gain a series of controversial verdicts en route to one of the most improbable gold medals in Olympic history. He saved the worst until last. His opponent in the final, nineteen-year-old Roy Jones of the United States, comprehensively outboxed him, landing 86 punches to the South Korean's 32. In addition, Park took a standing count of eight in round two. Yet incredibly the judges awarded the decision – and the gold medal – to Park by three votes to two. As he raised Park's arm in triumph, even mystified referee Aldo Leoni whispered to Jones: 'I can't believe they're doing this to you.' To his credit, Park, too, was faintly embarrassed by the decision and on the victory stand he raised Jones's arm. As if to underline the folly, Jones was subsequently voted the Outstanding Boxer at the Games. Rumours quickly began circulating that the three judges who had voted in favour of Park – those from Uganda, Morocco and Uruguay – had somehow been bribed by the Koreans, but an IOC investigation revealed no evidence of this. However, the Moroccan judge did later claim that he had only voted for Park so as not to embarrass the host nation!

Whenever a Korean lost in Seoul, there were angry scenes. On 20 September the crowd reacted badly after light-flyweight Oh Kwang-soo had been narrowly beaten by Michael Carbajal of the United States, but the real fireworks were reserved for the following day when Korean bantamweight Byun Jong-il tackled Bulgaria's Alexander Hristov. New Zealand referee Keith Walker struggled to control the fight from the outset. After warning Byun on three occasions to stop using his head as a battering ram, Walker eventually lost patience and instructed the judges to deduct a point from the Korean's score. And when Byun repeated the offence in the third and final round, Walker ordered a second point to be deducted. The two penalties cost Byun the fight, the judges returning a 4–1 verdict in favour of Hristov.

No sooner had the verdict been announced than Korean trainer Lee Heung-soo stormed into the ring and thumped referee Walker on the back. His action provoked a mini riot, with other Koreans – in the mistaken belief that Walker had also refereed the Carbajal–Kwang-soo fight – angrily surrounding the harassed official. As a barrage of chairs rained down on the ring, Walker's fellow officials came to his rescue and handed him over to security guards who, unfortunately, proved every bit as indisposed towards the referee as the Korean coaches and trainers. One guard immediately directed a kick at Walker's head, while the Chief of Security, after first taking the precaution of removing his uniform, chased Walker around the arena. When asked later about his actions, he declared proudly: 'I acted instinctively for the love of my fatherland.'

The Koreans then turned their anger on Emil Jetchev, the Bulgarian president of the Referees' Committee of the International Amateur Boxing Association, and attempted to hit him over the head with a plastic box. The blow was intercepted by American judge Stan Hamilton, who later needed treatment for his badly gashed hand.

When order was finally restored, twenty-year-old Byun, in scenes reminiscent of his compatriot Chon Dong-kih in 1964, sat down in the middle of the ring to stage a silent protest. He remained there for 67 minutes (for the most part in darkness after the lights had been turned off) before deciding that he had made his point. On leaving the ring, he bowed graciously to the near-empty auditorium.

The Korean Boxing Association lodged a formal appeal against the result, but it was rejected, their cause not exactly helped by the disgraceful scenes that followed the fight. Referee Walker, who caught the first plane back to New Zealand, said of the altercation: 'I am horrified. Korean coaches were kicking and punching and pulling my hair out.' Lee Heung-soo, three Korean team assistants and a Korean judge were subsequently suspended for 'appalling and unprecedented behaviour' while Kim Chong-ha, president of the Korean Olympic Committee, resigned, as did Kim Seung-yon, president of the Korean Amateur Boxing Federation. Sadly the scenes came as no surprise to many journalists covering the Games. As Colin Gibson wrote in the *Daily Telegraph*: 'Crowds have been well-behaved and uniformly impartial – until a Korean steps into the action.'

Another Korean, middleweight Ho Jong-ha, was an innocent bystander in one of the boxing tournament's more chaotic moments when America's Anthony Hembrick failed to show up in time for their date in the ring. US team officials thought that Hembrick was due to fight Ho at around 1 p.m. on 19 September, so even when they missed the 9 a.m. bus from the Olympic Village they were not remotely concerned. However, when they arrived at the boxing hall at 10.30 a.m., they found Ho standing in his corner waiting for Hembrick. Even then, instead of shoving the 22-year-old Marine through the ropes and telling him to get on with it, the Americans persisted in arguing at the official table while Hembrick stood around still wearing his tracksuit. Finally they sent Hembrick to his dressing-room to change, but it was all too late and the bout was awarded to the Korean who by then had been waiting for over seven minutes, thereby comfortably exceeding the five-minute maximum. American coach Ken Adams subsequently accepted blame for the blunder.

But it didn't always require the presence of a South Korean to cause confusion at Seoul. In the second round of a feather-weight contest, Canada's Jamie Pagendam felled his opponent, Tserendorj Awarjargal of Mongolia, three times, which, under amateur rules, should have made him the automatic winner. Alas, referee Marius Guiramo Lougbo from the Ivory Coast lost count of the number of knockdowns and allowed the fight to continue. Then in the third round Awarjargal produced a haymaker of his own and sent Pagendam sprawling to the canvas, whereupon the referee stopped the fight and declared the Mongolian the winner. The Canadian team protested immediately and eventually the decision was overturned, making Pagendam the winner by virtue of his three knockdowns in the second round. But since the punch that felled him (which, of course, was delivered after the contest should have been halted) was a blow to the head, Pagendam received a mandatory thirty-day medical suspension, meaning that he was unable to compete again at the Games. Referee Lougbo was also banned from further participation.

Meanwhile, spare a thought for bantamweight Eduard Paululum, who journeyed to Seoul as the first-ever Olympic competitor from the tiny Pacific island nation of Vanuatu. He was so excited by life in a foreign land that he tucked into a hearty breakfast before his first bout, but on arriving at the weigh-in he was disqualified for being one pound overweight. Thus he had to return home without having fought.

THE TEST THAT SHOOK
THE WORLD

SEOUL, 24 SEPTEMBER 1988

Over the past few decades drugs stories at the Olympics have become so commonplace as to scarcely warrant a mention in terms of the unusual. However, the downfall of Jamaican-born Canadian sprinter Ben Johnson at Seoul was something else. Here was a national hero, a gold medallist, being stripped of his title because he had been caught cheating. The reverberations rocked the sporting world and inevitably raised questions about how many other athletes owed their personal bests as much to steroids as to talent.

Although it was at the Seoul Olympics that Johnson spectacularly fell from grace, the seeds for his demise were sown seven years earlier. In 1981 Ben Johnson was a powerful nineteen-year-old whose sprinting potential had brought him to the notice of experienced coach Charlie Francis. At the previous year's Pan-American Junior Championships Johnson had been outgunned by another promising youngster, Carl Lewis of the United States, and became obsessed with beating him. Lewis made it all look so easy; Johnson began to despair. But Francis had an idea. He told his protégé that anabolic steroids represented one per cent of performance, or the equivalent of one metre in the 100 metres, and offered to put him in touch with a helpful doctor. Assured that most of the other top sprinters were taking steroids, Johnson worried about being left behind. A few days later he phoned Francis back. He wanted that extra metre.

Over the next few years all that Johnson saw of Carl Lewis was his back as the American sprinted away to yet another triumph. At the Los Angeles Olympics Johnson deliberately false-started in the 100 metres final in an attempt to unsettle his rival. The plan failed miserably. Lewis took gold – one of four he collected at the Games – while Johnson had to settle for bronze. The gulf between the two athletes was becoming as wide on the track as off it – Lewis educated, lithe, arrogant and American; Johnson brooding, bulky, shy and Canadian. The pedigree versus the mongrel.

Then in 1985 the balance of power began to shift. After seven consecutive defeats at the hands of Lewis, Johnson finally turned the tables. In the same year he gave an interview to Canada's *Athletics* magazine, in which he echoed Lewis's own anti-drug stance. 'Drugs are both demeaning and despicable,' said Johnson, 'and when people are caught they should be thrown out of the sport for good.' Noble words indeed.

In May 1987 Lewis's father died of cancer and at the funeral Lewis tenderly placed the gold medal from the Los Angeles 100 metres in his father's hands. 'I want you to have this,' he said, 'because it was your favourite event.' His mother was surprised at such generosity, but Lewis calmly replied: 'Don't worry, I'll get another one.'

Those words were beginning to look decidedly optimistic, because Johnson seemed to have got the measure of Lewis and was being hailed as the fastest man on Earth. Bursting out of the blocks with phenomenal pace and power, he sealed his newfound superiority at the 1987 World Championships in Rome, where his victory time of 9.83sec smashed the world record and left Lewis trailing by a metre – the precise advantage that Francis had told him steroids could provide. It was Johnson's fifth straight win against Lewis. All Lewis could offer by way of response was a television interview in which he launched a thinly veiled attack on Johnson. 'There are gold medallists at this meet who are on drugs,' said Lewis. 'That [100 metres] race will be looked at for many years, for more reasons than one.' Lewis was not the first to voice suspicions about Johnson, who was nicknamed 'Benoid' by other competitors on account of his yellow-tinged eyes and highly sculptured muscles – both indications of steroid use. But coach Francis was always quick to point out that Johnson had passed countless drug tests and the athlete himself dismissed it as a case of sour grapes by Lewis. 'When Carl Lewis was winning everything, I never said a word against him,' commented Johnson. 'And when the next guy comes along and beats me, I won't complain about that either.'

At the start of 1988 Johnson was the number one, but then a succession of injuries hampered his Olympic preparation. In February he pulled a hamstring, aggravating the same injury three months later. Meanwhile Lewis was returning to form and at Zurich in August, their first clash since Rome, he beat Johnson into third place. 'The gold medal for the 100 metres is mine,' boasted Lewis. 'I will never again lose to Johnson.'

In Seoul, Johnson appeared to have rediscovered his old spark and both he and Lewis reached the final in impressive style. The grand showdown took place on 24 September. Johnson got away to a typically strong start and this time Lewis was unable to overhaul him, the Canadian's breathtaking time of 9.79sec bringing him gold and a new world record. In an emotional little speech moments after finishing, he dedicated his gold medal to 'my mother, for everyone, for Canada'. Not wishing to be accused again of being a bad loser, Lewis kept his counsel about Johnson's run.

An hour after his win, the new Olympic champion and toast of Canada entered the doping control area for the mandatory test that was conducted on the first four finishers. Struggling to produce a urine sample, he found it necessary to drink three beers and some liquid from a flask that he had left in a bag during the race. Two days later the Canadian team received a letter from the IOC medical commission informing them that Johnson's first test had proved positive. Three hours later his second sample was also found to be positive. Richard Pound, Canadian vice-president of the IOC, said of Johnson when the news was broken to him: 'He sat there looking like a trapped animal. He had no idea what was going on all around him.'

At 3.30 the following morning Canadian Olympic chief Carol Anne Letheren visited Johnson to confiscate his gold medal. 'We love you,' she told him, 'but you're guilty.' Seven hours later his disqualification was confirmed by the IOC, who revealed that traces of the anabolic steroid stanozolol had been detected in Johnson's urine. Johnson protested his innocence and desperately tried to find an acceptable explanation for the positive tests. He claimed that he had received anti-inflammatory cortisone injections from the doctor a few days before the race. 'I was told I had to have the shots three to four days before the race so the pain would go away. I rested for a couple of days to let it take effect.' He said the only other medication he had taken was that mystery liquid prepared by his doctor Jamie Astaphan. Johnson said: 'I stayed in the hotel and Jamie mixed my drinks. He told me it was an energy builder and contained sarsaparilla and ginseng. I never mixed my own drink.'

Francis suggested that someone must have spiked that drink while it lay unattended in the flask. He went so far as to hint that the Lewis camp might somehow have been responsible. Johnson seized on the opportunity to play the victim, insisting: 'I'll pay back whoever did this to me. I never took anything. When I was a kid I never took drugs. People who know me in Jamaica know I wouldn't take drugs. I have never, ever knowingly taken illegal drugs, and I would never embarrass my family, my friends, my country and the kids who know me. I trained for thirteen years for the Olympics to watch my hard work disappear in a second.'

With the IAAF annulling his world record and banning him from competition for two years, Johnson slunk home to Toronto under cover of darkness. Instead of returning to the kind of welcome that he had envisaged straight after his victory, he found himself branded a cheat by the media in the form of headlines such as 'FROM HERO TO ZERO IN 9.79SEC'. The *Toronto Star* wrote: 'There are a lot of impressionable young Canadians, especially Jamaican-born kids, right here in this city, who were sitting at home in front the TV, their little hearts breaking.' Canada's prime minister, Brian Mulroney, said the decision to send Johnson packing was correct, but a tragedy for the athlete and a great sadness for all Canadians.

However, Johnson still had the support of his family and of Britain's Linford Christie, the man promoted to second place by the Canadian's disqualification. Christie, no stranger to drugs allegations himself (he would receive a two-year IAAF ban after testing positive for the anabolic steroid nandrolene in 1999), said Johnson had been a 'great ambassador' for the sport and called the Canadian's exclusion 'a very sad day for athletics as a whole'.

The Canadian government ordered an official inquiry into the use of banned substances at which Johnson's doctor, Astaphan, revealed the full details of the athlete's history of steroid use. Astaphan revealed that 26 days before the Olympic final Johnson was given an injection of a compound used to fatten cattle before they are sent to market. In June 1989 Johnson himself appeared before the inquiry and finally admitted to having taken steroids. Three months later the IAAF stripped him of his 1987 world record even though he had not tested positive in Rome.

Having served his two-year suspension, Johnson began racing again in January 1991 but his form deserted him and he failed to reach the final of the men's 100 metres at the 1992 Barcelona Olympics. In January 1993 he tested positive again for steroids at an indoor meeting in Montreal and was banned for life by the IAAF. Reduced to appearing as a novelty act, in 1999 he ran against two racehorses and a stock car at a charity event in Charlottetown, Prince Edward Island.

Johnson's guilt is not in doubt. Francis, Astaphan and the athlete himself have all admitted that he was on steroids. Yet, intriguingly, there are still unanswered questions as to how he came to test positive at Seoul. The IOC medical commission had dismissed Johnson's suggestion that his sample had somehow been sabotaged but witnesses reported seeing a mystery man seated alongside the sprinter in the waiting-room at the main stadium in Seoul as he was preparing to undergo his urine test. Rumours circulated that this individual – an unauthorised person in an area of supposedly high security –

may have slipped stanozolol into the beer that Johnson was drinking in order to produce his urine sample. And the speculation increased still further when the mystery man was revealed to be André Jackson, a friend of Carl Lewis.

Curiously, both Francis and Astaphan stated independently that within minutes of the race finishing, they heard a rumour that Johnson had tested positive. Yet it took him over an hour to produce his urine sample and another day for the testing to be completed. So was Johnson's fate pre-arranged? Furthermore, Francis and Astaphan maintain that the steroid Johnson was taking was furazobol, not stanozolol. Indeed stanozolol – a steroid that helps to build muscle – would have been more likely to hinder than improve his chances, yet the high level that showed up in his sample showed that he took it in the days leading up to the final. Again, this contradicts the evidence that Johnson's last shot was on 28 August 1988 – 26 days before the final. Taken then, it would have cleared his system twelve days before he lined up for gold at Seoul, thus enabling him to pass yet another drug test. Only a fool would have given Johnson anything in the immediate build-up to the biggest race of his life . . . and Francis and Astaphan were no fools.

So did someone fit Ben Johnson up in Seoul to make sure that he finally paid the price for his years of cheating? Was his drink spiked, his sample tampered with or, as Astaphan hints, did he really test positive at all? Johnson still feels bitter that he was the big fish that got caught. 'Regardless of what I did,' he said in a recent interview, 'I am still the best sprinter of all time. Most people loved the entertainment and know the game. The sport will never be clean. It's going to be going on until the end of time.'

HE WHO HESITATES

SEOUL, 25 SEPTEMBER 1988

The organisers at Seoul hit upon the idea of dividing the boxing hall into two halves with a ring in each so that two fights could take place simultaneously. To keep confusion to a minimum, they had decreed that the fights in Ring A would use a traditional bell and those in Ring B would be governed by a buzzer. The concept must have sounded feasible at the planning meeting, but in practice it proved no easy task persuading boxers who had spent their entire careers responding to a bell that suddenly they would have to listen out for a buzzer instead.

When 21-year-old Todd Foster of the United States met South Korea's Chun Jin Chul in a light-welterweight contest, they were told they would be fighting in Ring B and would therefore have to listen for the buzzer. Towards the end of their first round, the bell sounded in Ring A loud enough for Foster, Chun and referee Sandor Pajar of Hungary to hesitate in Ring B. Thinking that the round had ended (in fact there were still seventeen seconds remaining), Chun dropped his guard and took a step towards his corner, whereupon Foster, who was alive to the situation, caught him with a left hook to the head. Reeling slightly, Chun took two more steps towards his corner, then saw his trainer signalling him to fall. With that, the Korean slumped to the canvas, clutching his eye. Referee Pajar instinctively counted him out, but then paused, thinking that maybe he should disqualify Foster for hitting after the bell.

The place was in uproar. The harassed referee consulted with Emil Jetchev, president of the Referees' Committee of the

215

International Amateur Boxing Association, who, unable to find a rule that covered such a situation, made one up on the spot and declared the fight a 'no contest'.

The Americans claimed that Chun had gone down on instructions from his corner, hoping to win on a disqualification, and anyway, they said, it was Chun's fault. As an aggrieved Foster said: 'I threw a punch; that's what I'm in there to do. It was his fault, not mine. My coaches told me to listen for the buzzer and not the bell. I did just that. The whole thing's crazy!' Naturally the Koreans saw it differently and demanded that Foster be disqualified for ignoring the referee's orders to stop, but television replays of the incident showed that Pajar never told anyone to stop, even though, bizarrely, he stopped refereeing.

When everybody had finished having their say, the bout was rescheduled for three hours later and this time Foster stopped Chun in the second round. Justice was probably done.

INTERNAL STRIFE

BARCELONA, 31 JULY 1992

The Barcelona Games saw South Africa, having abandoned apartheid, welcomed back to the Olympic fold after a 32-year absence. Meanwhile, the break-up of the Soviet Union enabled Lithuania to field an independent team for the first time since 1928 and for Estonia and Latvia to do so for the first time since 1936. The IOC declared that while Lithuania, Estonia and Latvia could be represented separately, the remaining twelve former Soviet republics would have to be part of a combined squad known as the Unified Team. The title proved to be a misnomer. Squabbles broke out on a regular basis between the rival factions, with matters coming to a head in the weightlifting.

The man with the unenviable task of persuading the Unified weightlifters to pull together was head coach Vassily Alekseyev, a Russian and two-time gold medallist. The Unified Team boasted the favourite for the light-heavyweight division in Turkmenistan's Altymurat Orazdurdiyev and also had a strong second entrant in Ibragim Samadov, the 1991 world champion, who, like his coach, was Russian. But a quarter of an hour before the official weigh-in, Alekseyev told a stunned Orazdurdiyev that he would not be allowed to compete because he might 'get in the way' of Samadov. To omit the top-ranked weightlifter in order to allow a supposedly lesser athlete a free run at the medals inevitably provoked huge controversy, expressed in the form of angry accusations from the Turkmenistan delegation that Alekseyev was favouring his fellow Russians. Orazdurdiyev was so distraught at the thought of not being able to participate that he pleaded with Alekseyev, even offering to lose to Samadov and accept silver, but the coach refused to change his mind.

The row placed enormous pressure on Samadov's broad shoulders. To justify Alekseyev's selection, the 24-year-old knew he had to collect the gold that Orazdurdiyev would surely have won if he had been given the chance. Nothing less would do. The rules of weightlifting stipulate that in the event of more than one competitor lifting the same final weight, the person with the lower bodyweight wins. It was Samadov's misfortune that he weighed one-sixth of an ounce (five grams) more than his two chief rivals, Pyrros Dimas of Greece and Poland's Krzysztof Siemion, so that when all three men tied on 814lb, Samadov was relegated to the bronze medal because he weighed that fraction of an ounce more. With the other two weighing the same, Dimas took gold by virtue of having been the first to lift his final weight.

Having incurred the wrath of Alekseyev and the entire Turkmenistan contingent, Samadov was not in the best of moods approaching the medal ceremony. He had already been jeered by Greek fans when making a mess of his final lift in the competition – the one that would have enabled him to overhaul Dimas and Siemion – so when a Greek Olympic official endeavoured to present him with the bronze medal, he saw red, first refusing to lean forward for the medal to be hung around his neck and then, when it was placed in his hand, hurling it to the floor and storming off. Dimas helpfully picked it up and tried to return it but Samadov simply threw it to the ground again in a fit of pique.

Retribution was swift. Dr Tamas Ajan, general secretary of the International Weightlifting Federation, raged: 'He did not respect the International Olympic Committee, the spirit of the Games, his colleagues, the anthems, the flags. He did this in front of 4,000 people and a television audience of billions.' The IOC disqualified Samadov (thereby depriving him of even a bronze medal) and ordered him to leave the Olympic Village. Samadov issued an apology the next day, attempting to justify his actions by claiming that he had been in a state of shock at the medal ceremony and remembered nothing about the incident except feeling 'bad'. His memory loss failed to cut any ice with the IOC, the Unified Team not helping his case by sending their appeal in the form of a fax on unofficial blank stationery and signed by a lowly secretary instead of their federation leader. After the IOC refused to reinstate him, the International Weightlifting Federation rubbed salt into Samadov's wounds by banning him for life.

THE 200-METRES HOP

BARCELONA, 3 AUGUST 1992

'It was,' wrote the *Observer*, 'sport's equivalent of watching Bambi's mother die.' It was a moving moment brimming with bravery and endeavour, one which, in its own heartbreaking way, encapsulated all that is best about the Olympic Games.

Derek Redmond was one of those unlucky athletes whose career was repeatedly blighted by injury, invariably at the most inopportune moments. At the 1988 Olympics he was forced to pull out just two minutes before his first-round heat of the 400 metres with an Achilles tendon injury and by the time he arrived in Barcelona four years later he had undergone no fewer than five operations – four on that troublesome Achilles and one on a toe.

But despite the fact that he seemed to spend almost as much time in hospital as on the track and that if he had been a racehorse he would have been put down years ago, Redmond appeared back to his best. In 1991 he helped the British 4×400 metres relay team to a shock victory at the World Championships and, injury permitting, he was confident of a bold show at the Olympics. Indeed, he was one of Britain's genuine medal hopes.

Everything in Barcelona started so promisingly for the 26-year-old. He recorded the fastest time of any of the runners in the first-round heats and then won his quarter-final in impressive fashion. As he lined up with seven other runners for his semi-final, he dedicated the race to his father Jim, who had made so many sacrifices and been such a tremendous support to him throughout his athletic career. Typically, Jim Redmond was among the 65,000 people seated in the stands that day.

Running in lane five, Redmond got off to a perfect start and was flowing smoothly until, at a point just beyond 150 metres, he heard a sudden pop. His right hamstring had torn and as the other runners sped past he crumpled to the ground, painfully aware that another major prize had eluded him through no fault of his own. With most eyes focused on the finish, the stretcher-bearers ran towards the stricken figure on the far side of the track. 'It was only when I saw the Red Cross coming out,' said Redmond afterwards, 'that it dawned on me I was going to be stretchered off from the Olympic Stadium and there was no way I wanted that. All that was on my mind was that I wanted to finish this race, even if it killed me.' So after a couple of unsuccessful attempts, he staggered to his feet and began hobbling around the rest of the course.

As Redmond, scarcely able to put one foot in front of the other, made his way painfully slowly towards the finish, a man broke through the cordon of security guards and ran on to the track at the far turn, dashing past the medical men who were still trying to encourage the athlete to get on a stretcher. It was Jim Redmond.

'You don't have to do this, you don't have to put yourself through this,' said Jim, who was wearing a hat with the slogan 'Just Do It'.

'I've got to finish,' replied Derek.

'OK,' said Jim. 'We started your career together, so we're going to finish this race together.'

With that, Jim Redmond put his arm around his son's shoulder, held his hand and together, like a scene from a three-legged race on school sports day, they headed for the finish. While tears streamed down Derek's face, Jim fended off security guards and overzealous track officials. 'I don't speak Spanish,' he said later, 'and I wasn't going to be stopped by anything.'

With the crowd cheering their every move, a few steps from the finish, Jim let go and allowed Derek to limp across the line unaided. The entire stadium rose spontaneously in a standing ovation. One Canadian TV producer described Redmond's actions as 'the purest, most courageous example of grit and determination I have seen'. *El Pais*, Spain's biggest-selling daily newspaper, put father and son on the front page. And at her home in Northampton Derek's pregnant sister Karen went into false labour.

Derek Redmond's gutsy performance turned him from being just another athlete into a figure of inspiration. Reflecting on the day's events, he said: 'I was feeling good and it [the injury] came out of the blue. It happened so fast. I wanted to keep going. It was all animal instinct – I kept thinking I could still catch the other runners. Then it dawned on me I was out of the final. No one was going to stop me from finishing the race. I pulled out of the 1988 Olympics because of an Achilles injury, and I wanted to finish the race here. I didn't realise it was my dad at first. I was saying to him, "Get me back in lane five. That's where I started and that's where I want to finish."

'It made quite an impact because everyone seemed to think I demonstrated the perfect Olympic spirit . . . not the winning but the taking part.'

From the sublime to the ridiculous. Another British competitor, women's 400-metres runner Phylis Smith, landed in hot water after breaking the IOC rules on advertising by scribbling in ink on her running bib a greeting to her local butcher. As Smith pulled up after qualifying for the final, the words 'Arthur Cackett hello' were clearly visible to anyone with a high-powered telescope.

The aforementioned Arthur Cackett was the owner of Cackett's the butchers (established 1904) of Wolverhampton, who had supported Smith in the build-up to the Games. 'When she qualified for Barcelona,' he said, 'I think we gave her a nice bit of sirloin and a couple of turkey drumsticks.' It hardly constituted powerful corporate backing, but Smith was so grateful for this sponsorship that she sent the greeting from Spain. However, the British women's team manager, Joan Allison, took a dim view of the matter and warned Smith that she would be for the chop if she repeated the offence in the final. And a dedicated IOC official vowed to have strong words with the athlete 'about defacing her uniform'. Smith finished last in the final.

Arthur Cackett was bewildered by all the fuss. He said: 'I know she did mention my name when she was being interviewed, but I did not know she had written anything on her vest. I do not really see how the Olympics people could say it was a bad thing because it is only a small firm. None of this was done to try to increase trade. It has not affected our business.'

A TALE OF TWO COUNTRIES

BARCELONA, 3 AUGUST 1992

In the early 1990s international 10,000-metre running was dominated by Kenyans and Moroccans. Eight of the eleven fastest men in the world over that distance came from Kenya, their chief adversary being Morocco's Khalid Skah, whose name means 'runaway' in Arabic. The rivalry between the two athletic nations was bitter and intense, often resulting in highly dubious tactics being employed by the one to thwart the other. At the 1991 World Championships Skah was pushed into third place by blatant Kenyan team tactics. The Kenyans Richard Chelimo and Moses Tanui set a blistering pace, leaving a third Kenyan, Thomas Osano, to hang back and harass Skah throughout the race. Whenever Skah put on a spurt, Osano would cover him or overtake him again to slow his pace. By badgering, hustling and generally making a nuisance of himself, Osano destroyed Skah's running rhythm, allowing Tanui and Chelimo to finish first and second. Similar tactics were employed in the 5,000 metres. The Kenyans were up to their old tricks again at the 1992 World Cross-Country Championships, this time blocking a dangerous Ethiopian, thereby allowing Yobes Ondieki to break clear and win. So come the 10,000 metres final in Barcelona, Skah and the Moroccans knew what to expect. What's more, they were gunning for revenge.

Although the Olympic final did not begin until after 10 p.m., the temperature in Barcelona still touched 29 degrees Celsius (85 degrees Fahrenheit). At first the Kenyans bided their time but then Chelimo and fellow countryman William Koech started

224

to step up the pace. By lap sixteen of the 25, Koech was struggling and the contest developed into what should have been a straight fight between Chelimo and Skah. Halfway round lap 22 – 1,400 metres from the finish – the two leaders prepared to lap Skah's team-mate, 36-year-old Hammou Boutayeb, who was back in next to last position – a surprisingly poor performance from someone who had finished eighth in the 1991 World Championships. As they approached Boutayeb, Skah, who was in the lead, deliberately edged wide to allow Chelimo to resume the burden of pace-setting. The pair both passed the back-marker but instead of falling away, Boutayeb kept pace with them for the next lap before suddenly accelerating and cutting in front of Chelimo, forcing the Kenyan to chop his stride. Chelimo now found himself sandwiched by the two Moroccans with Skah so close behind that he was repeatedly clipping his heels. Desperate to extricate himself, Chelimo managed to overtake Boutayeb but with 700 metres to go, the Moroccan put on another spurt and cut back in front of him for a second time. The crowd began to boo.

Chelimo succeeded in getting back in front on that lap but Boutayeb was still ominously running alongside, much to the Kenyan's discomfort. As the threesome approached the bell, Carl Gustaf Tollemar, chairman of the IAAF technical committee, decided to take action. Stepping on to the track, he made a grab for Boutayeb, but the Moroccan evaded his grasp and carried on running for another 200 metres before finally dropping out. His stride constantly disrupted over the last three laps, Chelimo had no answer to Skah's sprint finish and the Moroccan came home the winner by seven yards.

It was not a popular victory. On his celebratory lap Skah was jeered by the crowd and pelted with paper cups and assorted rubbish. *The Times* wrote indignantly: 'The appearance of two competitors from one country collaborating to disrupt the chances of another was a distasteful breach of ethics.' But the jeers turned to cheers when it was announced that Skah had been disqualified.

A law student by profession, Skah decided that attack was the best form of defence and angrily accused the Spanish officials of being racists and thieves. Nor did he spare his supposed accomplice, Boutayeb, whom he labelled ill-educated, 'an animal, an imbecile'. Chelimo claimed that the fact that Skah and Boutayeb had been talking constantly over those final laps was clear evidence of collusion. Initially Skah denied that he and Boutayeb had spoken, but when video footage of the race showed the two runners exchanging words, Skah explained that he had simply been berating his fellow Moroccan. Skah said: 'I told him, "Go away, go away. I have already won the gold or silver, and I don't need any kind of help from you."' Skah suggested that Boutayeb's bizarre behaviour stemmed from his desire not to be lapped because the race was being televised live in Morocco and Boutayeb was ashamed of his poor showing.

The Moroccan team appealed against Skah's disqualification and after studying the video of the race, the jury concluded that Chelimo's progress had not been physically impaired. Therefore Skah was reinstated as the winner. This change of heart did not exactly find favour with the Spanish crowd, who whistled and booed throughout the medal ceremony.

SYNCHRONISED MAYHEM

BARCELONA, 6 AUGUST 1992

Since the inception of the modern Olympics hapless competitors have inadvertently devised all manner of methods of missing out on their big moment. Some have overslept, others have overeaten, but Iranian boxer Ali Kazemi came up with a new one moments before he was due to fight in Barcelona. He announced that he had lost his gloves! With no suitable replacements available, he was duly disqualified.

Canadian boardsailor Murray McCaig saw his hopes vanish when he suffered a broken leg the day before the start of his competition. Cycling in the Olympic Village, he pulled out to pass a slow-moving bus and was hit by a police car.

Another boardsailor, American Mike Gebhardt, did manage to take part in his event, only to be robbed of the ultimate prize by a cruel twist of fate. The sailboard competition was staged in Barcelona's least attractive venue – the Parc de Mar in Barcelona harbour, where the surface was dotted with such interesting obstacles as dead rats, expired refrigerators and a range of garbage that would do credit to any council tip (garbage dump). Any competitor ending up in the water was in need of an instant health check. When the International Yacht Racing Union drew attention to the scandalous conditions in which their members were expected to contest an Olympic event, the Barcelona authorities, in an attempt to clean up their image as well as their harbour, assigned four boats to collect the floating debris on a daily basis. But inevitably these refuse vessels missed some items . . . as Gebhardt discovered to his cost.

The bronze medallist in 1988, Gebhardt was well placed going into the seventh race out of ten, but on the last lap of that race his board became entangled with a plastic garbage bag that had evaded the attentions of the clean-up brigade. While he frantically tried to remove it, he was passed by six of his rivals. Had he been able to remain ahead of just one of those six, he would have claimed the gold medal. As it was, he had to settle for silver, just 0.4 points behind Franck David of France.

Thankfully the synchronised swimming competition took place in more congenial surroundings, thus sparing spectators the possibility of one of the girls surfacing from a routine with a deceased rodent on her head. Yet it featured a heated controversy of its own when a judge's error deprived Canada's Sylvie Fréchette of an almost certain gold medal. And if any athlete deserved a lucky break at Barcelona, it was the 25-year-old from Montreal.

At 3 p.m. on 18 July 1992 – just a week before the Barcelona Games – she returned from a practice session and photo shoot to the Montreal apartment she shared with her fiancé and business manager, Sylvain Lake. The place was filled with the smell of exhaust fumes. All the windows were shut, but a door leading to the garage was open. Lake's car was in the garage, its motor running. Fréchette found his body in the bedroom. He had committed suicide by carbon monoxide poisoning. Lake, who ran the 400 metres for Canada at the 1987 World University Games, was scheduled to leave that night for Barcelona to work as a track analyst for a French-language Canadian television network. Fréchette, the favourite for the gold medal in the synchronised solo event, was due to follow four days later.

Lake did not write a suicide note, leaving Fréchette none the wiser as to why he had chosen to end his life. But she was never in any real doubt about going ahead with her plans to compete in Barcelona. As a former athlete himself, Lake would surely have wanted her to compete on the world's greatest stage, whatever the circumstances. She was still in something of a daze when she arrived in Barcelona. She later told *Sports Illustrated*: 'My body was in Barcelona, but my mind was somewhere else.

I felt like I was eavesdropping on someone else's life. I was like this little robot. The only thing I remember about the opening ceremony is it was long and I was sitting on the wet ground at the stadium.' Her quiet dignity in the face of such a tragedy earned her the affection of the Canadian public, who bombarded her with postcards offering sympathy and good wishes . . . apart from one or two who thought she was being cold-hearted and selfish by travelling to the Olympics.

Fréchette's principal rival for gold was the Californian Kristen Babb-Sprague, who had twice finished second to the Canadian the previous year, at the World Championships and in the World Cup. The Olympic competition was divided into two sections – the figures and the free programme, both counting for fifty per cent of the final score. The figures (where the swimmers performed four set movements, each of which was marked separately) were Fréchette's speciality, whereas Babb-Sprague excelled in the free routines. The first day of competition brought the figures. At the end of her compulsory albatross spin routine, Fréchette received marks ranging from 9.2 to 9.6 from four of the five judges, but the Brazilian judge, Ana Maria da Silveira Lobo, accidentally tapped in a score of 8.7. Realising immediately that she had made a mistake, she tried to amend her score but had trouble with her touch pad and merely succeeded in repeating the error. Flustered, she then tried to attract the attention of the assistant referee, Nakata Saito of Japan, but her command of English did not extend much beyond 'Where are the toilets?', as a result of which she was unable to make him understand. By the time da Silveira Lobo notified the referee, Judith McGowan of the United States, the 8.7 had been displayed to the public, and the rule stated that once the scores had been made public, they could not be amended. McGowan was happy for the rule to be upheld in this instance.

Although they refrained from suggesting that McGowan's nationality may not have rendered her wholly impartial over an incident that was sure to benefit an American competitor, the Canadians launched a formal protest, claiming that da Silveira Lobo had intended to mark Fréchette at 9.7 but had pressed the wrong button. The Americans disputed the Canadian version of events, saying that while the Brazilian judge had undoubtedly tried to correct her score, it was to lower than 9.7. The Canadian protest was heard by FINA, swimming's governing body, who, somewhat surprisingly, elected not to call da Silveira Lobo as a witness. In her absence, they voted 11–2 to keep the score of 8.7, the two dissenting voices being Canadian. An official statement admitted that there had been some confusion but said that Fréchette's score could not be altered because under the rules of the sport 'an issue of fact cannot be reversed'.

In the following day's free routines, Fréchette actually out-scored Babb-Sprague but the deficit was just too much for the world champion to make up and she missed out on the gold medal by 0.131 points. Had her albatross spin in the figures been rewarded with a mark of 9.7 or even 9.4, she would have finished in first place.

In post-Games interviews da Silveira Lobo, a university professor, refused to reveal what score she had intended to give Fréchette except to say that it was over 9.0. She also insisted that her blunder had not been costly because, she claimed, the other judges had marked the Canadian up during the free routines to compensate for the earlier confusion.

Fréchette accepted her silver medal with customary good grace, but the row rumbled on. Canada, led by Richard Pound, a member of the executive board of the IOC, campaigned for the result to be overturned and the following year, upon FINA's recommendation and with the IOC's blessing, Fréchette was informed that she had been awarded gold, although it would be as a joint-winner with Babb-Sprague. And in December 1993, before 2,000 cheering fans at the Montreal Forum, Fréchette traded in her silver medal for gold. For once, common sense had prevailed and the Barcelona Olympics had something approaching a happy ending for Sylvie Fréchette.

THE GREAT MARATHON FRAUD

BARCELONA, 9 AUGUST 1992

From Fred Lorz to Norbert Sudhaus, the Olympics have had their fair share of marathon impostors, but none to compare with Polin Belisle, the man who used his dual nationality to trick his way into the line-up at two successive Games.

Born in Honduras, Belisle was raised in Belize before becoming a naturalised US citizen. By 1988 he was living in California and dreamed of competing in the Seoul Olympics as a marathon runner. His modest ability ruled out any chance of making the American Olympic team, but he reasoned that Belizean standards would not be so high. So he approached the country's Olympic officials by sending them a wad of newspaper cuttings, which reported that he had run a highly impressive time of 2hr 36min 18sec at the Long Beach marathon. However, it was subsequently rumoured that he had run only the start and finish of the race, resting in between. Believing what they read in the papers, the Belizean authorities accepted his credentials and despatched him to Seoul, where they expected him to put on a performance that would be a credit to the nation. Instead, he trailed home a distant last of 98 in a time of 3hr 14min 02sec – over an hour behind the winner, Italy's Gelindo Bordin. It is fair to say the Belizean Olympic officials were none too happy with their new sporting discovery.

Doubts about the legitimacy of Belisle's earlier marathon times surfaced in 1991, when he was disqualified after finishing fifth in the Long Beach race because he had not been picked up on some of the key checkpoint videos. He tried the same trick

231

the following year in the Los Angeles marathon . . . with the same result. His eleventh place and time of 2hr 18min 38sec were struck from the records because he had not been visible on camera during the middle section of the race. What he lacked in talent he made up for in nerve and in 1992 he badgered the Belize Olympic Committee to send him to Barcelona, but they remembered him from four years earlier and turned him down flat. Undeterred and armed with an Honduran birth certificate and more fake marathon results, he offered his services to Honduras Olympic officials, having changed his name to Apolineria Belisle Gómez. Like their Belizean counterparts in 1988, the Honduran committee took him at his word and granted him a place in the country's Olympic team after getting him to sign a loyalty oath.

And so Belisle (or Gómez) found himself attending a second Olympic Games. His deception worked perfectly until, on the fifth day of competition, some Belizean athletes recognised his name on the entry list for the marathon and told the president of the Belize Olympic Committee. The Honduran delegation were promptly informed that their great marathon hope had run for Belize in 1988 and he was kicked off the team.

Yet his luck did not completely desert him. For some inexplicable reason he was allowed to keep his identity card and race number and his name was not removed from the list of runners. So he simply turned up on the day of the marathon, slipped unnoticed into the first line of runners on the start line and set off on his 26-mile odyssey. Except that Polin Belisle never did run the full distance if he could help it and here, after keeping the leaders company for the first mile, he quickly dropped back before disappearing altogether. The great adventure was over. For the record the race was won by Hwang Young-cho of Korea.

According to respected Olympic historian David Wallechinsky, Belisle was the first unauthorised athlete to compete at the Games since Margaret de Jesus of Puerto Rico secretly replaced her twin sister in the women's 4×400 metres relay in 1984. When Madeline de Jesus was injured in the course of the long jump competition, she asked sister Margaret, who was in Los

Angeles purely as a spectator, to assume her identity in the relay team. In the qualifying heat, Margaret ran the second leg and helped the team to reach the final but on finding out about the switch, the Puerto Rican coach promptly withdrew the girls from the competition.

A VAULT TO GLORY

ATLANTA, 23 JULY 1996

They came to be known as the Magnificent Seven – the United States women's gymnastics team who swept all before them to win an historic and emotional gold medal in Atlanta.

Shannon Miller was the star of the team, a former Olympic medallist and the first American gymnast in history to win two consecutive world titles. The daughter of Romanian parents, Dominique Moceanu became the youngest US national champion ever at the age of thirteen and was hailed by coach Bela Karolyi as 'a diamond'. At fourteen she took the stage at Atlanta and published her autobiography. Dominique Dawes was a former national champion and veteran of the 1992 Barcelona Olympic team. Her bronze on the floor made her the first African-American gymnast to win a medal in an individual event. Amanda Borden just missed out on making the team for Barcelona, but her perseverance won her a place four years later in Atlanta, where she was voted team captain. Amy Chow had four years of international competition under her belt and survived a nasty accident on the beam at the 1996 US Olympic trials. Jaycie Phelps was a relative newcomer to the team but was highly regarded. And finally there was Kerri Strug.

The daughter of a heart surgeon from Tucson, Arizona, Strug began her gymnastics career in 1982 at the age of five. She made rapid progress and at the 1991 US Championships finished first in the vault and third in the all-round competition. In the same year at the World Championships she finished fifteenth in the all-round. On the strength of these performances, she was picked for the Barcelona Olympics, where she helped the team to a bronze medal in the combined exercises and finished fourteenth in the individual all-round. Over the next four years she trained exceptionally hard, pushing her frail 4ft 9in frame to the limits, and these virtues just about earned her a second Olympic shot in 1996, but it was a close call. For despite her undoubted talent, she was very much the unsung heroine of the US gymnastics team, a bit-part player, destined, it seemed, to remain forever in the shadows of the streetwise Miller and the precocious Moceanu. Even her coach Karolyi admitted: 'Little Kerri, she always hung around at the back. She didn't have the self-confidence, but she had the ethic to work very hard.' That determination would see her emerge from the shadows in Atlanta in glorious fashion to become, overnight, the most famous woman in American sport.

Heading into the final event of the team combined exercises, the vault, the United States held a handy lead over Russia and looked set to win their first-ever gold medal in the combined competition. Then, in front of a tense crowd of 32,000, it all started to go horribly wrong. Moceanu, on whom so many hopes had rested, fell down disastrously on both of her vaults, so that everything rested on the slim shoulders of anchor girl Strug. Although the vault was her favourite event, she landed short on her first try and fell backwards. She said: 'The moment my feet hit the floor, I heard a pop. As I scrambled to stand, a fiery pain shot up my left leg.' Strug had sustained torn ligaments and a third-degree sprain in her left ankle. Barely able to walk, she limped down the runway and consulted with coach Karolyi. Was her score of 9.162 enough to secure gold? Should she limp away and rest for the individual all-round competition a couple of days later? She had only a matter of seconds in which to make up her mind. Nobody seemed to know for sure whether her score was good enough for gold, but Karolyi persuaded her that she needed to make another vault, regardless of the pain. 'Kerri, listen to me,' he said. 'You can do it.' She was aware that if she didn't go, the team might lose out to the Russians. It was an agonising decision for the eighteen-year-old to make, since further pressure on the ankle would almost certainly rule her out of the all-round event, the blue riband of gymnastics. Similarly, she knew she could not let the other girls down. There may have been bigger individuals in the squad but there was no greater team player than Kerri Strug.

Standing on the runway, her hastily and heavily strapped left ankle still throbbing from her stumble, she whispered a silent prayer. 'Please God, help me out. I'm just asking you once here. I've always tried to be a good person. I've always tried to do what's right. I've done this vault a thousand times. Let me do it one more time.' If the prayer had gone on much longer, she would have been in danger of being timed out.

The vault facing Strug was a Yurchenko one-and-a-half, a straightforward enough jump with two good legs in a practice meet. But Strug was in no fit state to make a vault on which the Olympic gold medal depended. The apprehension among the crowd was almost tangible. Karolyi shook his fist in encouragement: 'Give me one last vault, give me one last good vault!'

Gritting her teeth and defying the pain, Strug bounded down the runway and after landing on both feet, gently lifted her injured foot and balanced on her one sound foot to complete the vault to tremendous applause. Collapsing in agony on her hands and knees, she looked up to see the judges award her 9.71, thereby giving the American team the gold medal. In fact, it was later determined that her first vault *would* have been sufficient to guarantee gold, making her heroics unnecessary, but, as US coach Mary Lee Tracy said: 'We had no idea what the score was.'

While the NBC cameras, heavily criticised during the Games for their relentlessly pro-American coverage to the exclusion of all other countries, focused intrusively on the tears of the defeated Russian girls, the bear-like Karolyi scooped Strug up in his arms and carried her to the medal ceremony. To a huge ovation from the packed arena, she joined the other six gymnasts on the victory podium. Afterwards the other six jumped down, once again forgetting the quiet girl of the team, until Moceanu turned and helped her from the platform.

That one vault transformed Kerri Strug from shy supporting act into the darling of America. The whole country went Strug-crazy. Her foot still in plaster, she was paraded on countless television shows where, over and over again, she relived precisely what was going through her mind as she prepared to make the final vault. 'I have had to deal with so much pain before,' she said, referring to previous injuries, 'that I thought I could deal with one last vault.'

When she revealed that she was the only member of the team not to have an agent, she was inundated with offers. One said: 'Her ankle may ache, but that girl is worth millions.' President Clinton called her vault 'quite miraculous', she received a congratulatory letter from former president Ronald Reagan, praising her 'determination, perseverance, and unyielding sense of commitment to your team', and she received the ultimate accolade – an audience with Bruce Willis and Demi Moore.

She was headline news on both sides of the Atlantic. *Time* magazine wrote: 'It was fitting that Strug's moment of Olympic glory was the storybook climax to one of the most brilliantly managed team efforts in US Olympics history. She played through pain, convinced that she had to for the team, risking a worse injury and jeopardising her own chance for more medals. Maybe she shouldn't have done it . . . but she did, and America got another electrifying moment to put into its collective sports memory bank.' Over in Britain *The Times* wrote, with reference to the opening ceremony: 'If Muhammad Ali lit the Olympic flame, Kerri Strug has set the Games alight.'

But amid all the adulation, Strug had to come to terms with the fact that her injury would prevent her from competing in the individual competition. Her mother consoled her by saying: 'In life, sometimes you don't reach all your goals. You have to be thankful that you have already accomplished something unforgettable.'

At the end of the Games, Strug and Carl Lewis were given Olympic Spirit Awards. Before the media frenzy subsided, Strug appeared on the TV series *Beverly Hills 90210* and featured with the rest of the Magnificent Seven on boxes of Wheaties cereal. Such is fame. Afterwards she quietly returned to her studies and used her celebrity to help children's charities. Meanwhile, Dominique Moceanu was taking her parents to court over money . . .

Apart from the Kerri Strug story, there was one other heartwarming tale to emerge from Atlanta. Before the Games two marathon runners from impoverished Malawi were adopted by the residents of a Mississippi town, who took pity on the state of their running gear. John Mwathiwa and Henry Moyo arrived in Hattiesburg for pre-Olympic training with worn shoes, shiny trousers and threadbare luggage. The town quickly came to their aid and a department store presented them with new gym bags while local housewives offered to feed the pair for free.

CHRISTIE BLOWS HIS TOP

ATLANTA, 27 JULY 1996

The Atlanta Games were not the Olympic movement's finest hour. Poor security, indifferent organisation, blatant commercialism, and a general lack of graciousness and hospitality towards non-Americans added up to a sorry show, highlighted by the bomb blast at the Centennial Olympic Park on 27 July that left one woman dead and over 100 people injured. Less than 24 hours later, with the sporting world still in shock and the Atlanta Olympics in desperate need of some good publicity, another regrettable incident – this time one made in Britain – further blighted proceedings.

Those who sat apprehensively in the athletics stadium on the evening after the explosion were relishing the prospect of some top-class performances to take their minds off the turmoil and anger that had enveloped the city. Instead they were treated to a prolonged display of boorish behaviour by none other than the British team captain and reigning Olympic 100 metres champion, Linford Christie.

There has never been any middle ground with Christie; people either worshipped him or despised him. They either adored him for his physique, talent and powerful charisma or detested him for his perceived arrogance and persecution complex. What was undeniable was that he had put British sprinting back on the map and had become a role model to millions of black youngsters.

Due in part to the fact that his attitude endeared him to some while alienating others, controversy has never been far from his door. At Seoul in 1988 Christie was promoted to the silver medal spot following the sensational disqualification of Ben Johnson. Yet Christie himself only narrowly avoided the same fate as the Canadian when a drugs test following the 200 metres revealed traces of the stimulant pseudoephedrine. Hauled before the IOC's medical commission, Christie explained that the banned substance got into his system because he was drinking ginseng tea. The IOC took a vote and Christie was officially given 'the benefit of the doubt' after an 11–10 decision, although it was later alleged that two members of the commission had been asleep when the vote was taken. Four years later in Barcelona he reached the pinnacle of his career with a gold medal in the 100 metres. Even his detractors had to bite their tongues for a few days.

By the time of the Atlanta Olympics Christie would be 36. His very participation at the Games had been the subject of an athletics soap opera all year. He was still undecided as late as May, but to the relief of British Olympic officials he finally announced that he would be going to Atlanta to defend his title. Cynics suggested that his participation was never in doubt, that the delay was simply Christie showing off his importance, another illustration of his outsized ego. However nobody could honestly deny his value to the British team, as he proved at the Europa Cup Final in Madrid in early June when his double in the 100 metres and 200 metres represented half of the total number of British successes. He carried his form through to Atlanta and in the quarter-finals of the 100 metres recorded his fastest time of the season, 10.03sec. His semi-final run was less impressive but he still scraped through to the final, where he would face formidable opposition in the form of Canada's Donovan Bailey, Frankie Fredericks of Namibia, Trinidad's Ato Boldon and Dennis Mitchell of the United States. On his day, Christie was capable of beating them all, but the one obstacle he was unable to overcome on this particular day was a rule that he himself had pushed for five years earlier.

False starts are the bane of a sprinter's life. So much depends on a fast exit from the blocks, titles being won or lost in fractions of a second. Judging what does and does not constitute a false start has always been a moot point, from the perspective both of athletes and officials, so in 1991, in an effort to simplify matters, a rule was introduced whereby a false start would be called automatically if a runner left the starting blocks less than one-tenth of a second after the gun sounded. That fleeting moment between gun and departure is known as reaction time, but if that interval was under 0.1sec, it was to be considered an attempt to anticipate the gun, rather than a reaction to it. Christie supported the new proposals.

Settling down on his blocks that Saturday evening as part of what many believed was the finest 100-metres field in Olympic history, Christie knew that he had to get away fast if he was to have any chance of coping with his younger rivals. A number of people had dismissed his chances anyway, but Christie was a dangerous man to write off. As the gun sounded, the eight sprinters burst from their blocks, but it was a false start. Christie was called as the culprit. He had no arguments. 'It was definitely me,' he said later. They got in the blocks again, started and were at least twenty metres down the track when the gun went off to denote a recall. This time Boldon had broken early. For both he and Christie, one more false start would result in automatic elimination.

Nerves were beginning to fray. It was tough enough being in an Olympic final without the added distraction of two false starts. They took off for a third time, and once more the recall gun sounded. Another false start. All eyes waited to see who would be called. It was Christie again. The defending champion was out of the Olympic final.

Whereas he accepted the first false start, he bitterly disputed this, maintaining that he had made 'the perfect start'. Like a batsman who refuses to walk, he stood his ground. Then he marched over to the judges and stared at the replay. Still he was convinced of his innocence. There was no way he was going quietly. He paced up and down the track, arguing with the officials, raising his arms in gestures of disbelief and defiance, all the while keeping the other seven finalists waiting. 'He demanded to come back into the race,' said America's Mike Marsh. 'That defied logic. This is the Olympics.' The problem was that in the past Christie had seemingly been able to steamroller British officials, who were in awe of his popularity. At the 1991 national championships in Birmingham, Christie had finished only fourth in his heat, thereby failing to qualify for the semi-finals, yet although he didn't run in the semis, he was allowed to run in the final, probably because the officials realised he was the athlete that most people had come to see. But while British officials may occasionally have been 'flexible', it was a different case altogether in the United States, and no matter how long he ranted and raved, he was not going to be allowed back into the final.

A burly Jamaican official tried to call a halt to the one-man protest. 'It's time to go, son,' he said, but Christie still refused to leave the track. Eventually the running referee, America's John Chaplin, appeared on the scene, went up to Christie and showed him the red card, ordering him to leave. Petulantly Christie ripped off his jersey, tossed his running shoes in the garbage can, tore the offending red flag from the start box and skulked away. His argument had raged for 3min 40sec.

Chaplin explained afterwards: 'It's quite straightforward. There were two false starts. The officials asked Linford to go, but he stood there and didn't go. They did what they should do under the rules. They called the referee. I simply walked up and showed him a red card and I explained very politely, "You have two false starts and you have to leave."' Christie's reaction time on that second false start was measured at 0.086sec.

When the race at last got underway after what amounted to a seven-minute delay, Bailey took gold, ironically after having the worst start of the entire field, with Fredericks claiming the silver and Boldon the bronze.

There was no disguising his fellow athletes' contempt for Christie's behaviour. Marsh, who finished fifth, said: 'I very rarely think or say that somebody has acted immaturely, but Linford did.' Fourth-placed man Mitchell remarked: 'That was the most unprofessional race I have ever been in. I've never been so ready for a race in my life. The delay really messed me up.' NBC reporter Cris Collinsworth, who said it was 'about as poor a show of sportsmanship as I have ever seen in a major event', added: 'I practically screamed at Frankie Fredericks, "Was it unsportsmanlike? Did it impact the race out there?" He said, "I'm not going to say it, but you make sure that you say it."' Christie was then involved in a heated exchange with Boldon, and the two men had to be separated by Mitchell.

Unrepentant, Christie, in his last Olympic Games, proceeded to go on a lap of honour, waving farewell to his fans whose numbers were probably diminishing with every stride. As one American journalist wrote: 'It was a tasteless ending to a brilliant career.'

Facing the media, Christie insisted: 'I think I went with the gun. If it was anywhere else other than the USA, I am sure I would have been in. Who is to determine how quickly one reacts? They make a figure, but who is to say? It's a shame to go out that way. I'm just sorry for the people of Britain. But I'm still Linford Christie. I'll always be known as an Olympic champion.'

The anti-Christie camp suggested that he might have deliberately false-started so that he would not be embarrassed at finishing out of the medals, but it seems inconceivable that an athlete would sabotage his own chances in an Olympic final. As his training partner Fredericks said: 'He was really upset. He trained for this day.'

Christie retired from international competition the following year in order to concentrate on coaching but continued to run in lesser events. And after years of rumours (all strenuously denied), at a minor indoor meeting in Dortmund, Germany, in 1999, his urine sample revealed traces of the banned steroid nandrolene, measured at almost two hundred times above the legal limit. He was cleared by UK Athletics but the case was sent for arbitration by the IAAF, who banned him for two years. Christie vowed to clear his name, pointing out that he would have been mad to blacken his reputation at the end of his career in a meaningless competition. But the ban stood.

Christie, who has always been a vehement anti-drugs campaigner, still maintains his innocence. 'I never did it. I wouldn't do it. One problem is that there is a grey area over nandrolene. There's no test to prove what's there naturally, and what has got into our system another way. It's always been the case that the athlete's responsible for what's in their system. If you buy a loaf of bread and there's glass in that bread, that's not your fault, is it?'

However, there is no grey area over his disgraceful antics in Atlanta, even though he contests to this day that he was wrongly penalised. 'It was not a false start,' he pleads. 'My reaction time was positive, but it was less than 0.1, which counts as a false start. We train to react like that.'

Love him or hate him, you have to admire his self-belief.

SAILING INTO A STORM

31 JULY 1996

Most   adlines at the 1996 Olympics
surro   Irish swimmer Michelle Smith,
but t   ostscript to the Games when it
emer   's swimming team, which won six
meda   e strength of fictitious qualifying
times   as never held! As eleven of the
22-member team had failed to attain Olympic qualifying times
at national and regional meets, a phantom meet was held and
imaginary times entered. Two swimmers were even disqualified
for the sake of authenticity. After the deception was revealed,
Tamas Gyarfas, head of the Hungarian Swimming Federation
which had submitted the false records, wisely decided to resign.

The win-at-all-costs mentality produced a few unsavoury
scenes in Atlanta. Boxer John Kelman from Barbados was
banned from amateur boxing for a year after angrily throwing a
glove when beaten by Janos Nagy of Hungary in a first-round
featherweight bout. The contest had been stopped midway
through round three. And after losing to defending Olympic
champion Philippe Omnes of France in the third round of the
men's individual foil, Cuban fencer Elvis Gregory continued to
fight his opponent away from the duelling piste. The pair had
to be separated by police.

Yet one of the Games' most cut-throat duels was reserved for
the sport of sailing in what was to be the first of two ruthless
Olympic battles in the Laser class between Brazil's Robert
Scheidt and Ben Ainslie of Great Britain. The world champion

245

for the past two years, 24-year-old Scheidt from Sao Paulo, was considered king of the Lasers. The young pretender was nineteen-year-old Ainslie, born in Macclesfield and based in Lymington. He started sailing from the age of four and entered his first competition at ten, but had yet to beat Scheidt and had recently finished third to the Brazilian at the world championships. Away from competition the two men were good friends, having stayed in each other's homes and shared hotel rooms, but in the heat of battle they were sworn enemies, both possessing a steely determination to win.

The Atlanta sailing events were staged at Savannah and Ainslie made a disastrous start to his challenge, finishing 27th in the first of the eleven races – his worst placing of the year. He made partial amends with a third in race two, and a second in race five, followed by a victory in race six, moved him to second place overall, a point behind Scheidt. Ainslie continued his charge and by the end of race eight he held a commanding five-point lead over Scheidt, having recorded two wins, three seconds, a third and a fourth with only that opening catastrophe blotting his copybook. But Scheidt was made of stern stuff and, in the manner of a true champion, rallied to win races nine and ten. Ainslie could only finish sixteenth in race nine and although he followed up with a second, he was stranded two points adrift of his great rival going into the final race on 31 July.

Since he needed to beat Scheidt by two places, Ainslie knew that it was imperative that he got away to a good start. It was equally important not to let Scheidt get free and the pair indulged in a series of aggressive pre-race manoeuvres with Ainslie, the chief instigator, staying close to the Brazilian in the hope of luring him into committing a foul, which would require him to perform two full circles and thus enable Ainslie to establish a commanding advantage. The start was a messy affair and there were two recalls for multiple infringements, obliging the race officials to raise the black flag to indicate that all boats crossing the start line early the next time would be automatically disqualified. Scheidt and Ainslie continued to jockey for position, the Briton sticking to the Brazilian like a limpet. With the seconds ticking away before the gun, Scheidt made a rush for the line. Fearing that he might be left behind, Ainslie went with him. It was a dangerous tactic by Scheidt, for if he was disqualified and Ainslie was not, he would almost certainly hand the gold medal to the youngster. Realising too late that he was heading straight for disqualification if he followed Scheidt, Ainslie tried to slow down but was unable to do so and was sucked over the start line in a thick crowd of boats just four seconds before the gun went off. Scheidt, Ainslie and nine other boats were disqualified, leaving the Brazilian with gold and the Briton with silver. It was a terrible way to miss out on a gold medal, outwitted by a ploy straight out of the Michael Schumacher handbook.

Scheidt's gamble in luring Ainslie over the line had paid off handsomely. Experience had won the day. 'Ben put himself in a bad position,' said Scheidt. 'I told him he'd sailed a great regatta, and I was sorry the way it ended.' Licking his wounds, Ainslie admitted that he would have done the same to Scheidt if the positions had been reversed. 'Robert was slightly in front of me as we came up for the third start. I particularly needed a good start. I had to keep pace with him, though it was clear there was a danger of going over. It was an easier way for him to beat me than going round the race track again.'

What some old hands saw as youthful naivety was defended by Ainslie's team-mates. Fellow Olympic sailor Ian Rhodes said: 'He had no alternative. When Scheidt turned for the line in the manoeuvring during the last minute before the gun, Ben had to stay with him. If not, had the start been clean, Ben risked letting him get away.'

Ben Ainslie might have been feeling sorry for himself that evening in Atlanta but four years later he would exact a full and even more controversial revenge.

ERIC THE EEL

SYDNEY, 19 SEPTEMBER 2000

After the despair of Atlanta came the joy of Sydney. For whereas Atlanta had represented some of the worst aspects of modern sport, Sydney epitomised the best, much to the irritation of a handful of American journalists who, in their myopic desperation to prove that their country was still number one in everything, sought to dig out and file only negative stories from Australia. Their feeble attempts at influencing public opinion were water off a duck-billed platypus's back. Generally reckoned to be the most successful and most enjoyable Olympics ever, the 2000 Games brought together world champions and no-hopers and, for the most part, treated each with courtesy and dignity. And when it came to no-hopers in the swimming pool, none made a bigger splash than 22-year-old Eric Moussambani of Equatorial Guinea, the man who became known throughout the world as 'Eric the Eel'.

Moussambani was invited to the Olympics through a programme that allowed a few athletes from smaller nations to compete even though they didn't meet qualifying standards – an initiative promoted by IOC president Juan Antonio Samaranch as a way of spreading sport around the world. Moussambani was part of an eleven-person team from Equatorial Guinea that also included an eighteen-year-old swimmer, Paula Barila Bolopa, who offered an insight into what it was like to prepare for the Olympics in a West African country not exactly renowned for its sports facilities.

Bolopa started swimming just three months before the Olympics after being asked to enter a national competition. She won, beating thirty others, and was then put forward for a trip to Sydney. 'There is only one swimming pool in Malabo, our capital,' she revealed. 'It is in the Hotel Urecha, so our head coach asked if I could use it without paying. It is a very basic pool. Sometimes I cannot use it because hotel guests are in it. There is not a single Olympic-size pool in the whole of my country and that makes it very hard for me to prepare. I try to swim for two hours when I am in the swimming pool and two hours each time I am in the sea. On the days I am in the sea, the coach and another friend always accompany me because it can be quite dangerous at times because of the tides and also the sharks – they are known to swim in the sea around Malabo. They do not come very often, but it is a danger I have to take into account when I am out there.'

Like Paula Barila Bolopa, Eric Moussambani was a latecomer to competitive swimming. One of five children of a Guinean cocoa farmer, he tried his hand at basketball and football before opting for swimming. He adopted the crawl as his chosen stroke in January 2000, his first race being two laps of that twenty-metre hotel pool with no lane markings in his hometown of Malabo. At weekends he would train in a crocodile-infested river, which, if nothing else, presumably sharpened his speed. Now in Sydney he was given the honour of carrying his country's flag in the opening ceremony and was about to come face to face with a fifty-metre pool for the first time in his life. He was due to compete in the men's 100 metres freestyle – a tall order, since he had never previously swum even half that distance in a race.

The 18,000 spectators in the Sydney Aquatic Centre had been weaned on world records and the achievements of Australian star Ian Thorpe but soon they would be cheering on an unlikely new hero – a people's champion. In baggy blue trunks more suitable for a day on the beach, the gangly Moussambani lined up for his heat alongside just two opponents – Karim Bare of Niger and Farkhod Oripov of Tajikistan. One could have obtained decent odds on any of this trio ending up as medallists, but at least the other two looked the part in their sleek bodysuits. However, that was as far as their expertise went, for just as the starter was about to set them on their way, Bare and Oripov overbalanced, fell into the water and were disqualified. This was a stroke of luck for Moussambani who, after reaching Sydney without achieving the qualifying standard, now found himself with nobody to beat. However, he still had to complete the course and that in itself would prove a monumental challenge. Two lengths of a fifty-metre pool was a journey into the unknown.

He set off with a belly flop that owed more to a grey seal than an Olympic athlete and gamely embarked on the first length. His lazy-looking strokes propelled him slowly but surely towards the halfway point, at which he managed something resembling a distant relative of a flip-turn. But on the way back he began to tire dramatically. His strokes became increasingly uncoordinated as he thrashed about in the water, his arms flailing wildly. His legs sagging visibly by the second, it was a now a struggle to stay afloat, to keep his head above water. Lifeguards hovered, ready to dive in and rescue him if needed. About ten metres from the finish, by which time he was barely able to raise a splash, he ground to a virtual standstill. Yet with the crowd, many of whom were on their feet, cheering him on, he summoned just enough energy to make it to the wall, and once there he clung on for dear life. He eventually emerged from the water to thunderous applause marking the birth of a new Olympic hero in the mould of Eddie 'the Eagle' Edwards, Britain's wonderfully inept ski-jumper from the 1988 Winter Games.

Then, in time-honoured fashion, Moussambani relayed his feelings to the world's media. Speaking through an interpreter, he said: 'I really do not understand what all the fuss is about because I have not won anything. But I am very happy that everybody now knows my country. I was very tired in the pool but the Olympic spirit meant that I had to finish the race. My muscles were hurting. I had never been in a pool that big before, I was very scared. I feel as if I have won a gold medal. Many people thought that I would not be able to finish the race.

I would have been ashamed had I not been able to finish. I would not have been able to live with myself. I want to send hugs and kisses to the crowd. It was their cheering that kept me going. I saw that I couldn't leave the race. In my mind I said to myself, "You must keep going."' He added that he hoped the world would not forget him once the Games were over. 'I would like somebody to sponsor me and pay for a coach.' Such was his sudden popularity that after the race it took him an hour to reach the changing-room.

Moussambani's time of 1min 52.72sec was over a minute outside the world record. It was also more than seven seconds off Pieter van den Hoogenband's world record in the 200 metres! And even though he didn't have anybody to beat, he still failed to make it through to the next round as his time – thought to be the slowest in Olympic history – was not fast enough to qualify for the next stage. He was mildly aggrieved on learning this. 'They should let me back into the event,' he suggested, 'because I did win my heat.'

But that was certainly not the end of Eric Moussambani's Olympics. His fame spread like a bush fire, boosted by constant re-runs of his race on Australian television. Moussambani mania swept through the Olympic Village as Eric became the most sought-after athlete at the Games. A giant flag draped outside the Equatorial Guinea team residence declared: 'Eric the swimmer lives here.' The day after his race he gave more than a hundred interviews. A German television crew took him on a cruise around Sydney harbour and he was featured as the main item on NBC's Olympic coverage. And he won his first taste of sponsorship when swimwear manufacturers Speedo presented him with a blue shark suit.

Speedo also gave one to Moussambani's compatriot, Paula Barila Bolopa, and it was her turn to take centre stage three days later. Competing in her heat of the 50 metres freestyle – half Eric's distance – she struggled home last in 1min 03.97sec, nearly forty seconds slower than the fastest qualifier, Inge de Bruijn of the Netherlands. She was immediately dubbed 'Paula the Crawler'. Team manager Enrique Roca Nguba was full of praise for her efforts, pointing out that she had never seen starting blocks before arriving in Sydney and that her fear of heights had not helped her make a good start. 'It was a long way down to the water,' he admitted. 'She wasn't used to that.'

PÉREC DOES A RUNNER

SYDNEY, 21 SEPTEMBER 2000

Nicknamed the 'Black Gazelle', triple gold medallist Marie-José Pérec was France's big track hope at the 2000 Olympics. Fans were almost salivating at the prospect of her clash with Australia's Cathy Freeman in the women's 400 metres. Yet before even stretching her legs in Sydney, Pérec had mysteriously done a runner and fled back to France. While Freeman took gold, Pérec took only flak.

Born at Basse-Terre on the Caribbean island of Guadeloupe, Pérec was raised in humble circumstances, but her world changed when at the age of sixteen she was spotted by French athletics trainers on the lookout for fresh young talent. She moved to Paris with her mother and four years later represented France in the 200 metres at the Seoul Olympics, only to be eliminated in the heats. Victory in the 400 metres at the 1991 World Championships made the long-limbed 5ft 11in-tall Pérec the darling of the French media, a symbol of the new, multiethnic France. In the build-up to Barcelona she was rarely out of French magazines, who even took her back to Guadeloupe so that they could photograph her visiting her grandmother. She repaid the devotion of the French public by winning the 400 metres gold in 48.83sec. Afterwards, when asked whether she thought she could ever break the astonishing world record of 47.60sec set in 1985 by East Germany's Marita Koch, she cast aspersions on the latter's time, hinting that it was a product of the East German doping system. Pérec told an Olympic press conference: 'I think the world record is the race I ran today. I don't think that anyone has run under 49 seconds until now. To run this race today I didn't need any "biological preparation".' Four years later she went one better, completing the 200 and 400 metres double in Atlanta, thus becoming the first athlete of either sex to win the Olympic 400 metres twice. Her time in the 400 final (in which she beat Cathy Freeman) was 48.25sec, the fastest time for ten years.

With her modelling work for Christian Dior and forthright personality (President Jacques Chirac was said to be a big fan), Pérec's profile was higher than ever. Even before Atlanta she had become such a huge name in France that she had been forced to leave the country and train in California in order to obtain a little respite from the media circus. It was a scenario that would reoccur with dramatic effect in Sydney.

In the meantime her form took something of a puzzling dip post-Atlanta until in 1998 she was diagnosed as suffering from Epstein-Barr disease, a viral disorder that leaves victims feeling chronically exhausted. 'I couldn't walk up the stairs without being out of breath, it was that bad,' she said. 'When you are used to running 400 metres in 48 seconds and you cannot walk up the stairs without being in pain, it is hard.'

As part of her struggle to regain fitness, she shocked the athletics world in January 2000 by splitting from her Californian coach John Smith and teaming up with the controversial Wolfgang Meier, husband and former mentor of Marita Koch. The irony was not lost on Pérec. 'I asked him if he had given drugs to his athletes,' she said. 'He answered by telling me I should come and train with him to find out.' So she swapped sunny California for the less obvious delights of the Baltic port of Rostock. 'I didn't come here to hide and take drugs,' she said at the time. 'I have nothing to be ashamed of and I don't have to justify myself.'

For the next few months she kept an uncharacteristically low profile, venturing out of her Spartan apartment at Rostock's dilapidated stadium only to train. 'There's nothing else to do,' she sighed. Although her image still adorned Paris buildings, that was about all the French people saw of the country's most famous sports personality – bigger even than the World

Cup-winning footballers. She shunned interviews and refused to train with her French team-mates all summer. In July – just two months before the Olympics – she made a rare track appearance, finishing a disappointing third in Nice in what was her first competitive run at that distance since 1996. But as she continued to pull out of races, speculation mounted that she would not be going to Sydney.

She finally laid those fears to rest by announcing that she would be defending her Olympic 400 metres title and was confident of a good show. 'For me, Nice was a victory,' she said. 'I'll be ready for the Olympics, believe me, I know what I'm doing. Before the Olympic final, there will be three heats. I will use every one of them as a warm-up session.'

Pérec's problems began as soon as she arrived at the airport. She immediately ran off to avoid waiting journalists and pushed a photographer out of the way. Once in Sydney, the woman labelled a 'diva' by former coaches, shut herself away from the outside world. Highly strung at the best of times (she had a tendency to vomit at the finish of races), the 32-year-old refused all contact with athletes from other countries. She refused to stay in the high-security Olympic Village at Homebush Bay and instead checked into a city centre hotel. She repeatedly cancelled press conferences and via her Internet site – her only link with the outside world – accused the Australian media of hounding her in what she claimed was a deliberate ploy to unsettle her before her clash with Freeman, the aborigine who had been elevated to the status of national icon.

'I have the impression everything is being fabricated to destabilise me,' she wrote. 'I have never seen anything like this. It is not right. It has affected me. They just make up rumours. I do not know what to do with these journalists who do not stop following me wherever I go. After three days I have not yet gone out of my hotel room and I have not even trained.'

The Australian press continued to speculate on her reasons for avoiding competition all year and on her training regime under Meier. One newspaper even extended the personal attacks by suggesting that she was wearing a wig. Meanwhile, reports from France said that she had recently made telephone threats to the two technical directors of the French national team. Pérec's paranoia was further fuelled when she learned that a number of French journalists were staying at her hotel – a fact she discovered when she found herself seated next to a reporter at breakfast on her first day. After that, she relied on room service. The pressure was clearly getting to her and her Internet diary entry for 19 September – three days before she was due to start the defence of her 400 metres title – pointed to a woman on the verge of a breakdown. 'The Games have hardly begun,' she wrote, 'and I am so frightened, I wish they would end. When I see the other athletes appearing for competition I really crack up.'

Her erratic behaviour came as no surprise to François Pépin, one of five coaches she had dumped since 1987. 'Marie-Jo has a difficult temper,' he said. 'She's egocentric and often behaves as if she were the centre of the universe. She needs to hate someone to run at her top level. I much prefer Cathy Freeman as a person. Her attitude is more noble. She's always nice to the public and the media because she knows how much she owes them.'

Then on 21 September, the eve of her opening-round heat, Pérec finally cracked and fled Sydney after claiming that a man had threatened her in her hotel room. Joined by her boyfriend, American 400-metres runner Athuan Maybank, who had failed to qualify for his event, she flew to Singapore on a London-bound flight, leaving her agent, Annick Averinos, to attempt to explain her sudden departure. 'A man came to her room, saying he had a package for her. When she realised he had nothing for her, she asked him to go away but the man kicked at the door so he could enter her bedroom. He told her he would find her wherever she went and there was no point calling the police because there was little they could do to protect her. She is a strong person but she was in tears and clearly alarmed when she called me.' Averinos claimed that Pérec had been threatened and insulted on several occasions since arriving in Australia. 'Once a man told her she might get run over. She just can't take any more.'

However, the hotel owners said there was no evidence to back up the intruder allegations and insisted that their high-level security arrangements had not been breached.

But controversy continued to dog Pérec's every footstep. At Singapore's Changi airport Maybank was involved in a scuffle with an Australian TV cameraman. Pérec joined in and the pair were quizzed by police for over eleven hours before being released without charge. While Pérec and Maybank resumed their escape to Europe, the French Olympic authorities confirmed that their star athlete had withdrawn from the Games. 'This is my worst nightmare,' said a rueful Philippe Lamblin, president of the French Athletics Federation.

A week after returning to Paris, Pérec broke her silence in an interview with the French sports daily *L'Equipe*. 'I missed the most important rendezvous I ever had with myself,' she said. 'I cracked when I shouldn't have cracked. I was defeated. I could think of only one thing: go far away. Fast. There wasn't a day that I wasn't tracked like an animal. Several times I went to a supermarket and each time there were problems. I was so afraid. All of a sudden, that morning, I grabbed my bag and nothing else mattered, not even the gold medal that I came for. The only time in my life that I really made every effort, everything needed to go all the way, the time that it counted the most for me, I didn't make it. Life is really bizarre.'

WE HAVE LIFT-OFF

SYDNEY, 22 SEPTEMBER 2000

Sports Illustrated correspondent E M Swift pretty much summed up the drawbacks of race walking as an Olympic sport. 'TV hates it,' he wrote. 'Spectators won't pay to watch it. And no one who isn't in the Olympics practises it, since that ridiculous shamble leads to the utter ruination of your hips. It's so contrived. It isn't fast. It isn't graceful. It isn't even natural.'

Swift suggested that the farcical scenes that marked the climax of both the men's and women's 20-kilometre walking races in Sydney represented the sport's nadir – no mean feat in itself. And certainly the cruel manner in which a Mexican and an Australian had gold medals ripped from their grasp indicates that this pastime is barely more civilised than trial by ordeal . . . and nowhere near as entertaining to watch.

While the curse of bodybuilding drugs has apparently yet to infiltrate race walking (although there are rumours of competitors being fitted with artificial hips), the lifting rule, which determines when a walk becomes a run, results in no end of disqualifications. Three transgressions of this rule bring about automatic elimination.

The men's race, on 22 September, produced what walking aficionados described as the best finish in Olympic history. Try telling that to Mexico's Bernardo Segura. He received his first warning for illegally losing contact with the ground early in the race and a second, of which he was not aware, as he chased the leaders. The third was apparently delivered near the finish, but Segura, thinking he had been given only two warnings, kept going and crossed the line just two seconds ahead of Poland's Robert Korzeniowski. To the delight of Mexican fans both in the stadium and watching at home on television, Segura completed a lap of honour to celebrate what he believed was his country's second gold medal of the Games. The third-placed finisher, fellow Mexican Noe Hernandez, joined in the joyous scenes and fifteen minutes later Segura was taking a congratulatory phone call from Mexico's president, Ernesto Zedillo. 'Your race is an example for the youth of Mexico,' gushed the President. 'It is proof that discipline, dedication and the love of sport can give results.' But as the Mexican people watched Segura take the call by the side of the track live on national television, an Olympic official walked up and showed him a red card to indicate that he had been disqualified. The gold was now awarded to Korzeniowski who, ironically, had himself been thrown out of the 50-kilometre walk at the 1992 Olympics as he entered the stadium in second place.

Mexico's elation turned to indignation. 'OLYMPIC ROBBERY' screamed one headline while a former medallist wrote: 'They've got it in for Mexicans.' As public outrage increased, Mexicans insisted that there was a conspiracy against their athletes and claimed that if it had been an American or a German who had crossed the line first, they would never have been disqualified. The anger was so vehement that the Australian embassy in Mexico City even felt compelled to issue a statement denying any conspiracy against Mexican athletes by the Canberra government.

When the fuss eventually died down, one last question remained: why had it taken so long after the race to inform Segura of his disqualification? The official line was that only the chief judge could inform a competitor of disqualification and he was too busy eliminating another walker first!

The women's race five days later was equally eventful, with all three leaders being disqualified for lifting over the final kilometre. The drama began as the reigning world and Asian Games champion, Hongyu Liu of China, approached the stadium with barely fifteen minutes' walking between her and the gold medal. Then, having earlier received two white paddles – or discs – to denote cautions, Liu was sensationally shown the red paddle for disqualification. Her exit handed the lead to Italy's Elisabetta Perrone (a silver medallist in the 1996 Olympic 10-kilometre race) but within fifty yards she, too, was disqualified for a third lift. After stopping and waving her arms in the air in disbelief, the 32-year-old Italian caused wholesale confusion by setting off again and overtaking the new leader, Australia's Jane Saville. It seemed that Perrone was intent on defying her disqualification, but once she had passed Saville, she left the course in utter dejection.

So now the 100,000 crowd inside the stadium had the prospect of cheering on a home winner. Even those who weren't remotely interested in race walking began to get animated for, as one spectator remarked, 'They'd cheer a monkey if it was wearing green and gold!' With an unassailable lead of fifty metres, it appeared that nothing could deprive the 25-year-old Australian of glory, even though she had already received two warnings for lifting. But as she headed into the stadium tunnel, just 150 metres from the finish line, the applause ringing in her ears, the judge suddenly produced the fateful red paddle.

Saville, the 1998 Commonwealth Games 10-kilometre champion, threw up her hands in horror. 'No, no, not me,' she cried. 'Yes, you,' replied the judge coldly. The Australian was led away in tears.

The lucky beneficiary of all this was China's Wang Liping who, having seen all three walkers in front of her disqualified in the closing stages, now kept her nerve to claim an unlikely gold. Norway's Kiersti Plaetzer took silver and Maria Vasco of Spain collected the bronze. It was China's first athletics gold medal of the Games. 'I feel proud for my country,' said a surprised Wang, who had only received one warning during the race. 'I raced for a silver but finished with a gold.'

Home sympathies lay very much with Saville, who recounted her nightmare to the world's media. 'I saw the chief judge and he started touching his paddle and I thought, "No, no". Then he had to check the number and it was me. What can you do? Nothing. I was embarrassed and upset. It has been a dream of mine to walk into the stadium first. As I was approaching the tunnel, I was thinking, "I can do this". This was a dream. I could hear the crowd. I knew that my family and friends I haven't seen for years were there, waiting for me. I was going to smile at them on the finish line . . . but it wasn't to be.'

When a TV reporter, presumably hinting at an appeal into her disqualification, asked Saville what she wanted, she answered simply: 'I'd like a gun, so I can shoot myself.'

That's how many people feel at the thought of having to watch an hour and a half of race walking.

AINSLIE'S REVENGE

SYDNEY, 29 SEPTEMBER 2000

In the four years since Atlanta hardly a day went by without Ben Ainslie thinking about that emotional afternoon when Brazil's Robert Scheidt controversially pipped him for the gold medal in sailing's Laser class. It still rankled, Ainslie feeling that he had been outsmarted at the start line. By the time of the Sydney Olympics Ainslie was 23 and had acquired the experience and maturity required to play the four-times world champion at his own game. Now in scenic Rushcutters Bay against the picturesque backdrop of Sydney Harbour Bridge, the young Briton was out to erase the memory of Atlanta once and for all.

The method of scoring for the eleven-race series gained an added complication in Sydney with each sailor able to discard his two worse scores from the final totals. Consequently, a pocket calculator became almost as essential an item of sailing equipment as a compass.

There were 43 competitors, hailing from such diverse locations as Peru and the Seychelles, but as expected, Ainslie and Scheidt dominated the event from the outset. After four races, the Brazilian led by a solitary point. Both men had won twice but also had a 23rd place counting. Clearly each would hope to discard this as the competition progressed. Going into the final two races, Ainslie had opened up a four-point advantage but Scheidt was carrying a 21st place counting from race seven, which he would be able to discard if he finished higher than that in the last two races. Ainslie struggled in race ten and although he eventually fought his way through the pack to finish fifth, Scheidt's second place allowed him to discard the 21st and theoretically to build a lead of six points with just one race remaining.

After poring over the complex calculations, Ainslie reckoned he had two ways of snatching the gold. Either he could try and win and hope that Scheidt finished at least seven places behind him or he could attempt to sail the Brazilian 'down the fleet' into such a lowly position that Scheidt would be forced to count that 21st place after all. Ainslie, too, would almost certainly have to discard the last race but the finish he would have to reintroduce to his overall score was higher than Scheidt's. With the wind shifting and varying in strength, Ainslie and his coach John Derbyshire decided on this latter tactic, to sail Scheidt out of the race.

In the pre-start period, Ainslie shadowed Scheidt everywhere. 'I decided to attack Robert,' he said later, 'because even if I had won the last race there was a very big chance of Robert finishing eighth or better. I was guaranteed a silver medal even if I did not sail the last race.' The first start was recalled and just before the restart Ainslie attacked again, only to see the race postponed due to lack of wind. It was an action replay of Atlanta, where three attempts had been needed to get the boats away.

They did set off at the third time of asking, but not before protest flags were hoisted by Ainslie who had forced Scheidt into fouling him, thus requiring the Brazilian to turn his boat in a full circle twice before continuing. Ainslie explained: 'We had a start line incident for which Robert did a 720 turn but I don't think he did it correctly.' Already delayed by his penalty, Scheidt now found his progress impeded by Ainslie, who hung back from the rest of the fleet to monitor his rival's every move. By staying just in front of Scheidt on that first windward leg, Ainslie was able to slow him down by blocking his access to the wind. Altogether they tacked or changed direction through the wind up to thirty times as Scheidt tried to wriggle free. He tried dummy tacks and sudden changes of direction, but Ainslie anticipated his every move. Ainslie was in complete control and as they approached the first windward mark, where the boats turned to run before the wind, they were already right at the back of the fleet, ninety seconds behind the previous boat and over three minutes behind the leaders.

At that mark Ainslie set out to frustrate his rival still further, hoping to delay Scheidt to such an extent that he would find it impossible to make up the lost ground. For several minutes he held off the Brazilian by dint of clever positioning. Finally Scheidt's nerve cracked and in a desperate bid to go for the mark, he gybed into Ainslie, committing a foul. The protest flags were raised again, but Scheidt knew that, free at last from Ainslie's shackles, he now had to sail on and take his chances in the protest room. Above all, he somehow had to finish 21st or higher.

Scheidt began attacking the back markers but as the wind dropped he failed to make much impression. For seven legs Ainslie continued to chase Scheidt, covering him on the downwind and shadowing him on the upwind legs. At the second last downwind gate Scheidt was a seemingly hopeless 34th but then, with the light wind having shifted, the race committee signalled a course change. Scheidt tacked immediately on rounding the downwind mark and started to scythe his way through the fleet. Ainslie remarked afterwards: 'Robert found a wind line, which I missed, and all I could do was watch him sail away.'

By the penultimate mark Scheidt had moved up to 22nd, just one place off his gold medal position. Ainslie was now back in 36th and powerless to act. The only sailor standing between Scheidt and a second Olympic title was Stanley Tan of Singapore who was three seconds ahead, but in the light wind there were no passing opportunities and as he crossed the line, the Brazilian was frantically counting the number of boats ahead of him. When Ainslie crossed the line a minute and a half later, he, too, was unsure of where Scheidt had finished, with the result that there were no immediate celebrations. Eventually it was confirmed that Scheidt had finished 22nd and Ainslie 37th, and with both men having to use these positions as discards, Ainslie had taken the gold medal by one point on the count-up.

However, the drama was not yet over. Scheidt protested about the incident at the first windward mark and Ainslie protested about the Brazilian's penalty turn at the start. Scheidt also tried to launch a counter-protest regarding the start, only to be informed that he was too late in submitting it. Hearing this, Ainslie withdrew his objection. For the next four hours the jury studied the collision at the first mark from all angles. Ainslie not only had to wait for the outcome of Scheidt's protest but also for that of other protests on boats finishing above the reigning champion. For if any of those boats were eliminated, Scheidt could have been raised the place he needed for gold. Eventually the jury announced that Scheidt's protest had been thrown out – indeed, it was he who was disqualified from that last race although he still took the silver medal.

Despite being outwardly confident of holding on to the gold, Ainslie was mightily relieved at the verdict. 'It was an amazing race,' he said, 'very tough. My only option was to try to do what I did. It is a shame that it came down to doing it that way. I would much rather that I had won with a race to spare, but sometimes you have to use the rules to beat someone and there is no question of any unfairness here. That is sailing. But it's always 50–50 when you go into a protest room.'

He insisted that the rivalry with Scheidt remained 'respectful and friendly' and although the Brazilian pointedly declined to attend the post-race press conference, he did later send his congratulations. Scheidt made no attempt to hide his disappointment at Ainslie's tactics. 'I think it was a bit too much,' he said. 'I'd rather see the Olympic final be more sportsmanlike.' He had obviously forgotten what had happened four years earlier.

Ainslie hadn't. Referring back to that final race in Atlanta, he smiled and said: 'I guess it's really a case of what goes around comes around.'

BIBLIOGRAPHY

Brant, Marshall. *The Games*. London, Proteus, 1980.

Buchanan, Ian. *British Olympians*. London, Guinness, 1991.

Greenberg, Stan. *Olympic Facts and Feats*. London, Guinness, 1996.

Hart-Davis, Duff. *Hitler's Games*. London, Century Hutchinson, 1986.

Hauman, Riël. *Century of the Marathon*. Cape Town, Human and Rousseau, 1996.

Phillips, Bob. *Zá-to-pek* – Bob Phillips. Manchester, Parrs Wood Press, 2002.